Praise for *Your Divorce Advisor*

"*Your Divorce Advisor,* written by a seasoned lawyer-and-psychologist team, is a gem of a guidebook that empowers divorcing adults to take control of their own divorce—legally, financially, and emotionally. It walks the reader through the divorce process, step by step. Vital information about financial matters and state-of-the-art research about the needs of children allow the reader to make constructive decisions for themselves and for their children, setting them on the pathway toward solutions that work for everybody involved. All of this is presented in a manner that is compassionate, sensible, and most comforting."

—Janet Johnston, Executive Director, Judith Wallerstein Center for the Family in Transition, and author of *In the Name of the Child*

"We know that divorce creates problems—for the couple, their children, their family, their friends. . . . Mercer and Pruett have done something other experts have failed to do: They have created rock-solid solutions based on their recognition that financial and legal decisions are inextricably influenced, even governed, by emotional feelings. The result: They offer a rare combination of legal, emotional, personal, and financial advice that makes this guidebook must reading, not only for anyone going through divorce but also for anyone knowing someone who is."

—Nancy Dunnan, author of *Dunnan's Guide to Your Investments, 2001*

"*Your Divorce Advisor* brilliantly and compassionately deals with the common challenges facing anyone going through a divorce. If your marriage is in trouble, you should buy *Your Divorce Advisor* before you hire a lawyer. Lawyers and therapists should recommend *Your Divorce Advisor* before the very first client meeting."

—Forrest S. Mosten, President, Mosten Mediation Centers

"*Your Divorce Advisor* is the most comprehensive divorce book on the market. It covers the legal issues extensively and is the only book to also tell you what you can expect to feel along the way. It offers an invaluable strategy for coping with the emotional demands of divorce, and has the best advice on talking with your kids about the divorce that I've read anywhere. It is the one book I will recommend to my divorcing clients."

—Louis Parley, author of *The Ethical Family Lawyer*

YOUR
DIVORCE
ADVISOR

A Lawyer and a Psychologist Guide You Through

the Legal and Emotional Landscape of Divorce

DIANA MERCER, J.D.,
AND MARSHA KLINE PRUETT, PH.D., M.S.L.

A Fireside Book
Published by Simon & Schuster
New York   London   Toronto   Sydney

FIRESIDE
Rockefeller Center
1230 Avenue of the Americas
New York, NY 10020

FIRESIDE and colophon are registered trademarks
of Simon & Schuster, Inc.

Designed by William P. Ruoto

Manufactured in the United States of America

10

Library of Congress Cataloging-in-Publication Data

Mercer, Diana (Diana Lee), date.
Your divorce advisor : a lawyer and a psychologist guide you through the legal and emotional landscape of divorce / Diana Mercer and Marsha Kline Pruett.
p. cm.
"A Fireside book."
Includes bibliographical references.
1. Divorce—Law and legislation—United States—Popular works.
2. Divorce—United States—Psychological aspects.
I. Pruett, Marsha Kline, 1960–   II. Title.
KF535.Z9 M47 2001
346.7301'66—dc21
00-052082
ISBN-13: 978-0-684-87068-1
ISBN-10:   0-684-87068-7

ACKNOWLEDGMENTS

We wish to acknowledge a few of the many people who have contributed to the writing of this book.

From Diana Mercer . . . Without the assistance and encouragement of her steadfast colleague, Nancy A. Noyes, Esq., this book would not have been possible. Christina Kelly Hunter, L.M.F.T., and Robert Stone, L.C.S.W., M.Div., are gratefully acknowledged for their patience, ideas, and enthusiasm, especially in the early stages of this project. I also thank Carl M. Porto, Esq., because without his guidance, mentoring, and confidence I could not be the lawyer I am today. And, of course, I thank my writing partner, Dr. Marsha Kline Pruett, for her dedication to improving the lives of the children and adults who experience divorce.

From Dr. Pruett . . . I wish to thank first and foremost the children and their parents who have taught me what we professionals do right and wrong from their perspective, and how we can always do more to assist them. To my first colleagues, Judith Wallerstein gave me my first job in the field, and Janet Johnston has remained mentor and friend. Jan's passion and loyalty to the ideas and emotions contained herein have always inspired me, and she has provided invaluable support and assistance throughout my career. Thanks to Albert J. Solnit for his encouragement in initiating my return to research in this field. The Honorable Anne Dranginis has run alongside me as we have tried together to better the lives of divorcing families; she possesses a rare courage in the ways she tackles the issues in this field, and she carries supporters in her wake. I warmly acknowledge Diana Mercer, my coauthor, for persevering. And to my family, from my parents to my children, and all extended family members in between, thank you for believing in me and cheering me on in the wee hours of the morning. Elizabeth and Emily, daughters though not children, thank you for holding on tight, and talking when it would have been easier to be silent.

Both authors gratefully acknowledge the assistance and support of their agent, James Levine, of James Levine Communications.

To Steve, my husband, my partner, my sweetheart
—Diana Mercer

For Olivia, whose smile and laughter remind me every day why I do this work. And for Kyle, who makes everything possible and worthwhile in life.

—Marsha Kline Pruett

CONTENTS

FOREWORD

Your Divorce Advisor is the first book of its kind, a comprehensive legal and psychological resource. The authors recognize that for couples going through divorce, the legal and psychological processes operate in tandem, though often pulling in opposite directions.

As a Family Court judge, I have long recognized the myriad problems we face in trying to serve the needs of families within an adversary system that was not designed to meet the social and psychological problems engendered by divorce. For most families, the legal system itself becomes part of the problem. We use arcane language and procedures, which only serve to exacerbate the feelings of insecurity and lack of control emanating from the failure of one's marriage. Of equal concern, however, is that the mental health world is without the authority or the decision-making capacity to meet the multilayered needs of divorcing families. One important lesson I have learned from my experience is that the process works best when people are empowered to make decisions for themselves. This book provides a comprehensive guide through the legal and emotional quagmire of divorce, and can serve as an armchair resource, providing on-the-spot invaluable information and strategic advice.

Clearly, the book is not intended to replace the counsel of an individual lawyer, but the legal blueprint it provides serves several very important purposes. It is readily available to answer questions when a divorcing party may be unable to reach his or her lawyer. It provides enough background information to enable the reader to do some of the legwork, thereby reducing legal costs and increasing a sense of individual control. And above all, it provides sound and sensible ways to prepare in the event that settlement is not possible, while never losing sight of the value of settlement.

Equally valuable advice is offered for dealing with emotional crises. The authors' identification of the most common reactions to divorce should provide comfort. The emotional and legal checklists in these pages, together with the strategies for dealing with your spouse as co-parent, will help to keep the reader on course and focused on long-term goals.

Divorce is recognized as one of the most difficult life events a person endures, second only to the death of a spouse. Most people are understandably overwhelmed when trying to deal with the personal trauma of divorce at the same time they are required to navigate the legal process. Notwithstanding this personal challenge, parents are asked to recognize the real needs of their children, who are faced with the dissolution of family and security as they have known it. *Your Divorce Advisor* is written by a lawyer/mediator and a psychologist, both outstanding, experienced, and insightful professionals who recognize the emotional roller coaster that divorce represents and who are capable of articulating valuable strategies for dealing with virtually every situation an individual might encounter.

I wish every parent going through divorce could have the wisdom contained in the following pages. If divorcing parents arm themselves with the practical psychological and legal wisdom provided by Diane Mercer, Esq., and Marsha Kline Pruett, Ph.D., M.S.L., in this book, they will help to stem the rising tide of adults carrying with them the effects of their own parents' hostile and highly conflicted divorces.

Honorable Arline S. Rotman
Retired Justice
Probate and Family Court
Massachusetts

INTRODUCTION

The idea for this book evolved from years of practice as a matrimonial lawyer and as a clinical psychologist. Our clients would repeatedly ask us questions we could not answer to their satisfaction, because although the questions were related to divorce, the client was asking the lawyer a question about family interactions, or the client was asking the therapist a legal question. We gradually realized how much our fields overlap not only in subject matter but also in strategy. The old-fashioned idea of legal strategy, with its "take no prisoners" tactics, does not work for families. The best strategy from either perspective is to take care of yourself and your family (for you are still a family), especially your children.

As simple as it sounds, this is truly your mantra. You need to know more than postdivorce recovery strategies or tactics for "winning" your divorce, because neither is enough in itself. You need to know about the process as it unfolds, from the time you decide to separate until after the divorce is finalized. The legal aspects of a divorce simply cannot be separated from the emotional aspects. Writing a book that puts everything in one place seemed like the natural solution.

Over the years, we've learned that divorce is a land of misinformation. Sources of misinformation include parents, bitter friends, neighbors, sitcoms, and soap operas. These people may attempt to help, but their circumstances are so different than yours that their advice just doesn't apply to you and your situation. Each family is unique.

In this book, you'll learn how to recognize issues, both legal and psychological, that pose a problem for you and your spouse. You'll learn how to minimize their negative effects, while maximizing the benefit you receive from the court by dealing with such issues appropriately. You will learn to consider legal issues from the perspective of their likely emotional impact on you, your ex-spouse, and your children. We will consider children's developmental needs and how they can be taken into account in decision making or negotiating. This book will help you with practical tips and solutions for dealing with both the legal and emotional facets of divorce, so that you don't let one sabotage the other in your own case. We've organized it chronologically, so you can skip through the sections and use it as a reference manual, or start at the beginning and work to the end of the book.

This book takes you along the entire journey of divorce as it unfolds from predivorce decision making and planning through the final settlement or trial. It addresses the simplest to the most complicated legal issues in divorce, as well as the emotional tugs that weave their way through each and every legal issue. It is written from the premise that taking care of yourself and your family is the way to "win" your divorce. It offers practical information, advice, and options at each crossroads during the divorce. It lets you see the whole picture before your divorce is completed, and before you are left in the aftermath to figure out what happened and what could have been done differently. By understanding the relationship between what you are thinking or feeling versus what you need to know and do, you and your children will come out ahead.

This book is meant for those want to proceed but don't know how to begin. It is also for those who are in the middle of the legal proceedings but find that they have more questions than either a lawyer or therapist alone can answer. Divorce is a complicated process, both legally and psychologically, and we hope to reach anyone who has a question about how the two parts of the process can work together for the best result for their family.

Use this book to supplement the advice you receive from your lawyer or therapist. It can be used as a handbook you can refer to at any time, especially at 2 A.M. when you can't sleep or when your lawyer can't call you back fast enough. It can help you wind your way through the maze of divorce with a minimum toll on you and your children, so that you can move ahead with your life with as little disruption as possible. It will let you emerge from your divorce as a healthy person who has lost a minimum of dignity, money, property, and time with your children, not to mention sleep.

Divorce is not just a legal change; it is a very personal transition that happens not only to you but to your children and your extended family. Handled clumsily or with venom, it can have devastating effects that last for years, or even generations. Handled appropriately, it can take its place among other important family events. It can be the path to a new and better life.

1.

The Legal and Emotional Landscape of Divorce: A View from the Summit

BEGINNING AT THE END

Divorce is now a commonplace phenomenon in our society. Almost all of us have familiarity with it, either personally or through family or friends. As a result, you begin your own divorce with some knowledge about how to approach it. You have heard horror stories about the legal system, but you have also heard about couples who managed their own divorce without hostility and high costs. Each divorce has threads in common, yet each is unique, reflecting the particulars of two people and their balance of personality, resources, hurts, and desires.

When you're thinking about beginning a divorce, it's also useful to think about your goals for the *end* of the divorce. Thoughtful planning, anticipation, and goal setting will help you stay on the path to a successful divorce: one which dissolves your marriage, but not your sense of family or financial security.

Looking back after your divorce is finalized, you will feel a combination of the sorrow, anger, hurt, relief, exhilaration, and exhaustion of reaching the top of a long, hard climb. The perspective from the top of any peak is often startling, as you see the view below with a clarity that eluded you during the journey. At the same time, the details become distant and the sights and sounds along the way become memories, each one giving way to the next, until only a hazy watercolor landscape is fixed in your mind. How you feel at the top of the summit depends on the way in which you approached the path. Did you have the right gear? Did you have a positive attitude? Did you work well with your partner? Did you take enough water and emergency supplies? Did you choose a good map? Did the weather cooperate? Some aspects were out of your control, but many were not.

Both the legal and emotional processes of divorce mark your path. How you arrived at the decision to end your marriage matters less than how you plan for that ending and beginning your new life. How you care for yourself during the process can mean the difference between a bad situation that never ends, and a future that permits you to move ahead and grow. You can set either a positive or a negative course that will influence your family through a lifetime. Much of your experience will be colored by how you prepared, and how you responded to hardships and curves in the road.

This chapter outlines for you the path you'll follow through the legal forest, and what you can expect to feel at every turn. At the beginning of a divorce, you need to have a picture of the whole journey, so that you will be confident that at the end you'll know:

- You made the best decisions for your children and yourself
- You made agreements based on sound decisions rather than emotional responses
- Your choices minimized the inevitable hurts and losses for you and your family
- Your actions are leading you in healthy directions toward the next phase of your life, whatever that turns out to be

OVERVIEW OF THE LEGAL PROCESS OF DIVORCE

In most states, the legal divorce process is clear-cut and simple, which is ironic, given the number of emotional roadblocks that can complicate and slow the process. How long it takes to complete a divorce case depends on your local rules and court systems. Variables such as court scheduling times and judges' vacation schedules can also delay your case.

The basic process begins when one spouse files the divorce by submitting the necessary forms to the court. This can be done with or without an attorney. This basic process includes:

- completing the forms required, typically a divorce petition or complaint, with general requests for resolution, i.e., "joint custody" or "fair division of assets and debts"
- official notice to the other spouse
- either a response from the other spouse, or proof that the other spouse has received notice
- filing the papers with the court

Once the papers have been filed, a mandatory waiting period begins. Each state has a different waiting period, from six weeks to one year. Some states require actual physical separation; others anticipate that you and your spouse will live together until the waiting period expires. During this waiting period, however, the court has the power to make preliminary orders about certain aspects if they are in dispute:

- payment of household expenses
- custody and visitation
- child support and alimony
- use of certain possessions during the case, usually the house or the car
- whether or not a custody investigation will be necessary
- whether or not there is a possibility for reconciliation
- relief from spousal abuse

During this preliminary phase, the court becomes involved only if these matters are disputed. The court's goal is to stabilize the situation, ensure that necessary bills get paid, and protect children from unnecessary or excessive disruption to their lives.

Court intervention is not necessary if there is agreement on the interim issues. These matters, along with the final settlement of the issues in the case, can be mediated, negotiated, or settled out of court at any time. Often, parties and/or their lawyers are able to settle some or all matters on a temporary basis, with the understanding that these agreements may be renegotiated before the case is finalized. When the interim arrangements are settled, they may be written up and presented to the court for approval, or agreed upon informally. When the court approves this agreement, it becomes a court order, and is enforceable by the court. An informal settlement that is not approved by a judge is not enforceable by the court.

If court intervention is necessary for these temporary provisions, the court holds a hearing, a sort of "mini-trial." The judge will hear limited evidence, either through testimony or documents, about your finances, needs, and issues concerning the children. The judge then makes temporary court orders designed to stabilize your living situation while the case proceeds and the waiting period expires. The result of the hearing becomes a court order and is enforceable by the court.

After the initial filing and interim issues have been resolved, several things must happen before the case can be finalized:

- you and your spouse prepare and exchange financial disclosures
- decisions are made about who will keep each asset and who will pay each debt
- decisions are made about who will continue to live in your home or apartment, or whether other living arrangements are necessary
- determinations as to how much spousal support and child support are appropriate, if any, and whether either spouse or a child has special financial needs that must be considered
- if disclosures are not forthcoming, or if financial records are unclear, additional investigations may be necessary
- if custody and visitation are issues, a custody evaluation or investigation must be completed

Once the waiting period has expired, and any necessary disclosures or investigations are completed, your case is ready to come to a final judgment. There are three ways in which this may happen:

- **Uncontested trial:** all matters are agreed upon, and a written agreement is presented to the judge for review on the final hearing date
- **Limited contested trial:** some matters are agreed upon, such as custody and visitation, or certain matters about finances, but other issues remain unresolved, requiring a court trial limited to those issues

• **Fully contested trial:** all financial matters are in dispute, or custody and visitation are not agreed upon, and a court trial will need to be held on all issues.

While most cases begin with unresolved issues, over 95 percent of these cases are settled prior to a divorce trial. Sometimes resolution takes only a few hours; for other cases, it takes months or years. Only about 5 percent of all divorce cases end up in fully contested trials.

Once the case has been concluded either by a court-approved agreement or by a judge after a trial, the matter goes to final judgment, and you are divorced. The agreement or judge's orders become the court orders that govern your case. In some cases, this conclusion is final, but in others, parts of the court orders may be modified in the future.

Property orders are not modifiable by the court after the final judgment except in extraordinary circumstances, such as the discovery of fraud. Other issues, such as spousal support, child support, or custody and visitation, may be adjusted to account for changes in circumstances upon proper motion to the court.

Orders that are made by the court but not followed by the parties may also be enforced by the court through contempt proceedings.

EMOTIONAL GUIDEPOSTS FOR DIVORCE

Your success with the legal process will depend in large part on the decisions you make at each stage along the way. As you enter and complete each phase of the legal process, intense emotions may create obstacles at any turn. You can learn to understand these feelings and get past them to act constructively and rationally.

At the same time, you will also have to meet the challenge of independent living. This is no small task, but it is important if you wish to stop feeling lost, helpless, or angry. The checklist below summarizes the emotional guideposts that will lead you through the legal system. As this book proceeds, you will see how you must walk the legal path and the emotional path at the same time.

1. Recognizing anger, hurt, distrust, revenge, fear, and other emotions associated with loss
2. Learning to assess and manage household finances and responsibilities
3. Developing practical job and career options
4. Finding legal advice and expertise that counsels but does not inflame
5. Establishing a safe environment for yourself and your children
6. Negotiating firmly but fairly to obtain a financial settlement that maximizes family assets
7. Handling anxiety without unduly burdening the children, your spouse, or significant others
8. Using the legal system as a means of protection and structure, not intimidation or blackmail
9. Maintaining a respectful distance from your ex-spouse without creating unnecessary alienation
10. Creating legal and financial documents that establish your new independence and preserve family assets over time

Depending upon your role in the divorcing family, you will face some additional challenges, legal and emotional:

If You Initiated the Separation or Divorce

1. Informing your partner of your decision with consideration for its consequences
2. Preparing for upcoming events without resorting to sneak attacks
3. Negotiating generously but with sufficient attention to your needs in the future
4. Checking your impatience to finish the divorce and allowing enough time for clarity, processing, and acceptance without diverting from your goal
5. Adopting patience with your partner's grief responses, including his or her rage

If You Are Faced with a Separation or Divorce You Did Not Want

1. Recognizing the many sides of anger, shame, and sorrow as you experience them
2. Checking for signs of depression, and treating them if needed
3. Identifying the use of helplessness as a defense or to punish your spouse
4. Refraining from wielding children, financial information, or resources as a weapon
5. Knowing when you need more support, and from whom and where to get it

If You Have Children and Are Divorcing

1. Developing ways of working together as parents that maintain the distance desired or needed
2. Determining children's needs jointly
3. Communicating to and about the children with the details needed to assure consistency and stability in their lives
4. Providing adequately for your children's financial, emotional, and parental needs even when doing so deprives you of personal satisfaction
5. Setting up decision-making and custody agreements that are developmentally appropriate and sufficiently flexible to benefit your children
6. Maintaining parental boundaries, authority, availability, and expressions of warmth
7. Restraining your desire to minimize your partner's access to the children
8. Minimizing the court's role in your family's and children's lives
9. Checking for signs of stress in your children and yourself and obtaining timely psychological, medical, or educational assistance
10. Establishing new family routines, celebrations, and traditions that are respectful of each of your child's families

If Your Friends and Family Ask How They Can Help

When people volunteer to help, you can ask them to:

1. Listen more often than sharing advice
2. Refrain from "spouse-bashing" and help think of ways to make the situation more tolerable
3. Provide practical support by babysitting, house sitting, running errands, or planning a night out with friends
4. Keep you company when loneliness sets in
5. Serve as a buffer during transitions and family events
6. Reinforce the importance over time of extended family and continuity of relationships

With these guideposts to mark the way, you are ready to embark on the path through the legal and emotional process of divorce. Along the way, look for the signs indicating that you are headed in the right direction, and aim to reach the summit with a better understanding of yourself and a sense of control over your destiny.

2.

Planning for Success: Your Success Depends on the Path You Choose

THE FIRST STEPS

How Do I Start the Legal Process?

You actually start the legal process with your emotions. The movement toward divorce from feelings of disillusionment, despair, anger, or emotional withdrawal is a process that can happen unconsciously. It creeps up on you, or pounces, catching you seemingly unaware. When the notion of separation forms in one partner's mind, the divorce process has already started.

Some of our most powerful emotions dominate at this stage: anger, fear, hurt, and pride. It is essential that you acknowledge these feelings in yourself and/or your spouse as much as possible at the beginning rather than the end of the legal process. Reconciling what you *feel* with what you *want* from the divorce takes years for some people, but if you can begin by separating out your feelings from what you know to be fair, you are on the road to a successful divorce and a faster route toward a brighter future.

How Could This Be Happening to Our Family?

It is tempting to fight against the emerging realization that your marriage is over. You ignore what's happening between you. You insist that things go back to the way they were, or the way they "should" be. You protest. You threaten. You sulk. You cajole, criticize, pressure, browbeat, beg. You read books and magazines on the subject. You talk to family and friends. You go to counseling. You try this or that, alone or together. You keep wishing and thinking, "If only . . ."

The divorce may feel unreal at this stage. "How could this be happening?" . . . you ask yourself over and over. "Where did he, she, we, or I go wrong?" The shock, shame, and the rage you feel all make the idea of divorce hard to accept.

We all have periods in relationships that are less satisfying than others. The critical juncture isn't just feeling unhappy or out of sync with each other. It occurs when sacrifice stops happening reciprocally, so that one person believes he/she is doing far more of the giving and the compromising than the other person. Unhappiness reaches a critical point when a sense of hopelessness sets in, and one or both partners are not motivated to work at it. People who begin drifting toward divorce because they are disillusioned are in for a rude awakening, because divorce is often an infinitely greater disillusionment.

WHY ARE MY FEELINGS SO COMPLICATED?

Although some people approach divorce with obvious and uncomplicated relief, most people are more uncertain, moving alternately toward and away from divorce. This is a natural process. Your feelings are understandably ambivalent. You are torn for a variety of reasons, some obvious and some less so:

- Once-close families are torn apart
- Untangling your lives is complicated
- You must now share your children
- New relationships form
- You have continuing attachments to your spouse

You have time, love, and energy invested in this marriage. Your families know each other, and they may enjoy being an extended family. Perhaps you adore your brother-in-law. Or you finally have the father you always wished for in your father-in-law. Or you have been through some tough battles with your mother-in-law and have made your peace, the kind of resolution that brings with it a sense of accomplishment and acceptance. This is all hard to give up. And you do have to be ready to give it up. Some people stay close to their ex-spouse's family or friends, but the majority of people lose these close relationships. Some in-laws and friends do not know how to deal with the change, and they fade away. Others take sides. Still others remain neutral in theory, but succumb to pressure to support their family member by avoiding the ex-spouse.

Linda's family loved Carl and were dependent on him in a variety of ways, but they agreed to turn completely away from him in order to gratify Linda's need for revenge against him for leaving her. Understandably, Carl was confused and upset. He'd had such a good relationship with Linda's family, and their marital problems had nothing to do with the rest of her family. How could they ignore their amicable history? Why were they treating him this way now?

When children are involved, the choices are vastly more complicated. Do not underestimate the difficulty in sharing your children for many years as ex-spouses. You cannot predict how such sharing will work.

For some, the divorce is a wake-up call to change their behavior. For example, research shows that fathers who were less involved with their children before the divorce sometimes become more involved afterward, not to gain revenge or advantage, but because they realize they have so much to lose and the stakes are higher than they were in the security of the marriage. On the other hand, some men who were very involved with their children may become less so, because they are so hurt, because the divorce is so painful, because they become involved in new relationships that demand their attention, and for a host of other reasons. Whether the moms and/or the kids think the reasons are good or not, the fact is that you cannot predict how father-child relationships will change. And the same holds true for moms. Researcher Christy Buchanan and her colleagues found that, among teenage children, regardless of which parent the child spends more time with, the child who has close relationships with *both* parents is likely to feel closer to each of them (see page 345).

Sometimes people move away from a marriage as they become involved in a new relationship. Often the new relationship is an affirmation during a vulnerable time that you are lovable, fun, and sexy, contrary to how your spouse is treating you. It can be a chance to act on fantasies that were irresistible to think about, all but compelling action. After several months of an affair or an open relationship within a separation, the new relationship may begin to deteriorate. It was a bridge through a transition, but not a good choice for a long-term commitment.

For all of these reasons, it is natural to have conflicting feelings. Long after love fades away, attachments can continue. The dependency, the comfort of the familiar, as well as the memories all contribute to difficulty in letting go. Angry feelings often coexist with longing for the familiar spouse. It is not unusual to experience a flurry of intimacy with your ex-spouse, when you turn to each other sexually for some of the needs both of you have, to hold on to the past, or just to release some tension between you. While such activity is common, and natural, be aware that it can be very confusing. One of you can easily get hurt when you attribute more meaning to the intimacy than was intended, or sustainable. You may also experience guilt and renewed pain. You may sleep together one night and wonder bitterly what is wrong with you in the morning.

Greg and Pam had been separated for three months already, and Pam was seeing someone new whom she liked a great deal. Yet when Greg dropped off their two children, he stayed around to make sure they got off to their various sports practices and activities. Alone in the house afterward, Pam and Greg made love with deep emotion and wild abandon. Later, as Pam drove to her new boyfriend's house, she pulled to the side of the road and sobbed, overcome with guilt and confusion.

As you struggle with your ambivalence, your spouse will sense it and respond. He or she may be experiencing similar feelings. Perhaps your spouse's reaction will stay at the unconscious level, unexpressed underneath layers of denial and fear. Perhaps he or she will try to stall the progress of the divorce. Or perhaps your spouse will surprise you by going along with the divorce process, as he or she begins to anticipate the possibility of life outside of this marriage.

Being aware of your feelings gives you *options*. As you begin the legal process of divorce, you can make conscious decisions about how to handle it and yourself. You do not have to be a victim, a passive recipient of circumstances, or even the perpetrator of coldness and secrecy. Perhaps most significantly, you do not have to drown in your own bitterness. Such bitterness starts with a desire for repentance from your spouse and then punishment for him or her. But these feelings can end up hurting you, leaving your heart feeling smaller and stingier. Bitterness not only poisons your life; sadly, it can affect everyone you care about, so that they, too, have to distance themselves from your negativity. Your children are likely to experience your bitterness most acutely, deepening their own sense of loss with fear about how you are feeling and a desire to figure out what you need and provide it for you.

WHAT WILL MY FAMILY AND FRIENDS THINK ABOUT ME?

One of the first things people wonder about is "What will everyone else think? My mother, our friends, his family, the people next door?" While no one can make a decision for you or fairly judge your behavior, it remains human nature to worry about how a decision to divorce will affect other people's opinions about you. Some people will think you are doing something awful, and others will say, "I'm not surprised, we always thought you were taking too much crap from him" or, "She always seemed controlling and unstable. You couldn't be yourself with her, and your family missed who you used to be." Everyone will have something to say, and you can't please them all. Making a decision based solely on others' opinions, or ranking everyone's opinion as a way to fashion a decision for yourself is stressful and unproductive. In the end, it may be for naught. You cannot predict how people will react to the news you are divorcing, especially from their first declarations. Trust those you love, trust yourself, and allow time its healing powers.

How people will feel about your decision is often a product of *how* you divorce rather than *if* you divorce. Divorce unofficially begins when one spouse leaves or announces an intention to do so. Out of embarrassment, fear, or impetuousness, many people handle leaving poorly. How you handle the leaving stage is a major factor in how the rest of the divorce proceeds. Leaving or being left is one of the hardest things you will have to face in your lifetime. It takes great resolve, integrity, courage, and grace to manage it well.

One way people begin their divorce on the wrong foot is by leaving without adequate explanation, or under circumstances that cut off communication at a time when more, not less, is needed. You might feel that because you are not sure what to say, it will be better not to say the "wrong" things. If you are unsure about what to say, tell your husband or wife that you do not know exactly what you want to say or how to say it, but that you have made a decision to pursue your life separately. If your spouse doesn't seem to hear you, keep repeating yourself until you are heard, and keep on trying to make yourself understood. He or she may not see it your way, but can only begin to understand if you communicate what you have been feeling and how you hope to behave in this transition.

Another way people divorce poorly is that they manage the legal process in hostile or underhanded ways—hiding assets, engaging a ruthless attorney, or fighting tooth and nail in the legal system. The theory seems to be: Take what I can get now, and worry about what's fair later because if I leave it up to my spouse to be fair, I'll never get my share.

All of these ways of behaving may bring comfort in the short run, but hurt you over time. Resist at all costs. It may be painful to address the issues squarely, but in the end you can negotiate hard and bargain fairly, and come out ahead in terms of your mental health and well-being without sacrificing your financial security. Facing these challenges honestly will ensure your best chance of maintaining the respect of those around you, and will likely shorten the time it will take you to focus optimistically on the future. Since you will feel good about yourself, you will be freer to expect a positive future for yourself and your family.

THE NEXT STEPS

WHAT SHOULD I DO BEFORE LEAVING?

When you first decide to separate or divorce, some preparation can save time, money, and aggravation. Because you're thinking about the possibility of a divorce prior to the time it actually happens, you can do planning that will assure both partners' self-sufficiency and financial autonomy.

In many relationships, one partner has taken on the role of financial planner by paying the household bills and taking care of the family finances, and/or one partner has taken over most of the household responsibilities. As time passes, each partner becomes more entrenched in his or her role, and a divorce can present a real challenge to the spouse who is not in the financial role, just as it does for the spouse not in the primary child care role.

Identifying that you have become entrenched in a world that puts you in a financial prison is easy. The housewife who does not have a job, the house-husband with primary child rearing responsibilities, or the spouse who is employed at a much lower wage than the other spouse can face a real disparity in income and autonomy. If you are considering a divorce, it is important to get out of financial prison by finishing your education, updating your skills, taking steps toward a more advanced degree or training, and following other suggestions discussed in this chapter.

Your ability to support yourself means independence, and that you will not have to rely on the other spouse's payment habits. If you do not know how to manage a checkbook, budget, or pay your family bills, now is the time to learn. Look through your old tax returns and through the checkbook. Perhaps take over the bill paying responsibility yourself. Take a money management seminar at the local adult education program, or consult a financial planner to get a better understanding of your financial circumstances. Knowledge is power, and the more preparation you do in this area, the better prepared you will be for the day when you are living on your own.

Much of the legal advice in this book is designed to help you think ahead, but also to protect your interests in the worst circumstances. Despite your best efforts, both of you may say and do nasty things to each other during the divorce. It may have seemed unimaginable that either of you were capable of such things. Divorce creates a transient craziness in many people. You feel lonely, frightened, and perhaps more vulnerable than you have ever felt previously. In response to the intensity of these emotions, people do crazy things.

Entering the legal system often magnifies such feelings. People enter the system expecting fair and reasonable treatment, but once the legal process begins, their feelings may change. Attorneys become part of the process, and the bureaucracy of the courts involves even more people in an already complex situation. Because your life can seem suddenly out of your control, people become secretive in the divorce to gain an upper hand and to reestablish a sense of control. They feel they are protecting themselves, or their children. But in these situations, *less is more*. Actions that you think are protective can be provocative, signaling "I don't trust you!" to your spouse. Perhaps he or she deserves it, but perhaps not. Once you head down the path of distrust and self-protection at any cost, you are embarking on a much longer, wilder hike than you may have planned when you started.

Because the *legal* process of divorce is more about financial separation than about emotional or psychological resolution, this book will help you become familiar with your own property and the things you need to do to ensure a fair division. Any of the preparation tasks can be carried out openly or in secrecy. Secrecy often leads to a nasty divorce. While it is important to take stock of your property, doing so in secrecy can drive you and your spouse farther apart, and fuel feelings of anger and betrayal that distort the whole process. These feelings create an atmosphere of distrust that leads to more animosity, distrust, and anger . . . all of the emotions you would be wise to minimize. Preparation tasks should thus be tackled only after you have thought about the most decent way to accomplish them.

Ideally, the tasks discussed below would be accomplished in consultation with your spouse. Try to accomplish the tasks in the least adversarial manner. That does not mean discussing every action with your husband or wife. It means acting on your own behalf and informing the other. Be gentle if your relationship enables you to do so. If not, remain factual, and try to keep your emotions removed from the tasks at hand.

Here are some of the first things you'll need to do:

- Start financial record collecting
- Make an inventory of your household items
- Get a copy of your credit report and establish credit in your own name

- Consider closing joint credit card and bank accounts
- Open a post office box
- Think about your career plans
- Open your own checking account
- Investigate your health insurance situation

Start Financial Record Collecting

Many clients come into their lawyer's office with no idea what assets and debts they have, what their pension plans offer, or even where their tax returns are located in their home. Other clients *had* a good idea about the assets but a spouse stopped sharing financial information, or even removed records from the house and hid them. For your case, you'll need your financial information. Ideally, couples and their lawyers would freely share financial information; without cooperation, there are plenty of ways that a lawyer can obtain these documents from a spouse, a bank, or an employer, but that's both time consuming and expensive. With a little bit of planning, you can assemble these records yourself. In the case of a small account or a few bonds, it may not even be worth it to have your lawyer pursue the matter if you are unable to do so.

If you can locate your financial records, make copies of all documents you think you or your lawyer might need for the divorce. Some typical examples are: your pay stubs and your spouse's pay stubs; the last five years of tax returns; bank statements; credit card statements; brokerage account statements; stock and bond certificates; the closing statement and deed to your house; the 1098 mortgage statement that came with your last year's tax materials; and the addresses, telephone numbers, and account numbers of anyone to whom you owe money (credit cards, mortgage, personal loan, IRS). When in doubt, photocopy. You can always throw away copies you don't need, but you may not be able to remember where a bank account is located or how many savings bonds you have if you don't make copies.

Organize your copies into folders clearly labeled with the contents. It will be easier for you to do this than it will be for your lawyer; after all, you're the one who knows what each document represents. Organizing the

⚖

FINANCIAL RECORDS YOU'LL NEED

At least five years of tax returns: individual, business, gift tax

Personal property valued at over $350, with appraisals if available

Evidence of money owed to you or your spouse

Vehicles: title, registration, insurance

Stocks and stock options, bonds, mutual funds, brokerage margin accounts (account statements, stocks, bonds, limited partnership agreements, reports on investments)

Cash and bank accounts, such as checking, savings, safe deposit box

Life insurance (including cash surrender value)

Retirement plans: IRA, 401k, defined benefit pension plans, annuities (statements, plan documents)

Real estate addresses, including purchase information and appraisals, deeds, leases, tax assessments

Business interests: partnerships, sole proprietorship, corporate ownership

Miscellaneous other assets, such as lawsuits, patents, copyrights, trademarks, right to royalties

Evidence of debts: mortgage, credit cards, personal loans, car loans, tax liabilities

Any agreements between the two of you: prenuptial agreements, agreements to convert separate property into community property, and vice versa

Business records and employment agreements, particularly those related to ownership, assets, liabilities, income, and expenses

Loan applications, net worth statements, financing statements

Résumés (current and those prepared before litigation was initiated)

Personal and business bank statements and canceled checks

Trusts

Safety deposit box and vault records that reflect payment of lease, location of box or vault, and contents

Insurance records, including policies, applications, invoices, and beneficiary designations

Charge account records

Court record of cases in which you, your spouse, or your closely held business is or has been a party (including prior divorces)

Wills

Record of who has powers of attorney

records will take time, but it saves you money if you do it yourself. If you aren't sure what a particular record means, bring the copies to a lawyer or a financial consultant to figure out how they fit in your financial picture.

If after careful thought, you strongly believe that you cannot trust your spouse, put your copies in a safe place, like a parent's or a friend's home, or even your lawyer's office. The trunk of your car is not a safe or prudent place. Likewise under your bed. You don't want your spouse to find your stash of photocopied records, especially before you have had the chance to discuss your plans. If your spouse suddenly removes the original records from the house, you can calmly give your lawyer the copies you have stowed.

Some people are reluctant to start collecting records, which can hold up the divorce and anger the other partner. Ask yourself: Am I delaying to punish my spouse? If so, consider that you are also drawing out your own suffering. If you are delaying because the task seems overwhelming, break it down into small parts. Get help from an accountant; see the list provided of common types of financial sources (see page 40). Spend time becoming acquainted with the papers in your home or safety deposit box. If you do not have access to them, call the person who does (accountant, financial planner, lawyer) and ask for a lesson in managing the family finances.

Make an Inventory of Your Household Items

Be prepared for this process to consume you with ambivalence and grief. It is the first cold, hard accounting you are taking of what you have accumulated in your marriage. You are taking stock of the tangible fruits of your marriage, both sweet and bitter. You are dealing in dreams, some realized, some lost along the way. This is a good process to engage in while you are deciding whether you want to go through with divorce: dividing up your lives has a corporeal reality now, as well as the abstract one you've been mulling over in your head.

Once the divorce has become inevitable for either or both of you, make a detailed list of the property in your home. If you and your spouse can discuss these matters, decide which one of you will do this. Then have the other person check it and add any items he/she wishes. Append photos if you can, especially of the more valuable items. You'll be very happy to have those photos if your grandmother's silver mysteriously disappears after a big fight.

In the event that your spouse decides to move out unexpectedly (like when you are at work), the inventory will come in handy. If you are the one moving, you can use the list to sit down with your spouse and divide up the personal property.

Approximate values of items are always helpful, but be prepared for your spouse to disagree about what items are worth. Receipts are useful for giving the items material value, rather than a "guesstimate." In the unlikely event you are testifying in court about the items later, those values and photographs will be especially helpful.

Get a Credit Report

It is easy to obtain a credit report. It will show all of the charge accounts and loans for which you are responsible. It will also show those accounts on which you and your spouse are jointly liable. Knowing this information can help you:

- know whether you have credit, and if you do, whether it is good or bad
- know which of your credit accounts are joint with your spouse
- know all of your open credit accounts, even if they don't have balances due

There are several credit reporting agencies listed in the Appendix, page 340. The most popular one, which most credit card companies use, is Experian. You can contact Experian at:

Experian, NCAC
P.O. Box 2106
Allen, TX 75013-2106
888-397-3742
http://www.experian.com

There is sometimes a nominal fee (under $10) for a copy of your report. Along with the report you may request a credit dispute form. Use that to dispute any credit item that appears on your report and is erroneous. Experian will then investigate and respond to you within thirty days. Pursue this option, as even one late payment can affect your ability to get credit later.

One way to test whether or not you have credit is to apply for a credit card. If you are approved, chances are you have good, established credit; if you are declined, your denial letter will offer to have a credit report sent to you free of charge. Take advantage of this. Beware, however: multiple credit inquiries in a short period of time is one way to flag to potential loan sources that you are a credit risk. Credit bureaus keep track of the number of inquiries made for credit. If too many requests come to the bureau too quickly, you may appear to be a credit risk. Time your requests thoughtfully, and make no more than three requests every 90 days.

Establish Personal Credit or Preserve Good Credit

Whether or not you decide to divorce, it is very important to establish your own credit. All adults today need valid credit, and too many people use prior credit problems or housewife status as excuses for not having credit. This potentially hurts you in many ways, especially if you need to establish financial independence.

If you do not have any credit in your own name, establish credit immediately. You can do this by applying for one or two credit cards, or a small personal loan at a bank. A local department store where you shop may be a good way of establishing credit if you've never had credit before. Apply for a very small credit line with the store (or MasterCard or Visa, or whichever credit source you choose). Even if the credit line is only $100 or $200, it will be reported as *credit* to the credit bureau, and your timely payments will be reported as "good credit" irrespective of the maximum balance. A short letter accompanying the application explaining that you've never had credit before but are trying to establish credit in your own name may help your chances.

Your bank may have a credit card plan, and your ongoing relationship with the bank may encourage the bank to give you a credit card with a small credit line, especially if it's linked to your checking or savings account.

If you are having problems obtaining a credit card, you may apply for a secured card. With a secured card, you deposit the same amount of money you desire as a credit line, say $500, with a lending institution, and they give you a credit card with a $500 credit line. If you don't make your payments on time, the lending institution seizes your deposit to cover their losses. These cards report to credit bureaus, and can help you establish credit if there is no other way for you to do so.

For more suggestions about how to establish credit or manage money you may wish to consult your bank, a financial planner, or a book.

While you are establishing credit, your spouse might view this as a threat. Be prepared for questions.

If you already have good credit, you will want to preserve it. That may mean closing your joint accounts with your spouse, or making sure that those accounts are paid first. Joint liability on credit means that you and your spouse are *jointly and severally liable* for the outstanding balance on the account irrespective of who used the account. This means that the credit card company can sue either your or your spouse—the company's choice—for the entire balance! Although a divorce court judge may have the power to make one or the other of you pay the balance on the account, if your spouse is ordered by the judge to pay and fails to do so, that failure to pay will end up on *your* credit report *despite the court order.*

When you deal with credit lines, try to follow up every telephone call in writing. Keep a copy of the letter in case your account is not properly closed as requested.

If you don't feel comfortable closing your joint accounts, consider making payment in full on those accounts a higher priority than payment in full on other bills, *if* you think that your spouse may not pay his or her share of the joint accounts. Unfortunately, you may also have outstanding balances on your own accounts—and you are definitely obligated to pay them. This strategy is a balancing act, and you will need to decide how best to proceed. Your lawyer, therapist, financial advisor, or a knowledgeable friend can help you decide how to prioritize payment in your individual circumstances.

If you have bad credit, now is the time to address that problem. There are many ways to legally and effectively improve your credit. The Fair Debt Collection Practices Act and Fair Credit Reporting Act are the two main laws that protect you, and they provide for ways to correct incorrect information, and to have damaging information removed from your credit report. Your credit bureau can give you information about how to submit the necessary information to correct your credit report.

To dispute an item on your credit report, ask the credit bureau for a dispute form. Fill it out, and the bureau will investigate by contacting the reporting creditor asking for a response. The reporting creditor has thirty days to respond, and your credit report will be amended to reflect the dispute after the thirty days has passed. If the reporting creditor does not respond within thirty days, the disputed item will be removed.

Even if damaging information on your credit report is correct, you can add a statement to your file explaining why it isn't your fault. For example, if you cosigned a loan for a relative who failed to pay, your credit report will reflect that, but you can at least explain that you were not the person with primary responsibility for payment on the loan. These statements will then be sent with your credit report whenever it is requested. You may not be able to fix everything on your credit report, but you can begin to repair your credit.

Of course, the best way to fix bad credit is to pay off any unpaid bills, and keep current on new obligations.

Close Joint Bank Accounts

The designation of "joint" on a bank account means that either of you could take out all of the money, or that either of you could take out the maximum line of credit permitted by the joint account. Neither of you needs permission, a signature, or even notice from the other unless the account is designated "joint tenants with rights of survivorship"(JTROS). The most common JTROS accounts are stock and brokerage firm accounts. While not every spouse will seize money or run up credit cards as soon as the issue of divorce comes up, many will. Don't be caught off guard.

There are four basic ways to deal with joint accounts:

- Discuss closing the accounts with your spouse, and cooperate by dividing the money as agreed
- Don't discuss closing the accounts, but withdraw only half (or a fair portion) of the money, informing your spouse of your actions afterward
- Don't discuss closing the accounts, and withdraw all of the money immediately
- For JTROS accounts, write a letter to the bank or brokerage house requesting that the account be frozen and no monies released without both of your signatures on the request

Whenever possible, the safest route is to discuss closing accounts and work out a fair arrangement with your spouse. You can cooperate in doing this, and you can even go to the bank together. If you aren't able to discuss dividing the joint accounts with your spouse, it often makes sense to close the joint accounts yourself and put at least half of the money in a new account in your own name, leaving the rest in the old account for your spouse. You can always give all or part of the money back.

Many people are offended by the prospect of closing the joint accounts and putting some or all of the money in their own name. If you don't, however, you are at the mercy of your spouse, because he or she could seize all of the joint accounts at any time. There are valid reasons for removing all of the money from joint bank accounts and placing it all in your name. Examples: your spouse has a gambling habit, your spouse threatens to stop paying child or spousal support, your spouse has been controlling with money in the marriage, the money represents a gift made solely to you, or you are worried that your spouse would hide the money if given the opportunity. If you decide to withdraw all of the money and place it in your own name, be prepared to keep an accounting of every cent for the court. You are obligated to preserve that money, and not to spend it during the divorce unless absolutely necessary. Even if you could not tell your spouse of your plans to close accounts before doing so, let your spouse know afterward, including what you've done with the money. Don't fuel a feud by embarrassing your spouse with bounced checks.

This advice is critical from a legal perspective; it will protect you. But don't expect it to endear you to your spouse. Do not close accounts unilaterally unless it feels like your only option. Every action you take to protect yourself may be viewed as an antagonistic act. It undermines trust and enrages the party who chose not to close bank accounts in an effort to be decent. Do not make this decision lightly. Know whether your spouse can be trusted.

You will need your own checking account. Open your own account soon after making your decision to divorce, so you can order your checks and have the account established before any financial emergencies arise. If you have direct deposit into a joint checking account, have your direct deposit go to an account listed solely in your name. Remember, however, that your spouse may still be depending on you to contribute your share to a household account. Discuss how expenses will be shared before changing accounts, if possible.

Rent a Post Office Box and Establish a Private E-Mail Account

If you need to have confidential communications with anyone—bank, lawyer, financial institution, or friend—and you are afraid that your spouse will go through your mail, you need to rent a post office box or establish another mailing address. The $30 you spend on a post office box will be worth the peace of mind.

Stop using e-mail accounts that can be easily accessed and change your password. Too many times spouses unwittingly (or accidentally on purpose) allow their partners to find out information they didn't want known through an e-mail address. Computer literate spouses have been known to restore e-mail that has been deleted from an unsuspecting spouse's computer. If an e-mail is truly private, be mindful to keep it that way.

Consider whether you are taking a cowardly way of exiting your marriage by ignoring the possibility that your spouse will find out about your negative feelings or illicit behaviors through your private mail, e-mail, or other method. Many people secretly hope to be found out because they cannot face telling their partner the marriage is over, that they are having an affair, discovered they are gay, or are considering a job in another state. Telling your partner about your readiness to divorce is exceedingly difficult, but you owe it to your spouse and your children to be direct and honest about your feelings or plans. You would be devastated if the same thing happened to you, and it is more difficult to cope with a divorce when your sense of the person, the relationship, and the reality around you are shattered simultaneously. Ultimately, such behavior is likely to cost you financially, as the other person will no longer trust you and will insist that all actions be examined by an attorney.

Think About Your Career Plans

Unless you are independently wealthy, or you already have a salary that's enough to support yourself and/or your family with less than optimal help from your spouse, you need to get your career plans in order. You can't risk being unable to support yourself adequately after the divorce, even if you can expect to receive alimony and/or child support. Sometimes, people refuse to pay support amounts set by a judge despite court orders, and sometimes they aren't ordered to make support payments at all. You need to be prepared for all of these scenarios. Divorces can be startling in their expense. Keeping up two families is not one plus a little, it is two of everything or double what you need now.

If education is an issue because you don't have a high school diploma, didn't finish college, need to update your skills, or you have let a professional license lapse, now is the time to get busy. After the divorce starts in earnest, it will be much harder to begin, and you may have a hard time concentrating on school.

Ideally, if you've been out of the job market for a while you will receive enough money from your spouse to ease your transition back into your career. This happens very rarely in practice. Either the family doesn't have enough money for this to happen, your spouse disappears or doesn't pay, or your education or career move takes much longer than expected. There are other reasons to start now:

• Alimony orders are lower than they used to be, and for shorter periods of time.

• On the other side of the coin, alimony payments may require you to make more money than you do now.

• Unless you have a disability, the judge will expect you to try to support yourself and/or your children fully at some point, with that point determined by the length of your marriage.

• It will be easier to structure a settlement that includes tuition or retraining if you're already enrolled in a program.

• The court will be impressed that you are trying to support yourself, even if you can't do so immediately.

Fifteen or twenty years ago, lifetime alimony awards for housewives were commonplace. Not so anymore. Women are expected to work, even if they cannot support themselves fully. Several states have abolished alimony entirely. And, with changing sex roles, it is not that unusual for men to put their careers on hold for children and other responsibilities that would have previously been considered to be women's work. Nowadays, some men are awarded alimony, as well as child support, when they are awarded custody of children. This is happening more and more frequently. It is no longer a phenomenon only in liberal or progressive states, such as California.

Lifetime alimony orders were also common in fault situations in the past. Perhaps a housewife's husband had an affair with his secretary, and that is the reason the marriage broke down. Twenty years ago, that would have meant a huge alimony order. Not so anymore. Alimony is now based on the spouse's ability to pay, as well as the needs of the recipient (among other factors). Lifetime alimony is not only awarded less often, but usually only in circumstances where people have been married thirty years or longer.

In addition, the economic reality for most families is that maintaining two households will necessitate two incomes, even if one is smaller than the other. There simply isn't enough money to go around, no matter how deserving the recipient.

How to think about your career plans and what to do

If you have been thinking about reentering the workforce, you will want to do so as soon as possible. Brush up your résumé, update your wardrobe, and research job prospects. If you have been thinking about changing careers, make those moves before you discuss a divorce with your spouse. A court is less likely to upset your plans if you have already started.

For example, assume that you have been thinking about getting divorced but need to finish your college degree. You enroll in school and finish two semesters, but have two semesters left to complete. The chances that a judge will order your spouse to pay the remaining tuition are much better than your prospects of obtaining future tuition monies from your spouse for a college in which you have not yet enrolled. A clear plan can make all the difference.

Some people, especially those who've been out of the job market for several years, experience a sense of panic and concern regarding the financial future when they realize that they will need to be responsible for their own household. If you have not worked for several years, you may think about going back to your previous field. On the other hand, this is your chance to change careers if you're interested in doing something new, or if you find your old skills are hopelessly outdated.

Be creative in your thoughts regarding your career future. Low-paying jobs are going to be just as easy to obtain in six months or a year from now as they are today. Don't rush into a decision you'll regret later. Rather than assuming you will need to go back to work in a bank, retail sales, or another career that you left many years ago, begin to think about interests or activities that you have developed over the course of the marriage. The examples below help to illustrate this point:

Steve knew that he could not take the stress of his job as a department store manager for the next thirty years, until he retired. He'd always wanted to finish law school, but had only completed one year because he and Julie had gotten married when she became pregnant. His failure to realize his career goals had never stopped bothering him. Julie encouraged him to go back to school, but there had never been the time or money. When he realized that his marriage was shaky, and that in the event of a divorce, he'd never have enough money to support his family and retire at fifty-five, as he dreamed, he decided to apply to finish school.

This strategy made sense both for him and for Julie and the children, because although it would mean an initial sacrifice of earnings in the short run, once he finished school and got a job, they would all be better off. At the outset, this kind of cooperation and joint planning may seem impossible in the face of a failing marriage, but if you are able to work together to maximize your total income and assets, the end result will be much more favorable, and stable, than if you spent your time and money squabbling in court rather than paying tuition.

Susan's story may also help get you started in this new way of thinking about yourself.

Susan had been the primary caretaker of her three children, ages eleven, nine, and eight. Now that the children were older, and she had a little more time to herself, she began to realize that her marriage was falling apart but that she had no idea where to begin to build a new life. She had been out of the job market for so many years and knew so little about her and Ed's finances that she didn't really know what the future would hold.

She decided that she would like to finish college, and had two years to go after her previous, premarital, college credits were transferred. She found out from the college how much it would cost to finish her social work program, how long it would take, and when she could expect to be available for the children.

She also took some time to sort through tax returns and financial documents so that she could better understand the family finances. She was able to copy the documents without explaining all of her plans to her husband until she was ready.

As Susan educated herself and enrolled to finish school, she learned more about what her future might be like, what the possible division of assets would be, and what she would be able to count on receiving as part of the divorce. As a result of her research, she decided to wait a year before filing for divorce. Since she had already established herself in school chances were much better that she would be awarded the tuition money to finish than if she hadn't made these plans in advance.

In Susan's case, planning helped her gain self-confidence and a new career. Her financial research enabled her to feel comfortable about her ability to support herself with the assets from the divorce as well as her income. Her patience paid off.

⚖️

DAY CARE CONSIDERATIONS

The high cost of day care can undermine both your salary and child support orders. A poor choice of day care can also undermine your career progress. Part of your planning needs to include quality, cost-effective day care options as well as backup care for snow and sick days.

Mary Jane is another success story.

Mary Jane had been married for seventeen years and had four children. She had not worked since the birth of her first child. During the marriage she had developed an interest in interior decorating, color, and design. She had provided her husband and her family with a home that was warm, cozy, and comfortable. Her friends admired her sense of taste and design. Realizing that there would not be sufficient financial assets to maintain her lifestyle after her divorce, she enrolled in a local college, taking courses in interior design part-time. She applied for a job in a home furnishing design center. This enabled her to develop a talent that she had into a career that she thoroughly enjoyed.

Investigate Your Health Insurance Coverage Availability

Health care coverage is a critical issue and you need to know what your available coverage is as soon as possible. Many spouses are covered through their partners' insurance. This is a critical issue at divorce time because continuation of coverage for adults under their spouses' plan can be expensive and limited.

Typically, the spouse with the best coverage will continue to cover the children after the divorce. It is extremely tempting to make this issue one about power and control. Parents fight to have the coverage so that they are not subject to the other person's control over the reimbursements, or they fight not to have control because "she has custody, it should be her responsibility" or "he can do it as child support." These issues divert attention away from what your children need. Better to get your children into the best long-term plan, and then work out details about reimbursement procedures.

If you have coverage available through your own employer

Find out when you can sign up for health coverage, and how long you have to wait before your coverage becomes effective. Find out if the company has a waiting period for preexisting conditions, and its length. Find out what your coverage is, what kinds of care will and won't be insured, and how much the premiums will cost.

If there is a long waiting period for coverage or for preexisting conditions to be covered, sign up as soon as possible, if you can afford to do so. If coverage is very expensive, you may want to wait until a few months before your case is finalized before you sign up.

If you do not have insurance available to you through your employer

If you don't have other coverage available to you, find out how long you can stay on your spouse's insurance plan after the divorce. You can continue your spouse's employer-provided insurance through a federal law called COBRA. If you need to sign up for COBRA coverage (currently provided for a maximum of three years) investigate how much it will cost. COBRA coverage is the same coverage that you now receive from your spouse's employer, only the employer doesn't pay the premium after the divorce is finalized. Either you or your spouse must pay the COBRA premiums if you elect to take COBRA coverage. Often these costs are high. Figure out whether the coverage will be worth it, or whether you can procure a comparable policy at a cheaper price. Ask a lawyer or human resources personnel if state laws will permit you to stay on your spouse's insurance longer than COBRA permits.

For your children

Decide which parent has the most comprehensive health care coverage. Some insurance plans allow children to stay covered longer than others, for example, until the child turns twenty-five years old. Covering your children under *both* plans, if both you and your spouse have coverage, can also be cost-effective. Know what kinds of coverage are available, and do your best to decide jointly what is best for the children's health.

Some employers provide medical coverage for children free of cost, and others require such a small contribution toward the premium that insuring your children under both your and your spouse's policies may be less expensive than insuring them under one policy and paying the deductible or co-pay expenses.

When children are covered under two policies, typically you will submit bills and expenses to the primary policy (determined by each policy's provisions). The primary policy will process the claim. Any uninsured or unreimbursed expense can then be submitted to the secondary policy, which will typically pay any remaining amount. Therefore, if you can cover the children on two policies inexpensively, you may save money, especially if your children have chronic conditions which require ongoing treatment.

Another advantage of keeping the children on two separate policies is that if one of you loses your medical coverage, the children still have medical insurance in place. You won't have to wait for an open enrollment period in order to sign them up for coverage with the second policy, and their ongoing conditions won't be "pre-existing medical conditions" subject to an initial waiting period for coverage.

WHAT IF I CAN'T MOBILIZE MYSELF TO DO THIS PLANNING?

Sometimes when you know that a divorce is inevitable, yet feel you cannot face all the preparation that starting the process will take. You procrastinate and postpone. Consider these possibilities:

1. You are afraid to start the process, because you are not emotionally ready.

If this is the case, take a step back and spend time with yourself, family, or a professional to evaluate whether you need more time to give the relationship another chance. Ambivalence is natural at early stages of separation, so don't rush this phase. A divorce with children involved does not end the spousal relationship but changes it, requiring a different form of parental entanglement until the children are grown (and beyond!). Think until you have no doubts about your decision. Err on the side of taking time to prepare yourself and your loved ones; it may feel like wasted time, but it will ease the transition.

2. You are afraid of your partner's anger once he/she finds out.

Ask yourself what is your greatest fear. If it is hurting your spouse, know that there is no way to divorce without causing pain. However, think of the pain you have each endured to bring you to this point. Write down what to say and how to say it so that you will be as kind as possible when you inform your spouse of your decision. This will begin to free you both from the angers and hurts of the marriage so that you may lead a happier life. If you just can't stand to make *anyone* unhappy, especially your spouse, get professional assistance from a pastor, rabbi, or counselor to examine whether such inclinations are undermining your ability to act in your own best interests.

If your spouse has a problem with anger, and berates or hurts you when he or she feels vulnerable, refer to Chapter 10 of this book to take precautions to protect yourself and your children from abuse.

3. You have no idea how to proceed because you do not know or understand your family finances.

If possible, begin to take an interest in your financial affairs and have your spouse teach you what he/she knows. Be explicit about wanting financial independence for both of your sakes. If you cannot talk to your spouse, make an appointment with your attorney, accountant, or financial advisor and have your assets explained to you. Such persons will probably be named on your taxes, wills, or their names will be found in an address book at home. If you have a friend or family member whom you trust to understand your finances and not to inflame the divorce, ask that person to give you a lesson in reading and understanding your documents.

4. You are too depressed to proceed in the planning phase.

Do not try to manage this alone. Get yourself support and advice from trusted friends or from professionals. Join a divorce support group if you can find one, with a positive focus, but beware that some groups are full of bitter men and women who lead you down an adversarial path in the name of helping you. Their experience is not yours—not yet.

Once you have evaluated what is preventing you from acting, get back to business. Many journeys seem daunting at the beginning, but preparing yourself and maintaining a sense of readiness support you for the rest of the climb.

PERSONAL ASSESSMENT

This section, in Chapters 2 to 12, is a chance for you to check your progress. Ask yourself:

- Have I thought through my own or my spouse's reasons for wanting a divorce? Am I taking adequate responsibility for how my actions contributed to where we are now? If I maintain a balanced view of the divorce, even through my distrust and anger, then I am more likely to get my spouse to act in reasonable ways.
- Have I been careful not to let my anger lead me to trash my partner with family and friends with whom he or she was close? Have I found ways to begin letting people know how unhappy we were or are now, without needing to vilify our whole life together? If I do not present myself as embittered and my spouse as the villain, I will maintain greater support and I can call on family and friends to help when things get heated between us.
- Have I thought enough about my career options for the future? Am I headed in a direction that will enable me to support myself and my children to the maximum extent possible? I should be thinking beyond teaching my spouse a lesson, using this time to enhance my skills and opportunities to pursue meaningful employment now or in the future when my children are older. If I am the primary breadwinner and I am considering a career change, I must set up my life so that I can take care of my own needs without neglecting those of my children.

- Have I taken careful stock of our family assets and household possessions, cataloging them in order to create a fair division with less room for "he said, she said" in a void of facts or concrete information? I want to be reasonable and fair and receive the same treatment from my spouse.

- Have I collected all the information I need about our financial situation, so that I can negotiate from a fully informed position? Have I learned what I need to know about our family finances and how they have been managed? The more I know, the better armed I am to protect myself and my family, and to contribute to creative solutions for complicated economic issues. Knowledge has great preventive power against making decisions based on emotional needs, especially transitional emotions such as fear and anger.

3.

Making the Initial Decisions: Charting Your Own Course

On any trip, once you have decided where you are going, you then assemble what you need to take, and decide whether you'll need a guide to steer you in the right direction. The "gear" required for your divorce journey includes legal and financial information. Whether you need an advisor or counselor depends on the complexity of your situation and how well your spouse and you can work together. The type of guide will depend upon the difficulty of the trip and your familiarity with the territory.

WHAT ARE MY LEGAL OPTIONS FOR ENDING A RELATIONSHIP?

You have several options for legal ways to end your marriage. We will refer to divorce, legal separation, and annulment simply as "divorce," but typically the same rights and responsibilities apply to each.

Divorce

Divorce is a full and final settlement of your property and money issues. A divorce also resolves custody and access to both parents for children. Typically divorce judgments stand as final decrees, meaning that they cannot later be modified except under special circumstances. Those parts of

HOW TO LEARN THE LAWS IN YOUR STATE

There are many ways to learn about the laws in your state:

- Consult a knowledgeable family lawyer on an hourly basis
- Visit your local law library, public library, or law school library
- Martindale-Hubbell, a legal publication that lists lawyers by geographic area and specialty, also contains a digest of each state's laws. These books can be found at most local libraries as well as law libraries and online.
- Check the Internet: A huge database of legal topics can be found at Cornell Law School's legal research site, found at http://www.law.cornell.edu. For a direct link to the law of each of the fifty states, check out http://www.secure.law.cornell.edu/topics/Table_Divorce.htm.
- Many local bar associations and court clerk's offices maintain a list of state-specific and local resources, as well as not-for-profit divorce assistance organizations
- Consult with your local Legal Aid Society

the decree pertaining to children will always be modifiable as the circumstances change for the children. It is extremely unusual for property decisions to be revisited by the court.

The only situations in which the property divisions will not be final are: (1) either or both of you have made a fraudulent misrepresentation about your assets, in which case the judgment may be reopened; (2) the case is appealed and is remanded for a new trial, which only happens if the judge made a serious error; or (3) you and your spouse specifically reserve the authority for the court to reconsider an item in the divorce at a later time. Examples of when the court may retain authority are: to review a court order for division of pension assets, or for disputes that may arise in connection with the sale of a home. In order for the court to retain jurisdiction over these matters, the judgment must specifically delineate that these matters may be revisited. If it does not say so, the court will not retain jurisdiction and settled matters are permanent.

At the end of a divorce, your marriage is dissolved, and you are free to remarry.

Legal Separation

Some states still provide for legal separation, which is a legal decree that falls someplace between getting divorced and staying married. The court will make orders about alimony, support, and asset division, but you are not divorced at the end of the process. You are, therefore, not free to re-marry. This is a potential solution for those people who do not wish to live as a married couple, but for religious, health care, or other reasons do not consider divorce an option. It often enables spouses to stay on each other's health insurance. Under certain circumstances, you may also be able to in-herit from one another's estates, should one of you die while you are legally separated.

Typically, legal separation orders may be converted to a divorce at the request of either spouse, or revoked at the joint request of both spouses. The orders can be used to formalize a separation period while you make up your minds about whether to get divorced.

Many people ask if a legal separation is necessary before a divorce can be finalized. In most states, the answer is "no," but a notable exception is New York, which requires that parties live apart for at least a year before a divorce can be granted. Most other states have a waiting period require-ment (three months to a year), but not a physical separation requirement.

You may separate without filing in court for a legal separation, and you do not need the blessing of the court to do so. You may wish to establish temporary orders for child support, alimony, and use of assets during a sep-aration if you and your spouse are unable to negotiate these things your-selves. To do so, you must file papers in the court requesting these orders. This is typically done in either a divorce or legal separation, but court help is also available in informal separation situations.

A physical separation is not the same as a "legal separation." A legal separation is a specific court order that is made after filing papers with the court. A physical separation may be done informally, by one spouse simply moving out. In a legal separation, the court has the right to oversee your case, to make and enforce orders about how the separation will work.

Annulment

There are two types of annulments: religious and legal. A religious annulment is handled through your religious institution, and is usually unrelated to the legal process by which your marriage is dissolved. Therefore, it's possible to be legally divorced, yet eligible for a religious annulment. Check with your religious institution about the requirements to have your marriage annulled.

Eligibility for a legal annulment is very rare. Each state has its own criteria. Being married only for a short period of time is usually not sufficient to qualify. If you think you qualify for an annulment, you will need to find out the exact circumstances under which your state permits this procedure. Examples of circumstances that may warrant an annulment: you or your spouse were not legally divorced from a prior spouse (irrespective of whether you were aware of this problem) and you remarry; your spouse fraudulently induced you to marry promising children, and you find out that he or she is incapable of having children; or, you are married to a close blood relative. Simply finding out that your spouse is gay or a drug addict does not qualify for an annulment in most states. Thus, annulments are available only for specific, rare circumstances.

If an annulment is granted, your marriage is considered legally never to have happened. It's as if the court travels back in time and prevents the marriage from happening. Although the court may make orders concerning alimony, child support, and asset division similar to a regular divorce case, with an annulment you may represent yourself as "never married" because you haven't been legally married.

WHAT ARE MY OPTIONS FOR DIVORCE REPRESENTATION?

In most states, there are several options:

• *Pro se* or *in pro per* **divorce**: you can handle the divorce yourself, without the help of an attorney, or hire an attorney only to review your settlement but not to represent you in court

• **Mediation:** you can use a mediator or arbitrator to settle the case, and either file *pro se* or hire an attorney to file the papers, review the settlement, and escort you to court for the final uncontested court judgment

• **Hiring an attorney:** you can hire an attorney to represent you in court, from start to finish

You can use any or all three of these methods in any combination. These days, many people represent themselves or settle cases in mediation rather than hiring an attorney. As attorney fees rise and court case loads allow less and less time for each case, many people find that settling the matter between themselves saves time, money, and aggravation.

Pro Se . . . On My Own

You aren't required to hire a lawyer to handle your case. Filing a divorce without the help of a lawyer is called *pro se* or *in pro per,* which is Latin for "on my own." If you don't have children or issues such as alimony or property settlement in dispute, filing a *pro se* divorce can be an effective and economical way to end your marriage. Although you can file without a lawyer, the court will hold you to the proper procedures for filing a divorce. You must follow each of the court's rules and procedures exactly, so it's important to educate yourself about the process.

If you have questions about your rights, tax ramifications of property settlement, or you are in an unequal bargaining position with your spouse, you should consult with an attorney. You don't necessarily need to hire an attorney, but you do need to be informed about what you're entitled to have after the divorce is finished. This advice needs to come from a qualified professional—not your spouse, a neighbor, or a divorced coworker. Guilt, confusion, and feelings of powerlessness can lead you to make poor decisions, and divorce decisions will be with you the rest of your life. It's worthwhile to at least consult with a qualified professional. A lawyer can tell you the pros and cons of using an attorney or filing *pro se* in your particular case, to help you decide whether or not an attorney is necessary. And, if you decide during your *pro se* divorce case that you need an attorney's help, you can hire an attorney at any time before your case is concluded.

If, after consultation, you decide that a lawyer is not necessary, you can learn how to file a divorce on your own. The court clerk's office can help, and many community groups offer seminars on filing your divorce. There are "do it yourself" divorce books in each state. Select a book that is written specifically for your state's laws and procedures, as they vary from state to state. You can find these books through your local courthouse clerk's office, your courthouse's law library, a local law school's library, your local bookstore, or the Internet. Although the exact procedures vary across states, they all follow the same basic steps from start to finish, which are outlined in Chapter 4.

Mediation

Mediation is designed to help you and your spouse resolve issues without having to involve a court in your decision-making process. It can save money, time, and hurt feelings. If you want to do your divorce without hiring a lawyer, you may want to consider mediation. Many lawyers are "mediation friendly," meaning that they will cooperate with your mediator and keep the court process to a bare minimum while you work through your divorce.

Mediation is becoming increasingly popular as a method for resolving disputes concerning custody, asset division, and child support. In addition to saving money, time, and stress, it allows families to fashion their own court orders tailored to their unique circumstances. Because there are not immediate court pressures to resolve the case, mediation sessions can be scheduled at your convenience. And, if you want more information about a specific topic, such as taxes or your children's visitation needs, you can bring an accountant or psychologist into your mediation session.

Research indicates that it is a cheaper, faster, and less adversarial way to approach the end of a marriage or a custody negotiation compared to court intervention. It also tends to result in fewer returns to court for modifications after divorce. Most parties report high satisfaction with the process, and despite myths to the contrary, it is not more advantageous for either women or men. Partners who opt for mediation tend to select joint legal custody more often than spouses who utilize the court system, partly because of how well the partners got along to begin with, partly because of a slight bias among mediators toward joint custody, and partly because mediation helps parents learn to communicate. Mediation can be handled in a variety of forums, with a variety of professionals assisting.

Basically, a trained mediator acts as an impartial third party and assists in reaching resolution on relevant issues in the divorce. The mediator serves as a master communicator, referee, and problem solver, working to balance both parties' interests and to assist them in reaching fair decisions. A mediation need not resolve every issue: you can choose to consult a mediator to resolve custody and visitation issues, but not asset division. Or, you could decide to mediate asset division, but not child support and alimony. Mediation helps narrow the focus of the problems and lets you resolve what you can prior to court intervention. Even if you are only partially successful in mediation, the process enables you to keep much of the divorce in your own hands.

How Do I Find, Choose, and Use a Mediator?

Typically, both parties will jointly choose a mediation service. This may be a therapist, a lawyer, or both. Who you select depends upon the issues you wish to mediate. Issues about children are often best mediated by a mental health professional, while economic issues may best be mediated by an attorney. Both attorneys and therapists may be trained to mediate all issues, but be careful to select a professional based on experience and expertise. Mediation training isn't licensed or regulated in all states, and the title "mediator" may be used irrespective of one's background or training.

Ask a lawyer or mental health professional you trust for recommendations, look in the yellow pages, or call the Academy of Family Mediators (781-674-2663) for a list of members in your state.

Ask questions to determine if the mediator's style fits your needs and if he or she is qualified to mediate your case.

1. What is your style of mediation? Do you see couples separately or together? How long do you expect a typical mediation to take?

2. How many mediations have you performed? How long have you been a mediator?

3. Have you been through any special training? What kind of training have you had, in addition to state or board mediation certification? (mental health, child expertise, family law experience, economic expertise in matters of real estate, investments, pensions, specific tax knowledge).

4. If the mediator is a therapist, how does he or she keep up with the law? Is the mediator affiliated with a lawyer or group of lawyers? If the mediator is a lawyer, does he or she understand the psychological implications and dynamics of negotiating a divorce? Given that lawyers are professionally trained to argue, how has the mediator overcome that original bias? Is he or she affiliated with a therapist or therapy groups?

5. How do you work with spouses who retain individual attorneys?

6. What is the initial fee, are phone calls billed and charged, what is the hourly rate, and is there a retainer? Who is responsible for paying? Is there a special division of fees if one spouse calls without the other's knowledge? If either of you wishes to cease the mediation process, how will that be handled?

7. What does the mediator recommend if the mediation process breaks down?

8. How are other referrals made to professionals such as accountants, individual therapists, and attorneys?

9. How is confidentiality handled?

10. Is the mediator willing to testify in court under any circumstance? Is there a written agreement as to whether or not the mediator may testify, so that there are no misunderstandings?

The mediator typically will contract for a certain number of sessions, or a specific time period. A fee will be determined and set, and usually billed by the hour. Both parties should be encouraged to speak with a lawyer so that they each understand the legal options available, and whether or not the mediation is proceeding in a way that is fair for him or for her.

Once the agreement, or partial agreement, is finalized, both parties are encouraged to have a lawyer review it, and formalize it for the court to review and approve. Be cautious about agreeing to a mediated settlement that is not examined by an attorney. Some mediators accept the parties' decisions without informing them about the settlement's unfairness to either party. Whether it is best to reach an uncontested settlement or to have an agreement that is beneficial to both parties in the long-term is a matter of personal preference, but it is one that should be carefully considered to avoid regrets at a later date.

An uncontested divorce date is set, both parties appear in court, the judge reviews and approves the agreement. If the judge does not approve the agreement, then it's back to the mediator, or a review with an attorney, but typically mediated agreements are approved by the court without modifications.

In the past twenty years, more and more courts have set up alternative dispute resolution procedures. Family Relations Offices, Mediation Services, Judicial Pretrial Procedures, Conciliation Services, and special mediation programs exist throughout the country to help divorcing couples resolve their disputes outside of court. Oftentimes these programs are free of charge, or operate on a sliding scale, and may be an alternative to private mediation services.

How Do I Find, Choose, and Use a Lawyer?

Some people prefer to use a lawyer in their divorce case. Aside from preference, it's best to be represented by a lawyer from start to finish in your case if you have unresolved custody issues, or if you do not have equal bargaining power with your spouse. An example of this is a spouse who has been dominated or abused by the other spouse. If threats figure into your marriage, you'll probably need a lawyer in your divorce.

Most people fall someplace between not needing a lawyer at all, and needing to have a lawyer handle the entire case. It's always a good idea to be informed about your legal rights, and an initial consultation with a divorce lawyer is typically either free or reasonably priced. It's worth it to find out your state's child support laws, position on alimony, tax ramifications of your possible asset division and support scenarios, and factors that determine property division. You can consult with several lawyers to get several opinions.

You could also find a lawyer who would be willing to review a l̶ agreement or mediation proposal, and to discuss the concrete terms with you in the context of what you are entitled to under your state's laws, on an hourly basis rather than representing you fully. Of course, such a lawyer will not be as intimately familiar with your individual circumstances as he or she would be if representing you throughout your case, but an ongoing consultation relationship with a lawyer will keep you abreast of the laws and general considerations that affect you. You can then supplement this information with research on your own, or with an accountant.

You may also wish to hire a lawyer to represent you fully while you pursue different negotiation alternatives. This is a popular divorce attorney/client relationship because it keeps you under the protection of an attorney, yet it allows you to try and resolve your case on your own to the extent you can do so. As issues are resolved outside of the attorney's office, you can discuss the agreements with your attorney to be sure that they're fair given your particular circumstances and the law that applies to your case. If you intend to pursue mediation or other out-of-court settlement methods with your spouse, be clear with your lawyer that you don't want conflicts to escalate in court unless absolutely necessary. Oftentimes clients feel more comfortable having an attorney "on retainer" so that they can call and ask questions, make appointments, or have court papers filed upon request, without having to reestablish a relationship each time a service is needed.

How to Find the Right Lawyer

Among the many qualified family lawyers in your community, choosing the right lawyer for your particular circumstances is crucial. In most states, the family laws are not terribly complicated, but the details of how those laws might apply to you and your individual family situation can get tricky. Although many lawyers who are general practitioners do a fine job with divorces, your best bet is to hire a lawyer who specializes in family law. That person is more likely to be up-to-date on the most recent changes in the law, tax ramifications, the finer points of your states' divorce laws, as well as the personalities of the judges and courthouse personnel in your

at person will spend most of his or her time in domestic
nces of having your matter expedited are improved be-
nay be more available to you. Although the law itself
ely few pages in the law books, tricky issues such as
whether an inheritance or gift from your family is a marital asset, how best
to handle disputes pertaining to children, and how to divide up assets such
as pensions are best handled by the specialist practitioner.

Your local bar association has a lawyer referral service. You could also
ask your therapist or accountant for a referral. If you know a lawyer, ask
him or her for a referral. Lawyers tend to know who among them is the
most talented, and most will refer you to someone they respect. Speak to
friends or family members who have gone through a divorce for referrals.
Remember, however, that the way that person reacted to the process may
influence whether he or she gives a lawyer a good review.

What should you be looking for in a lawyer? Obviously, you want to
select a lawyer who knows as much as possible about family law in your
state. The manner in which the lawyer conducts the interview will tell you a
great deal about that, but do ask questions:

1. How long have you been practicing in this state? What portion of
your practice is family law? How do you keep current on changes in the
law, taxes, and emerging issues like stock options?

2. What is your policy on returning telephone calls, fees, and billing?
How much will it cost?

3. How long will this take? What is the basic process?

4. How is support determined? What if we can't resolve custody or visitation?

5. How do you feel about working with mediators?

6. What percentage of your cases are resolved without having to go to
trial? If the lawyer tells you that more than 5 percent of his or her cases end
up in a trial, beware. A good, ethical lawyer is able to settle most cases.

Have a list of questions ready to ask your lawyer at the initial appointment. Pay attention to how your lawyer responds to your questions. Does
he or she treat your inquiries with respect? Do you get a complete answer in
terms that you understand? If he or she doesn't know the answer, does the

lawyer admit it, and offer to get back to you—and does he or she follow through? The way in which the lawyer responds tells you a great deal about how the lawyer operates, and how you'll be treated as your case goes on.

Choose a lawyer who is responsive to your questions and needs. Divorce is a very personal process. You will live with the choices that you make in your case. Your lawyer will not. A good lawyer is also a good listener, explainer, advocate, negotiator, and barometer of the pros and cons of the decisions you'll have to make in your case. If a lawyer doesn't have time or patience to answer your questions or to explain the legal process to you, then you shouldn't hire that person.

Don't Let Fear Guide Your Choice and Use of Your Lawyer

Divorce is one of the top three stressors people encounter in life. In an attempt to protect yourself, it can be tempting to choose an aggressive lawyer to protect you. There are various ways of being aggressive, however. Some are constructive and some are not. Positive lawyers are known for being fierce advocates and paying attention to all details, yet advocating for settlement and compromise at the same time. Negative lawyers are known for being aggressive, and not settling a case. They've built a reputation on being difficult with opposing clients, other attorneys, and even judges. People flock to them to protect themselves, or to seek revenge. Few of these people stop to ask how the families who have used such an attorney have fared a few years after the divorce. Know the informal reputation of the lawyer you choose.

Using Your Lawyer Constructively

Fees

When you telephone to make an appointment to meet with an attorney, ask if there is a charge for the initial consultation and be prepared to pay at the appointment if there is a charge. In many communities, free initial consultations are a thing of the past for experienced divorce practitioners. One of the reasons for this is that the initial appointment can often last an hour or more, depending on how many questions you ask and how much you need to tell the lawyer at first blush. In addition, once you have consulted with the lawyer, the lawyer cannot then represent your spouse because it would present a conflict of interest for the lawyer.

Often, less experienced practitioners will not charge an initial consultation fee, or even a retainer fee. In some cases, that's because they have not built up a clientele, and would like to encourage business. In other cases, they are simply less qualified. It's hard to know whether a novice is going to do an extra good job on your case to develop a good reputation and encourage referrals, or whether the less experienced lawyer simply won't know enough to handle your case effectively. That's why it helps to get references from friends, family, other lawyers, and the local bar association.

Once you have hired a lawyer, ask for a written fee agreement. Most states require that this be done, but even if it's not required, it helps to have it in writing how much money you can expect to pay. Read this agreement carefully before you sign it. Your lawyer should also send you a monthly itemized bill so that you can keep track of your retainer, and the amount of time your lawyer is spending doing different tasks associated with your case.

If you have hired the lawyer on a flat-fee basis, meaning that you pay one fee for the lawyer to handle the case from beginning to end, the agreement should state what will be covered by the flat fee, and what will not be covered. For example, if you pay a flat fee for an uncontested divorce, what happens if you and your spouse cannot agree on whether or not to sell the house, or how to set up a visitation schedule with the children? And at what point will you be notified that you're no longer being covered under the flat-fee agreement?

Whether you pay by the hour or on a flat-fee basis, you should expect to pay a retainer fee, which is a fee paid in advance from which the lawyer's hourly costs are billed. When the lawyer sets the retainer fee, he or she is trying to guess in advance how long your case will take in billable hours to complete. Most matrimonial lawyers bill cases on an hourly basis, and you are charged for all of the time that the lawyer spends on your case, including telephone calls, travel to and from court, and preparation time.

Be careful if you price-shop for a lawyer. Your divorce is one of the most important events of your life. If you can find a lawyer you think is qualified at a reasonable price, great. But remember, if the lawyer you consulted asks for the lowest retainer fee in town, there's probably a reason for that. The most experienced lawyers are usually the most expensive, and that is no coincidence.

When the retainer runs out

Sometimes the retainer fee paid runs out before the case is completed. The divorce has become more involved or time consuming than originally anticipated, and ends up requiring more time. Your lawyer asks you to pay an additional retainer fee, and you suddenly feel as if he or she is more interested in money than in the progress of your case.

You should expect to pay for your lawyer's time, however, even if your case takes longer than expected. If your retainer has been exhausted, you need to make arrangements with your attorney to continue to represent you. When clients do not honor their obligations to pay fees, loyalties can feel divided. If your lawyer must pressure you to pay the fee, you may feel that he/she is no longer supportive. Going through a divorce with an attorney is a very personal process. It is not unusual for you to feel very close to the person who is representing you and that your lawyer is more than your advocate. You need to remember that your attorney is a paid professional, and is not representing you as a favor.

Generally, if lawyers are not being paid they can request permission to withdraw from your case. This kind of withdrawal requires the court's permission. Don't put yourself in the position of begging the court to force your lawyer to stay on your case. You and your lawyer need to work as a team, and underlying money issues shouldn't get in the way of your relationship. Meet the financial situation head on, and make an honest effort to abide by whatever payment arrangements you and your lawyer negotiate.

In the event of a dispute concerning your fee, most local bar associations have fee dispute committees that will look at such disputes and determine whether or not the fees charged were reasonable to that point. If you are at such odds that you do not understand how the fees are billed or you don't think your lawyer has earned the fees charged, you should hire a different attorney to represent you.

Working with your lawyer

Your lawyer should send you a copy of everything that crosses his or her desk. That way, you can stay up-to-date on what is happening with any pleadings, briefs, documents, letters, and any and all correspondence concerning your case.

Remember, you are the one living with the results of your case, not the lawyer. Therefore, it is important that you feel that you are being kept informed about the facts in your case, the pros and cons of each step that might be taken, including settlement negotiations and other matters in the decision-making process.

The most common complaint heard from clients is that the lawyer doesn't return phone calls. Waiting for a call back when you're in distress makes minutes seem like hours, and hours like days. You can help your lawyer by being organized:

1. Write down your questions. Save up several questions to ask your lawyer all at once since he or she may have a minimum charge for phone calls. Leave enough space between questions to write in the answers.

2. Consider faxing, e-mailing, or mailing your questions instead of telephoning. This gives your lawyer a written record of your question, prompting a clear, well-organized written response to which you can refer later.

EMOTIONAL RAMIFICATIONS OF EARLY LEGAL DECISIONS

Once you've decided to pursue a separation or divorce, conflicts with your spouse are inevitable. Even if you mutually decided to end the marriage, communication is difficult. Learning how to handle this part of your changing relationship is an important step toward establishing a new, less stressful way of working together.

How Do I Handle the Conflicts That Arise Between Us as We Prepare to Divorce?

While you are initiating a divorce, or bracing yourself for a divorce that's been initiated by your spouse, it helps to keep arguments to a minimum. While you sort out how to proceed legally, you need to take a hard look at how you've been dealing with emotional conflicts that arise between you. It is not easy to change the way you communicate, but learning to break out of old patterns (which clearly aren't working) is part of adapting to your new independent life. Furthermore, it is necessary for the sake of the divorce process. Conflict will generally deescalate if there is a decrease in expressed emotion and perceived threat over time. In other words, things will calm down if you stop treating every discussion like an argument waiting to happen. Replace fighting with negotiation and cooperation strategies.

Be aware of your own anger. Do you clench your hands, grit your teeth, stand rigidly, cross your arms? Are you breathing with difficulty, or feeling a tightness in your chest or face or a headache coming on? Acknowledge your anger to yourself, and spend a little time trying to understand what set you off. Learn to distinguish when you are just irritated or annoyed from when you are furious.

Think before you enter into yet another cycle of endless arguing. Use self-calming strategies such as asking yourself whether you are making a mountain out of a molehill, or if this is an important argument. Are you considering your spouse's point of view? Think about all the indirect ways you express anger that lead to arguments: you may get aggressive and try to hurt your spouse's feelings with words; you may get quiet and let your spouse know you are very unhappy. Being silent is an attempt to grab and control all the power.

Choose a good time to initiate a discussion. Consider whether you can manage your anger without getting into an unproductive discussion with your spouse. If you are not getting along well, try to avoid speaking only when you are bringing up something you are unhappy about. When you really need to discuss something *and* you think there is a chance of improving the mood between the two of you, then try and talk about issues calmly.

Prepare yourself ahead of time. Know what you want to say, and when you will say it, and what you want to get out of a conversation. What do you want to have happen? Don't just blow off steam. Express your anger directly about the way he treats you in front of the children, or the fact that you are angry about her affair. Be clear about whether you are looking for an apology, a change in behavior, or empathy for your position.

These moments are about the two of you, and they will be resolved easier if they stay that way. Keep your discussions and arguments private; try to keep the children and others around you from becoming uncomfortably aware of your problems. You do not need affirmation that you are right, nor do you need others to see what a jerk your spouse is being.

Practice the art of fighting fair. Talk about the problem, not the other person. Make discussions focus on an issue, not a personality. Then practice being assertive and direct with each other. Be firm without provoking the other through sarcasm, raising your voice, angry body language (such as moping, rolling your eyes), or coming home an hour later than you said you would. Look at your spouse, speaking calmly and slowly, without wild hand gestures. Listen when your spouse is talking. Ask questions before you jump to conclusions. Repeat what your spouse just said in slightly different words and ask if you understood the whole message. State clearly what is bothering you, what you need and want.

> Encourage . . . Can you tell me what you mean?
> Clarify . . . When did I do that?
> Restate . . . So you wish I was more willing to see your parents?
> Empathize . . . You are very upset with me.
> Summarize . . . This is what you've said so far.
> Validate . . . I guess I do act helpless in front of the children, because I am hoping they'll see how poorly you treat me. I can see how that would feel demeaning to you.
> Affirm . . . I hear you saying that you feel I was inflexible about rescheduling last week's visitation.

Acknowledge that you hear the other person and understand what he/she is saying. Disallowing or debating with your spouse about who really has the right to be angry usually heightens the intensity of anger rather than diminishes it. But don't pretend to feel all right about something when you do not; don't give in just for the sake of peace. This kind of behavior usually leads to a recurrence of anger and conflict, because it resurfaces between you, having not been truly resolved.

Admit to your share of the problem and tell your spouse you recognize where and how you are part of the problem, emphasizing that you want to move to being part of the solution.

Stress the legitimate benefits of resolving this together. Be ready to compromise, but remember, compromise isn't just a fifty-fifty proposition; even a 10 percent compromise can lead to positive change in your relationship. Brainstorm many possible solutions rather than insisting on one ultimatum. Once you agree to a solution or at least feel that you have said your piece and listened to each other, then renegotiate. Plan together how similar situations will be dealt with in the future. Contract together to take certain actions that are different from how you normally behave with each other.

Even when your spouse and you are communicating directly and calmly, sometimes you cannot agree on a solution to a problem. Perhaps you have listened carefully to how he feels about your keeping your son home when he is sick, but your spouse still wants you to send the child to his house during his regularly scheduled time. When the two of you disagree about a situation, here are some basic steps toward conflict resolution:

1. Both people agree on ground rules of the discussion (no interrupting, no put-downs, no bringing up the past).

2. Agree on what the problem is, the source of the conflict. Identify what you agree on and what you disagree about in your views of the problem.

"You want to keep him home, and I think I should be the one to take care of him if he is sick and it is my time with him."

3. The first person tells his/her side of the story by describing what "I think, feel, want." Stay away from accusations about the other person ("You did."). Typically, all such statements should begin with the word "I."

"I feel you are not thinking about what he needs to get well, and how he will want to be in his own bed." "I feel that I'll never get to do some of the nurturing that lets him know I can take care of him, and that he can be comfortable in his room at my house too."

4. The second person restates what he/she has heard in terms of content and the feelings underlying it.

"You are worried that he will not get well as quickly if he is at my house, and you want to make him as comfortable as possible." "You want to take care of him, too, and you feel that having both parents caring for him can be more important than where he is when he doesn't feel well."

5. Steps 1 and 2 are repeated, changing positions so that the second person tells his/her side of the story and the other person rephrases what's been communicated.

6. Both people suggest possible solutions. Consider the pluses and minuses of each of the solutions that you would seriously consider together.

"Perhaps we can decide the best solution depending on what the illness is . . . so that when he has a stomach virus, moving him doesn't make sense. But when he has a headache, he can try going to your house."

This plan makes sense because it takes the child's needs into account, but it leaves open the need for negotiating each time the problem arises.

7. Both agree to try one of the proposed solutions, and to discuss it again in a few days or weeks, to see if progress has been made.

8. Keep any agreements you made, and if they are not working for you, make changes through negotiation. Try to resist taking unilateral actions.

In addition, try measures to change the dynamics of your arguments. Whenever a disagreement can be bypassed, let it go. If you are in the midst of a heated issue, such as how often one of you will spend evening time with the children, agree to explain what you want rather than what you have to get. Agree to take time apart and rethink your position when you hit a roadblock. Get second opinions from people you trust; perhaps you can even agree to talk to the same people so that you are less polarized by competing opinions. Most of all, focus your energy on the positives of your future: rebuilding your life, your new home, assets, career, and friendships rather than the arguments and failures of your past relationship.

PERSONAL ASSESSMENT

Have I considered all of my legal options? Am I sure I understand the pros and cons of each? If I take time now to learn about different ways to proceed, I am more likely to make a choice that accomplishes my goals both in the short run and in the long run.

Have I accurately assessed my personal circumstances, my willingness to learn about the legal process, and my emotional needs so that I can decide whether I need the help of a lawyer during my divorce? Have I been honest with myself about my own capability in handling this legal matter, especially since it is such an emotionally charged process? If I am confident that I have enough knowledge about the process to proceed, I can trust myself to ask for help when I need it.

Have I considered the different ways to approach this divorce? Am I confident of my ability to keep focused on my goals: a fair settlement, a sensible parenting arrangement, practical financial support orders, even when I am tempted to seek revenge? If I am able to see all of the options without losing sight of what's best for my future, then I am more likely to be happy with the end result.

Have I determined my goals in choosing professionals to help me with this divorce? If I understand my goals, I will be better able to pick the most appropriate people to help me accomplish them.

Have I recognized that the old style of communicating with my spouse is not working? Have I found ways to begin to communicate differently? If I am able to communicate with my ex-spouse, it will be easier for us to resolve our differences without unnecessary expense, delay, and stress. If we communicate well, it will be easier for us to focus on our children's needs rather than our own, even when we disagree.

4.

Steps to Success:
Taking One Hill at a Time

Once the decision to divorce is made, you reach a fork in the road where you need to make a series of choices about how you will proceed with your divorce. At each decision point, you choose your path: settlement or conflict. You can maintain a generous outlook toward your spouse, which fosters settlement, or you can respond to your more negative emotions, which fosters more conflict. In choosing conflict, you soon find yourself farther down the road toward adversarial divorce than you intended. Once several choices have been made that foster conflict over settlement, it becomes increasingly difficult to find resolution.

Choices that exacerbate conflict include acting with distrust and dishonesty, being aggressive or stubborn when reasonable compromises are available, or making the process difficult in order to satisfy your anger, desire for punishment of your spouse, or your fears. When each conflict is held on to with tenacity, feelings of affection from the marriage are eroded and are replaced by resentment that smolders into fury. These feelings often stem from grief that goes unacknowledged, your own or your spouse's. When grief is not worked through, it becomes a cantankerous emotional tumor, spreading its way through your heart and central nervous system. It hardens into bitterness.

Divorce is rarely easy, and bitter feelings make it more arduous. Although few couples actually go to trial, many go a long way toward trial before finally settling. These cases are characterized by added length and cost to the divorce process. On the other hand, if your priorities are clear, you

⚖

AM I READY TO START THE LEGAL DIVORCE PROCESS?

Emotional Checklist

- I know that my feelings will be complicated during this process, and I may be tempted to change my mind many times about decisions made. I am ready to examine my feelings and to resolve them, not to let them negatively influence my decisions in my legal divorce.
- I know that even in an amicable divorce, some conflict is inevitable, and I am committed to learning new ways to communicate with my spouse so that we are able to resolve the end of our marriage as peacefully as possible.
- I am committed to cooperating with my spouse in resolving issues that affect both of us, and I need to be forthright about informing my spouse of my decisions and the rationales behind them.
- I am emotionally ready to follow through on the legal requirements to obtain my divorce. If the divorce is not my choice, I am committed to accepting my spouse's decision, and doing what is best for myself and my children, legally and emotionally.

Legal Checklist

- I have started collecting my financial records, closing my joint credit and bank accounts, and establishing credit in my own name.
- I have established a confidential way to communicate with the people who advise me during this process.
- I have thought about how I will support myself after the divorce, and made plans to ensure that I am ready to do so.
- I have decided what type of case to pursue—Divorce, legal separation, or annulment—and whether or not I will need a lawyer to represent me.
- I have considered mediation as an alternative way to help settle our case.

are willing to compromise on most sticking points, you hired an attorney who is interested in settlement, and you are not hindered by emotional issues carried over from the marriage or the hurt of facing divorce, then you have an excellent chance of settling your disputes with minimum chaos to you and your family. Of course, you cannot effect success alone. Both partners have to participate.

Many spouses feel that they are the ones doing the compromising to achieve resolution, while their spouse is blocking it. Yet their spouse tells the same story, believing that he/she is the one doing all the work! When perceptions are so disparate, neither person can be acting in the "perfect" way the individual believes. If conflict is increasing rather than decreasing, take a hard look at what you might do differently. Most important, try understanding what's happening inside of you that is contributing to communication breakdowns. Assess whether you are acting out your feelings instead of experiencing and managing them.

Now that you have a better understanding of the ramifications of letting emotional issues hinder settlement, you are ready to move forward with the legal process. The steps outlined below take you through the legal divorce process from its initiation step by step and in more detail than the broad overview of the process outlined in preceding chapters.

FILING FOR DIVORCE

To begin, you have to file with the court. Basically, a set of forms will be filled out, served on your spouse (or you, if your spouse is the one initiating the divorce), and returned to the court with a filing fee. The filing fee varies, but is typically under $200 and can be waived by the court if you are unable to pay. You need to fill out a special fee waiver request at the courthouse if you wish to request that the fees be waived.

Typically, the forms require the date and place of your marriage, the wife's maiden name, and if there are children, their names and dates of birth, and whether anyone in your immediate family receives welfare assistance. The papers also request information regarding how long you've lived in the state, and the grounds upon which you're seeking a divorce, typically "irretrievable breakdown of the marriage" (no fault).

⚖

THE PRAYER FOR RELIEF

The general request for court orders which you will put in your divorce complaint will read something like this:

1. Dissolution of the marriage
2. An equitable division of the parties' assets and debts
3. Alimony (if alimony is being claimed)
4. Sole/joint custody of the parties' minor children (you need to select either sole or joint custody). If you don't have children, this request is omitted.
5. Child support
6. Restoration of the wife's birth name (option of the wife only)
7. Such other relief as may be appropriate in law or in equity

If you change your mind about your requests, they can be amended later by filing a new set of requests with the court.

The person who files the initial papers is called the Plaintiff. The recipient of the papers is the Defendant.

The forms also require you to state in general terms what orders you'd like the court to make. You must indicate whether or not you're requesting alimony, a property distribution, custody, joint custody or visitation, and a restoration of the wife's maiden name (wife's choice only). You don't need to state specifically what you're requesting, just the general categories.

Along with the initial papers, you can file a request to have the court make initial orders concerning custody, visitation, support, alimony, and use of certain items which belong to either or both of you. These orders are temporary, and last only as long as the divorce is pending.

To illustrate the procedure, let's outline a typical case:

Bill decided he wanted to file for a divorce from his wife, Anne. He contacted and retained an attorney, who agreed to represent him. The attorney filled out the necessary forms, which stated that Bill and Anne were married July 20, 1990, in New Haven, Connecticut; that they'd each lived in Connecticut for more than a year; and Anne's maiden name. It also stated that they have three children, Bill Junior, born December 1, 1992; Thomas, born July 5, 1994; and Julie, born September 21, 1997. The forms also stated that no one in the family received welfare assistance during the marriage, and that the marriage had broken down irretrievably (no-fault divorce). Bill asked the court to divide their property fairly between the two of them, and for joint legal custody and visitation with the children. He filed a request for temporary orders requesting that visitation be established on an interim basis, since he had already moved out of the house. The attorney arranged to have Anne served with the papers, and when they were returned to the attorney after service, the attorney filed them with the court. This started the case.

Cynthia wanted to divorce her husband, Ted. Because she and Ted had no children and little property, she decided she would file the divorce pro se, *without a lawyer. She purchased a book at a bookstore (oftentimes the courthouse clerk's office can provide a list of* pro se *books available) titled* How to Do Your Own Divorce in Minnesota *and followed procedures as stated above. She filled out papers she picked up at the court, arranged with the sheriff service at the courthouse to have the papers served on Ted, and after they were served, she returned them to court with a check for the filing fee. Thus, her case was opened with the court.*

DOES IT MAKE A DIFFERENCE WHO FILES FIRST?

In most cases, it doesn't make any difference who files first for the divorce. Your rights are not compromised by the fact that you (or your spouse) filed the divorce papers. In the event of a trial, the person who files tells his/her side of the story first, which can be advantageous. If you are the plaintiff and you change your mind about pursuing the divorce, you may stop the process at any time by filing papers to withdraw the case from court. If you are the defendant (your spouse has filed the divorce against you), you cannot withdraw the case without your spouse's cooperation. In a no-fault divorce, if the plaintiff represents to the court that the marriage has broken down without hope of reconciliation, the court will grant the divorce even if the other spouse wishes to remain married.

PREPARING YOUR SPOUSE TO RECEIVE DIVORCE PAPERS

Although it may be very difficult for you to broach the subject of divorce with your spouse, if you have decided to file for a divorce it is best to let your spouse know in advance that the divorce papers are coming. Even when the marital relationship has gone awry, the spouse served is often shocked and upset when the papers finally arrive. Try and soften that blow to the extent you can. It may set the stage for how much you and your spouse will cooperate throughout the process.

If, on the other hand, you feel that you may be in danger if your spouse knows in advance that the papers are coming, then make sure that your lawyer is aware of your fear so that he or she can help you take precautions before the papers are served. You will want to make sure that you and your children are in a safe place when the papers are served. If your spouse becomes violent or threatening after the papers are served, call the police. Then call your lawyer after you and your children have had a chance to get to someplace where you will be safe.

ARRANGING FOR SERVICE OF THE PAPERS

Sheriffs and registered process servers are permitted to serve divorce papers and then submit a "proof of service" affidavit, which sets forth the method, date, and time they used for serving the papers. Sheriffs' offices are located in most local courthouses, and the court clerk's office can direct you there. Many jurisdictions also allow "indifferent persons" to serve papers, which includes registered process servers, process servers, or indifferent persons (people who are not involved in the divorce action). Registered process servers may offer door-to-door pickup and dropoff service. Beware of using unregistered process servers or indifferent persons to serve these important papers. If they make a mistake, you could have to refile your entire case.

What the Sheriff or Process Server Needs to Know

In order for the service of process to run smoothly, the sheriff needs to know how, when, and where to find your spouse. The more information you can give your lawyer and the sheriff about where to find your spouse, and the best time to find him or her, the easier it will be for the lawyer to get the papers served, thereby expediting your case and saving you money.

Give the sheriff a written schedule of where your spouse can be found. Include his or her home address and telephone number, and the days of the week and times he or she is ordinarily available. If you want the sheriff to serve your spouse at work, list his or her work address and telephone number as well as hours and days worked. If your spouse can be violent, or carries a gun, the sheriff needs to know that. If you suspect that your spouse will attempt to avoid service, the sheriff needs to know that, too. If you don't want the papers served during certain hours when the children are home, be specific in your instructions. If you need to be notified before service so that you can make sure you're in a safe place when it happens, also let the sheriff know.

The sheriff will need a description of your spouse's appearance: height, weight, hair color, race, whether your spouse has facial hair or wears glasses. Attach a photograph to the written description. The color, make, and model of your spouse's car is also helpful information, as is the license plate number.

In some states, the sheriff may be able to simply leave the papers at your spouse's house, as opposed to handing the papers to your spouse personally. Each trip that the sheriff makes costs you money, so make it as easy as possible for the sheriff to successfully serve your spouse.

The appendix contains a Sheriff Information Sheet, which you may use as a guide for information to give the sheriff.

Your Role

How you handle serving papers on your spouse can be instrumental in how the rest of your case progresses. Most sheriffs and registered process servers can arrange with your spouse to deliver the papers so that it is not unduly embarrassing. If you inform your spouse in advance, usually he or she will be able to meet the sheriff to receive the papers so that service can be as private and nonconfrontational as possible.

THE MANDATORY WAITING PERIOD

One of the most confusing and least understood parts of the legal process is the mandatory waiting period: what happens and what is the timing?

Most states specify a waiting period of between three and twelve months from the time you file the papers until your divorce can be finalized. During this waiting period your lawyer, if you have one, will be pursuing financial discovery, that is, assembling all of the financial documents that are relevant to your case (in addition to the documents you've already provided). The discovery process is discussed in Chapter 5, Evidence and Pretrial Procedures. Your lawyer or mediator should also be helping you to formulate a settlement proposal for resolving your case. By understanding the settlement process, you can help to guide your case to a successful ending.

STAYING IN OR LEAVING THE HOUSE

Many states permit couples to live together during their divorce. Other states, such as New York, require a physical separation of a specific duration (New York is one year, most other states are three months to a year) before a divorce can be granted. All states permit separation during the divorce process. The question is whether a physical separation at this time makes sense for your family. Consider:

• Your finances: will you and your spouse be able to support two households right away?
• The stability of your children: where will they live, and how will they get to see each parent?
• Can you agree on who stays in the marital residence, or will this decision require court intervention?

• Is there a potential for domestic violence, especially now that tensions are escalated?

• Will both of you have adequate transportation and furnishings—e.g., are you sharing an automobile?

The most frequently asked legal question is *Is there a legal advantage to separating or staying in the same household?* The answer to this question varies widely across jurisdictions and lawyers. Many lawyers subscribe to the old adage of "possession is nine points of the law" and instruct their clients that if they hope to live in the house after the divorce is finalized, they should not move out of the house during the divorce. Similarly, if the client wishes to live with the children, the client should not move out without them. Even though orders made during the time the divorce case is pending are supposedly "without prejudice," meaning that the court has the authority to change the orders at any time, lawyers who subscribe to the "possession is nine points of the law" school of thought believe otherwise. While no statistics are available to support or refute this theory, imagine such a scenario as presented to a judge: if the arrangement has stabilized the children and seems to be working, why risk a change?

There are psychological and practical advantages and disadvantages to staying in the same house. The advantages include saving money, having time to organize your lives for an easier separation, having time to talk to your children, and providing support to each other on a daily basis. This way of living requires a friendly situation at best, or one in which tensions are squelched for your own or your children's benefit. If your situation is not civil, however, it is difficult and painful to face each other every day and manage the "good face" that such arrangements require. Staying in a tension-filled living situation can exacerbate stress and magnify the ways in which spouses annoy and frustrate each other.

Certain situations support separating sooner rather than later. If your spouse is continuously putting you down, berating you, abusing you, or manipulating you into being frightened, meek, or withdrawn from family and friends, then staying in the house is likely to have negative consequences for your children and for you. If your spouse is involved in illegal activities, or is self-destructive, such as a compulsive gambler or a cheat, then staying

WHAT TO DO WHEN YOUR SPOUSE WON'T LEAVE

- Concentrate on keeping relations as peaceful as possible, even if that means ignoring hurtful comments or doing more than your share of the work around the house
- Concentrate on the positive: you are saving money, you have backup help with the house and children, you can take more time to think about what you'd like from the end of the process without having to worry about living arrangements in the short term
- Protect your personal space and privacy, and respect your spouse's personal space and privacy
- Begin to implement separation behaviors: sleep in separate bedrooms, do not engage in sexual activity
- Agree upon what to tell family and friends so that there is no misunderstanding about what the living arrangement signifies

can have only negative consequences unless you both get professional help. If your spouse has a disabling mental illness that causes him or her to act erratically in ways that could put you or your children in danger, that is an unsettling but potentially necessary reason for leaving. Finally, if your spouse is hurting your children in any way, then you must leave immediately, even if you are not fully prepared emotionally to do so.

Separating might be temporary. Sometimes just taking this action breaks old patterns like taking each other for granted. It introduces fear, and provides an opportunity to experience what life will be like without your spouse. Is it relieving, barely noticed, or does it compel you to rethink all of your reasons for leaving? If you separate, you must stick with it long enough to pass through the immediate aftermath—the loneliness, demands, threats, promises for change, and bouts of intimacy that wreak havoc in the early separation period.

Ellen and Harry lived in the same home during their divorce process. Harry set up a bedroom in the basement, and the children moved freely between the two floors on which their parents lived. They each planned to stay out of the home on alternating evenings, so that they did not interact except when the children were asleep. Despite this plan, mounting tensions during the legal process were taking their toll, especially on Harry. He felt he did not have a real home, and that the children did not respect his being "banished" to the basement. Harry reported feeling depressed and anxious, to the point that he was not functioning successfully in the workplace. He wondered if the money he was saving was worth it, and whether being with his children in this way ultimately undermined his relationship with them.

WHAT ARE THE LEGAL ISSUES WE MUST SETTLE DURING THE WAITING PERIOD AND PRIOR TO DIVORCE?

During the waiting period, you begin to resolve each of the issues germane to divorce. You are thus working toward a fair settlement for the postdivorce period. Two categories of issues must be resolved: financial, and if you have children, issues related to legal custody and parenting arrangements.

We will discuss the financial issues first, followed by the custody, support, and parenting issues. Financial issues must be resolved in order to equalize both spouses' means of economic support. The primary considerations in these areas include:

ALIMONY

Alimony—or spousal support, as it's known in some states—is a legal mechanism by which the court acknowledges that two people make up a marriage partnership, and that the earning power of the two people is rarely equal. Sometimes one of those people sacrificed a career, education, or job track in order to fulfill an unpaid role in that partnership. In some cases, an injury or illness contributed to the lesser earning capacity of one of the two partners.

In recent years, however, alimony awards are more rare, and for shorter periods of time. All states reserve the right to make asset divisions based (at least in part) on the earning capacity and future prospects of the couple.

☩☩

SETTLEMENT POINTS CHECKLIST

Financial

- alimony or spousal maintenance support
- personal property
- division of liquid assets: cash, stock, and bank accounts
- division of retirement accounts and pensions, stock options, and less liquid assets
- whether or not to sell the house and other real estate
- who will keep the house and other real estate if it is not to be sold
- tax issues
- child support, medical insurance, and tax exemptions for children

Parenting Related

- legal custody and parenting schedules
- special provisions concerning children: medical expenses, college, extracurricular activities, private school, and the like

CONSIDERATIONS BEFORE SETTLING

- What do you believe is in the best interests of your children?
- Can you handle all of your new responsibilities?
- Have you considered all of the tax ramifications?
- Have you considered the mix of assets you'll be receiving: liquid versus nonliquid, and does the settlement meet your immediate needs?
- Does the settlement set you on the right path for your long-term needs?
- Can you live with the proposed settlement, even though you're not completely satisfied?
- Will a trial cost more emotionally and financially than what you hope to gain?
- If you cannot settle, will what you're fighting about matter in five years?

Even if a court doesn't favor alimony, it may allow other provisions in order to even out the spouses' financial positions—e.g., a larger share of the equity in the house or cash savings.

Both men and women are entitled to alimony in those states that permit alimony awards. Alimony awards are not gender-based, but rather, depend on broad criteria:

- age
- health, both mental and physical
- education
- income
- future prospects for income and employment
- separate property that may be used for support
- the desirability of a parent not working for a length of time (e.g., when children are young)
- length of the marriage
- reasons for the breakdown of the marriage
- contributions to the household, both monetary and nonmonetary

Alimony is considered to be an income substitute. You need not have children to be entitled to alimony. It is determined based on both spouses' incomes, the factors listed above, and a determination of the relative importance of each of the factors for each case. It's therefore impossible to predict how much alimony may be awarded in a given case. Some jurisdictions have a rule of thumb, and experienced lawyers can give you an estimate of the amount you might receive. But unlike child support, which is determined by law, alimony is completely negotiable. Alimony typically ends upon the death of either the payor or the recipient, but all other details are subject to your own design. Some (mix and match) provisions that can be included:

- alimony terminates upon the remarriage of the recipient
- alimony terminates upon the cohabitation of the recipient with another adult under circumstances that are tantamount to remarriage, but without the ceremony
- alimony terminates after a specific number of months or years

- alimony is for a decreasing amount each year (subject to some tax rules), i.e., $15,000 the first year, $10,000 the second year, $5,000 the third year, and terminates after year three
- alimony is not awarded at the time of the divorce but is an issue kept open for modification later if circumstances change
- alimony is modifiable in the event of a substantial change in circumstances, or modifiable only under certain, predefined circumstances, such as a physical disability
- alimony is not modifiable by either party for any reason
- alimony is not modifiable unless either party's income changes by a certain amount or percentage—e.g., to encourage a nonworking spouse to begin working, alimony might be modifiable only if that spouse's gross income exceeds $20,000 a year

Alimony thus can be tailored to fit your individual situation. In some cases, it may never terminate; in others, triggering events can be specified that will mark a termination. Think about what you want to accomplish through alimony, and then negotiate to fit those needs.

Emotional and Tax Considerations for Alimony

For most divorcing spouses in states that recognize alimony awards, alimony is a hot emotional issue. In a typical scenario, the husband pays the wife alimony. The longer the marriage, the more likely alimony will be awarded. If you are the husband, it is difficult to stomach paying alimony when you feel that you earned most of the money anyway. While you may feel that she never did much to help you at the office or with the children, she feels that she was your "right arm." As the wife, you may feel that you deserve all that he is worth and could be worth someday, since you supported the family during his education, early career, or even while he amassed his profits. You feel he couldn't have reached his current status without you, while he insists that you undermined him at every turn and did precious little to further his achievements.

Anyone who is required to pay alimony after his or her spouse decided unilaterally that he/she wanted a divorce tends to feel doubly hurt by the system. It is painful to pay someone a substantial part of your income while you are in the throes of divorce and related conflicts, and you'd prefer to spend your money on your children, new partner, or yourself. During the divorce process, almost all partners feel that *they* are the generous spouse, and their partner is being unreasonable. Therefore, the subject of alimony adds salt to wounds that are already searing. It helps to remember during this time that alimony is a potentially versatile and cost-effective way to help settle your case. Often clients say, "I don't want to pay a dime of alimony!" only to realize later that the "dime of alimony" is actually the cheapest, most sensible alternative. It is one method of equalizing assets over time; it is not the only way, and if it can be thought about calmly and with creativity it can be a useful tool for a successful divorce.

For example, what many people do not realize is that, for tax purposes, alimony is deductible for the person who pays the alimony, and included in income for the person who receives it. You must consider the tax ramifications of an alimony order before deciding whether it makes sense for you. An alimony order can save a couple a great deal of money.

For example, for someone in the 28 percent federal tax bracket, every $100 in alimony paid "costs" only $72 because of the tax savings. If the recipient is in the 15 percent tax bracket, each $100 received means $85 is truly realized because of the taxes owed. The couple saves $13 in taxes for every $100, which means the alimony order can be higher than if there was no tax savings. And the recipient pays less taxes on the money than the spouse would have in his/her tax bracket. Alimony thus keeps money in your collective pockets. Furthermore, many state laws provide for alimony deductions on top of the federal deductions. As much as spouses dislike giving alimony to each other, giving money to the IRS is even less popular!

If you have children, and paying alimony in addition to child support is a possibility, the IRS has another vehicle by which you may take advantage of tax provisions called "Unallocated Alimony and Support," which is a special combination of alimony and child support—*all* of which is deductible by the paying spouse and taxable as income to the receiving spouse. If your incomes are very disparate—for example, if one of you stays home with the children and does not earn an income—then this option may make sense for you. Where Child Support Fits In, on page 226, addresses this issue more fully.

Courts also have modernized alimony in creating "rehabilitative alimony" or limited-term alimony. Rather than have alimony continue for the rest of one's life, as was typical twenty years ago, courts nowadays are considering orders that last for a specific period of time and then terminate. For example, in the case of a woman who has taken time off from her career as a teacher to raise two children, now ages three and five, the court might award alimony for four years. During that four-year time period, the woman has an opportunity to renew her teaching license, look for a job, and establish the children in school. By the time the four years pass, she should be in a much better position to support herself, without further need for alimony. Without a reasonable reprieve (in this example, four years), she might be unable to find a job because her teaching license or education is out of date; she might be unable to find good, reasonably priced day care for the children; and the children would be forced to adapt to a sudden change of living circumstances. Even a few years of modest alimony helps this situation immensely.

On the other hand, there are also traditional cases in which women who have made their lives as housewives find themselves thirty years later without a pension, 401k, or even a job. Many of these women married in college, or before college, and never finished their education. Some have never worked outside of the home, and find themselves for the first time without financial support. Because of their wives' family work and skills, their husbands were able to further their careers without having to worry about keeping house or making daily arrangements for their children. At age fifty-five, finding a first job is extremely difficult. Alimony in this type of a scenario is more likely to be ordered for an indefinite period.

PROPERTY DIVISION

Facts and Factors

Courts in the United States fall into two categories: equitable-division states and community-property states. While some of the theories in each type of jurisdiction overlap, they are two distinct areas of the law.

⚖

CHECKLIST OF FACTS AND FACTORS FOR DISTRIBUTING PROPERTY IN AN EQUITABLE-DIVISION STATE

- age
- health
- education
- ability to earn income in the future
- ability to accumulate assets in the future
- special needs of children
- parenting needs of children
- contribution to assets
- separate property
- inheritances, gifts, and family loans
- appreciation of joint and sole assets over time
- liquidity of funds
- tax ramifications
- premarital contributions
- nonmonetary contributions

Equitable-division states

Forty-one of the fifty states are equitable-division states (i.e., every state except Arizona, California, Idaho, Louisiana, Nevada, New Mexico, Texas, Washington, and Wisconsin). That means that *any* property belonging to either you or your spouse may be subject to division by the court. The division is based on what the court determines to be fair, hence the name "equitable division" or "equitable distribution." All property acquired during the marriage is subject to division, *as well as* property that was acquired prior to the marriage by either of you individually, gifts from one family, inheritances, personal injury lawsuit settlements, bonuses, pensions, stock options, and other assets that have value to you.

Typically, most courts will focus on dividing the assets that accumulated during the marriage rather than those that accumulated prior to it. Premarital assets may be subject to division, however, depending upon the individual circumstances of your case.

For example, if you and your spouse have $150,000 in assets which accumulated during the marriage, both of you are in good health and have decent jobs, and your children are healthy and don't require any special care, then the court will focus first on dividing those assets. Assets that each of you accumulated prior to the marriage will be considered, but if dividing the marital assets will provide each of you with a reasonable settlement, then several thousand dollars of premarital savings or property is probably "safe" from the court's orders.

If, on the other hand, one of you has $100,000 in premarital savings, and together the two of you accumulated no assets and $20,000 in credit card debt, it is likely that a court will order a portion of that premarital $100,000 to the other spouse, or order that some of it be used to pay the credit card debts.

Other factors that can influence property division are how long you have been married, your health, your age, your educational backgrounds, your prospects for future income, whether or not the judge thinks that the spouse ordered to pay child support and spousal maintenance will actually pay the orders, and a variety of other factors. Inheritances and money that each spouse contributed to the marriage are often important as well. Be sure to bring these matters up with your lawyer and discuss what they mean in your particular case, given your state's laws. While each case is decided individually by the court, your lawyer can give you an idea of how judges in your state would consider the factors under your circumstances and how that would translate into property distribution.

Courts recognize nonmonetary contributions to families just as they do monetary contributions. Housewives, stay-at-home moms, stay-at-home dads, and spouses who contributed to the family in positive ways are recognized along with spouses who contributed to the home with salary, inheritance, or savings.

Don't expect the court to do a dollar-for-dollar accounting of all money earned and spent by each spouse. Most courts will assume that while you and your spouse were married, you made certain decisions together for the best interests of your family as a whole. The court will not second guess those decisions by punishing one spouse for not working, or for not earning as much, unless those are material issues in your case. For example, if the reason your spouse didn't work is because he or she had a drug problem, the court will likely consider that unfavorably toward your spouse in the property settlement. If your spouse didn't work because he or she stayed home with the children while you advanced your career, the court will view that spouse as an equal contributor to your family assets, even though his or her contribution was not monetary. It is not the court's purpose to unravel every financial transaction during your entire marriage to decide who contributed exactly how much money, who purchased which item of furniture, and who worked the most hours, thereby creating a disparity in earnings.

However, if you had substantial property prior to your marriage, or you

inherited substantial property during the marriage, you may be able to preserve this property as your own, separate property even in an equitable-
jurisdiction state. Be prepared to prove ownership and how you acquired
the property, and be sure to give this information to your attorney early in
your case.

Community-property states

The remaining nine states are community-property states: Arizona,
California, Idaho, Louisiana, Nevada, New Mexico, Texas, Washington,
and Wisconsin. In these states, only property that was accumulated during
the marriage will be divided, with a few exceptions, and that property will
be divided fifty-fifty, asset by asset, whenever possible. Wages, income, and
bonuses are community property, as is credit obtained during the marriage.
Therefore, homemakers are not penalized for not working outside the
home, and claims of "I earned all of the money, so all of the property is
mine!" aren't considered by the court. Property accumulated by either of
you prior to the marriage, or during the marriage through a gift or inheritance, or by virtue of appreciation or rents from other premarital property is
considered "separate property" and is not subject to division by the court
(again, with some exceptions).

In community-property states, the main exceptions are:

1. when one spouse receives a community-property–funded education,
the other spouse will be reimbursed for half of the educational expenses,
unless both spouses received a community-property–funded education,
more than ten years has passed since the education was completed, or the
marital community has benefited in some other way. Any educational loans
taken out for educational expenses are the responsibility of the person who
received the education.

2. when liabilities exceed assets.

3. when one spouse has misappropriated family assets. Oddly enough,
this does not include excessive gambling debts, as all debts incurred during
the marriage are considered marital debts, irrespective of whether one
spouse had the permission of the other spouse to incur the debt.

4. lawsuit liabilities for injuries. For lawsuit liabilities, who has to pay

depends on whether the accident happened in the course of "marital business." For example, if you are involved in an accident while driving to the store to buy groceries, then the liability is paid from community assets. If you get in an accident while on your way to meet a boyfriend for an affair, the liability is paid from your separate property.

5. For people with children and a family home, the family home may be awarded to the custodial spouse, and the other spouse may receive different assets to compensate for giving up an interest in the home.

6. Businesses started prior to the marriage present a special problem. The division depends upon whether any increase in the business value is due to the nature of the business, or the businessperson's special efforts. If the business has increased in value because of the nature of the business, then the business is generally separate property. To illustrate, California's leading case in this area of law is *Van Camp*, pertaining to the divorce of the Van Camps of pork and beans fame. Their business value increased drastically during World War II just because of the nature of the business, i.e., canned food during wartime. Such a business was maintained as separate property.

If a business increased in value during the marriage because the businessperson devoted time, skill, and expertise, then the business will be considered community property. Examples include an interior decorating business, software development, and other labor-intensive businesses.

7. Professional licenses are not subject to division, but can warrant alimony orders to even out the earning power of the spouses.

To the extent that you intend to prove that an asset is your separate property, or that although an asset was purchased while you were married it was purchased with separate property, be prepared to present documentation that traces the source of the funds used to acquire the asset. If you have kept your property separate, you have a good chance of it remaining separate property during a community-property-state divorce. If you've intermingled separate property with community property, the court may find that you intended to give a gift of that separate property to your spouse, or that, at best, you're entitled to reimbursement (without interest) for your separate property's contribution to community property.

For instance, if you owned a rental property prior to your marriage and kept the rental income separate from any marital funds, in a bank account in your sole name, and used only the rental income to improve the rental property, then the rental income will be considered to have remained separate property, even though it accumulated during your marriage.

While the details of property division can become a bit confusing, keep sight of the initial premise: if it accumulated during your marriage, it's probably community property. If you intend to claim otherwise, be prepared to prove it.

PERSONAL PROPERTY IN ALL JURISDICTIONS

The courts are reluctant to get involved in dividing up personal property, so if you and your spouse can do it yourselves, that is the best way to proceed. By the time you've argued in court about a two-year-old TV set and a sofa with a spot on it, you will have spent enough in lawyers' fees to purchase both items new.

Sit down with the Inventory of Household Items made in Chapter 2 and sort out the obvious items that one spouse or the other will want. The antique that came from your mother's family home should go back to you, and his favorite recliner should go to him. Narrow your list to those items which are actually in dispute.

Once you have determined which items are in dispute, make a list of them. From here, there are several ways to proceed. One frequently used method is to flip a coin, and the winner gets to pick the first item, the loser gets to pick the second item, the winner gets to pick the third item, and so forth. Another possibility is for one spouse to make up two lists of estimated near equal value, then the other spouse gets to choose which list he/she wants. A third possibility is to assign a dollar value to the property and have an "auction." The spouse who wants certain pieces of property the most will be willing to pay the other spouse more for them than the spouse to whom the property is less important.

Negotiate with your spouse for any personal property you want, but don't expect cash in lieu of property. The court will be reluctant to award one spouse money in exchange for giving the other spouse most of the personal property. Despite sentimental attachment to your furniture and personal items, unless they are antiques, oriental rugs, or paintings by famous artists, most of your items have more value to you personally than they would to someone else. A judge will be unlikely to place values on the items, and award one spouse or the other the commensurate cash value for the items.

If you cannot agree upon a fair way to divide up the items in dispute, at least you have narrowed the list, hopefully to a manageable length, for your lawyers or a mediator to deal with in negotiations.

⚖️

DON'T LET THE CD COLLECTION RUIN A SETTLEMENT

Emotions run high for certain possessions, and spouses sometimes use these hot buttons as an opportunity to retaliate against the other person. A good benchmark is to ask "will this matter in five years?" If it will not matter, then be prepared to give it up now.

ASSETS

Cash, Stocks, and Other Assets

Cash in the checking or savings account, CDs in the bank, stocks, stock options, bonds, mutual funds, 401k contributions, and pension funds are subject to scrutiny and division by the court. Consider how you hope to use these assets in the future before deciding how and when they are divided. If you need to put a security deposit down on an apartment, you'll want to have access to this money quickly. If you are saving for retirement, you won't need the money now, and it would be desirable to invest it. Your goals should dictate how important issues such as liquidity, immediate and long-term tax ramifications, and the safety of certain investments are to you.

Pensions

Your defined benefit pension, 401k plan, profit sharing or Keough plan, 457b plan, Individual Retirement Account (IRA), Roth IRA, and tax-sheltered annuities are all assets that may, depending on when you acquired them and the laws of your state, be assets that are subject to division by the court. You will need to know how much your pension-type asset was worth when you were married, how much you've contributed to it since your marriage, and how much it's appreciated during your marriage. Because these plans are typically funded with pre-tax dollars (with the exception of the Roth IRA), their value needs to be calculated with this in mind. If you liquidate these assets prior to age $59^1/_2$ (with some exceptions), you will pay the income tax due on this money as well as a 10 percent penalty. For that reason, they are not considered to be liquid funds. They are valuable assets, nevertheless, and in some cases they are the most valuable asset in the marriage.

Defined benefit pensions are those plans in which only the employer deposits money. The employee does not contribute to the plan. At a specified retirement age, the employee receives a monthly payment. The amount of the monthly payment is a function of years at the company, age of retirement, and ending salary. These plans typically cannot be liquidated, although when the employee leaves the company, sometimes they're offered a buy-out of the pension plan in exchange for waiving any future pension benefits.

Defined contribution plans are made up of funds contributed by the employee. The employee usually elects to have money withheld from his or her paycheck to fund such plans. This money is withheld as pre-tax dollars, which means income tax has not been paid on the money contributed. The most common defined contribution plans are 401ks, named for the Internal Revenue Service law which created them. Sometimes an employer will contribute funds to match a percentage of the money contributed by the employee. When these plans are liquidated before age $59^1/_2$, income tax plus a 10 percent penalty is owed on the funds withdrawn. IRAs are another form of defined contribution plan, although they are set up individually rather than by a company.

If your pension-type assets are subject to division by the court as part

PENSION INFORMATION TO GIVE YOUR LAWYER

PENSION INFORMATION

Name: _____

Date of Birth: _____

Official Name of Pension Plan: _____

Date Employment Started: _____

Date Employment Terminated: _____

Dates of Breaks in Service: _____

Normal Retirement Age: _____
(date upon which participant may retire without reduced benefits)

Estimated monthly benefits as of a recent date:

_____   _____
Date   Estimated monthly benefit

Whether or not the participant is eligible for postretirement cost-of-living increases: yes   no

Will the pension holder receive Social Security benefits for the years of participation in the plan?   yes   no

Is the pension holder fully vested?   yes   no

If not, when will full vesting occur? _____

Contact person, name, address, and telephone number, and fax for plan information:

Name: _____

Address: _____

Telephone: _____

Fax: _____

of your divorce, the court can issue a special order called a Qualified Domestic Relations Order (QDRO), which allows the plans to be divided without having to pay the tax that would be owed if the plan was liquidated. QDRO orders can be prepared for defined benefit plans, defined contribution plans, and even IRAs. Although a QDRO order will add paperwork to your divorce, avoiding the tax due on transfer of these assets often saves money and preserves the value of the asset.

Liquidity

When you are dividing up stocks, bonds, and cash assets, keep in mind that some investments are more liquid than others. Some may be available more easily than others in the event of an emergency. Your house and pension may be the least liquid of all of your assets. Be sure that you understand the ramifications of your choices for the mix of assets you are dividing.

Also consider tax ramifications. When assets such as stocks gain in value, that added value becomes taxable as capital gains. The tax becomes due in the year that you sell the asset. If you bought IBM stock at $25 per share, and now it's worth $75 per share, the taxable gain is $50 per share. A 20 percent federal tax rate (your rate may vary) translates to a tax of $10, so your $75 stock is really worth $65 if you sell it this year. Tax ramifications make a great impact on the true value of an asset, and should influence your choices. Contact an accountant if your lawyer cannot answer your tax questions.

How Do We Use Our Assets for Mutual Benefit?

During a divorce, many people feel that their spouse will receive monies in the settlement which the spouse will use inappropriately. A common refrain is "He'll just use the money on his new girlfriend, and forget all about our children" or "She is terrible with money and will waste it." Sometimes sentiments reflect a concern that parents who once used money for a common goal may lose sight of that goal, such as saving money for a child's college expenses.

A constructive way to control your money in a divorce is to use that money to advance a common goal. You may be thinking that you and your

⚖

DO NOT MAKE KNEE-JERK DECISIONS

During the early days of your divorce, beware the urge to squander assets or make impetuous investment decisions. Preserve your money so that the courts can help you and your spouse divide your assets appropriately. You can spend the rest of your life determining how best to invest your money, and what purchases to make.

Now is also not the time to make expensive decisions about how you want to live your life after the divorce. Too many clients exclaim, "Well, if my spouse gets the house, then I want a house that's just as nice, and just as big." That same client immediately buys a house that is just as nice and just as big, using every available dollar to do so, taking on a huge mortgage. What if your feelings change a few months after the divorce is over and you decide to pursue a job in another state, or meet someone new who already owns a house? Consider that your thoughts and feelings about where and how you want to live after the divorce will probably change when the divorce is concluded, and over time.

spouse no longer have common goals, but you'd be surprised at what you may be able to agree upon. One use for savings that you're afraid your spouse will spend frivolously after the divorce is to pay off joint credit card debt. The spouse with the highest income takes the largest chance that he or she will get stuck with the lion's share of the credit card bills, so this is a good strategy for that person to advance. Presumably, a judge will divide savings that accumulated during the marriage equally (at least somewhat equally) between the two of you. If you negotiate for those savings to go toward a credit card bill for which you owe money (or upon which your signature appears as an obligor), then you've reduced your after-divorce expenses (no more credit card payments). You've also restricted the amount of money your spouse has to spend on items you don't believe are important. Your spouse may even agree to pay off the credit card debt. This benefits both spouses unless the credit card you're paying off includes presents and vacation expenditures for your current single life or love interest, or was clearly only used for your benefit as opposed to your family's benefit.

Another way to put assets toward a mutual goal is to set up trust accounts for your children's college expenses, or a first car. Each party can be required to contribute a certain amount of assets or income into a fund that will be jointly administered. Neither party can take money out of the account without the agreement of the other. Expenses to be paid from the account are agreed upon in advance, such as "tuition, room, board, and books," or "an automobile at age eighteen costing not more than $10,000," or "travel expenses for a trip abroad after high school graduation, not to exceed $3,500."

Dissipating Assets

The court frowns upon dissipating assets during the divorce process. With respect to stocks, bonds, mutual funds, and other related cash assets, refrain from spending until after the divorce. If you suspect that your spouse may dissipate assets, write a letter to your broker, bank, or financial institution immediately informing them of your impending divorce, and that you will not authorize withdrawals on any accounts without both signatures verified against the original signature cards at the institution. Once you've initiated the divorce, seek a court order freezing the assets in all of your accounts except for day-to-day living expenses. In some states, like Connecticut, these orders are automatic upon the filing of the divorce.

You are under the court's microscope with respect to dissipating assets. If you need to use any of your savings to pay bills, make sure there is not a court order already in place prohibiting you from doing so. If there is, and you need to use some of the frozen monies, you must first obtain the court's permission. If you are permitted to use your assets to pay ordinary and necessary living expenses, keep records of how the money was spent, as well as a record of why the living expenses were ordinary and necessary. If the judge perceives you as dissipating assets, you may have a real problem at subsequent court proceedings or a trial.

Don't plan on being tricky by closing accounts and then diverting the money to an untraceable account. All a judge needs to see is a bank statement with, say, $5,000 two days before you filed divorce papers, and then a $5,000 withdrawal two months after, with no disclosure concerning the whereabouts of the money, to determine that you're a money-hider. If a judge believes you've hidden even a small amount of money, the next question will be "What else is this person hiding?"

Because you are under a microscope during your divorce, keeping a paper trail of how you spend your money is important. Keep a notebook in which you record all major financial transactions, including receipt or payment of child support, medical bills for the children, any savings that you utilize or any accounts that you cash out, bank statements, credit card statements, and so forth. You aren't necessarily going to need these records, but if you do need them, you aren't going to want to have to dig around the bottom of a shoe box or call MasterCard in order to find them. You can always throw the paper trail away later if you do not use it.

WHAT SHOULD WE DO ABOUT OUR HOUSE?

Sell or Keep the House?

One of your first big decisions in your divorce is whether or not you can afford your house or apartment after the other spouse moves out, and if so, whether you *want* to continue to live there. The last thing that you and your spouse need is property that neither of you can afford. By the same token, don't make any rash decisions. You can always give up an apartment or sell a house later, but you probably won't be able to rerent the same apartment or rebuy the house after you give it up.

Even if you can afford the house and want to live there, can you mow the yard and do the necessary repairs without your spouse to help? Is there too much space? Are there too many memories? If you are able to afford it, will it take so much of your monthly income that you won't be able to do anything besides pay the mortgage or rent and buy groceries? Is that a lifestyle you can accept?

When Edith got divorced, she wanted the house. She and Charles had renovated it themselves over the last ten years, and she'd personally picked out all of

HOW YOU'RE GOING TO FEEL WHEN IT COMES TIME TO THINK ABOUT MOVING OR STAYING

The house you have lived in during your marriage represents many memories and dreams from bygone days. The familiarity of the house may be desirable for you and your children, especially during the changes that accompany divorce. You may wish to preserve your familiar neighborhood, friends, local dry cleaners and grocery store; however, living in the house can also evoke painful memories that you would rather replace with new surroundings. You will have to weigh these factors internally, and also measure whether staying in the house will create untoward financial stress, to determine what is best for you and your family.

the details, from the paint color to the doorknobs. When Charles said he was leaving, she felt the house was her only solace. It was a comfort to her, but only for a time. Within two years she realized she was rushing home from her job every day to mow the yard, wait for the washing machine repairman, and to clean. She barely had enough money left every month to go to the movies, and most of her "savings" were tied up in the equity in the house. Two years ago, the house had been a comfort—now it was a liability! She sold the house and moved to a condominium, and as a result has free time and money to enjoy herself.

If either you or your spouse can afford to stay in the home, and there is a sentimental reason or attachment to it, or if you want your children to stay there, you will need to begin thinking about who will be living in it. Once that decision is made, then the question becomes how to divide the home equity.

Determining the Value of the House

Determining the value of your house will influence your decision about whether or not to sell. How much cash you each need and the net worth of your house must be weighed against other reasons for not selling (e.g., continuity for children and your preference for the neighborhood). Determining value is easy if the house is on the market for sale, and a willing buyer offers a price that both you and your spouse feel is fair. At the closing, the mortgage and any liens, as well as Realtor's fees, are paid off, and the leftover money is the net equity. That's the amount you and your spouse divide.

If you are not going to sell your house, or you are uncertain about whether to sell and would like to know the value first, you can have it professionally appraised. Since the 1980s real estate boom and crash, few people have a realistic idea of what their home is worth. Real estate agents may offer to appraise your home for free, but beware. These same agents may realize that you are divorcing, and may want the listing on the house in the event that it's sold. In order to entice you to sell, they may artificially inflate the value of the home in an effort to woo you into listing the property with them. Ask the Realtor for a list of comparable homes in your neighborhood that have sold recently. If those houses are indeed comparable to your house, you can then use these sales to estimate the value of your home.

How to select an appraiser with your spouse

If possible, select an appraiser with your spouse. Ask for a referral from a trusted real estate agent, a friend who has recently sold or purchased a house, or your lawyer. If you each know an appraiser but cannot agree on which appraiser to use, you may ask your appraisers to recommend a third party. If you can agree on an appraiser, you can split the cost, which poses an obvious advantage. By choosing one appraiser, rather than each hiring your own, you avoid "dueling appraisers" who testify against each other at a trial, a time-consuming and expensive approach.

If you cannot agree on one appraiser, and you each hire your own, choosing an appraiser who will assign a fair value to your home is generally the best strategy. If your case proceeds to trial, you'll need an appraiser who is respected in the professional community and who has experience testifying in court. An unscrupulous appraiser who assigns a disproportionately high or low appraisal value to your home to please you may not be able to justify that value in court. Judges do not take kindly to parties who try to unduly bias the court in their favor. Such shading of the truth then undermines your case.

Once you have a fair appraisal, you can determine the value of your home and decide how its equity fits in when dividing your assets.

If one of you is keeping the house and it won't be sold in the foreseeable future, the court will probably not take into account Realtor's fees and the costs of closing. If you plan to sell the house soon, credit for these fees can be negotiated.

Take into account the capital gains tax ramifications, if any. Recent changes to the law allow an exemption of $250,000 per person for gains in value on your home if it was your primary residence for at least two of the last five years. Therefore, if you sell your house while married, $500,000 of appreciation is tax-free. If you sell it after you divorce, $250,000 of the appreciation value is tax-free. For homes valued at more than $250,000, therefore, timing of the sale is an issue. You are able to use this exemption an unlimited number of times provided you adhere to the two-year residency rule in each house, so selling the house while married does not penalize either spouse should he or she buy or sell a house several years later. This is a dramatic departure from the previous capital gains tax law applying to the sale of houses. When you're considering equity, you need to take into account the tax ramifications because when they apply, they can significantly reduce the equity in a home.

Negotiations Once the Value of the House Is Set

Negotiating once the value of the house is set is a process that demands creativity and flexibility. Determine your priorities in advance of the negotiating process so that you and your spouse can develop a plan that works for both of you. Generally, judges will approve any agreement that is fair to both parties, which means you can be as creative as you wish with respect to the timing and provisions for the sale of the house and division of the equity.

If You Decide Not to Sell: Joint Versus Sole Ownership

You and your spouse have two choices concerning the ownership of the house. You can continue to own the home jointly, or one of you can own it in your sole name. Although joint ownership can be continued after a divorce, in practice this is sometimes inconvenient. It keeps one spouse

$$\triangle\!\!\!\triangle$$

Reasons to Sell

- cannot afford mortgage payments
- too much upkeep
- too much money tied up in equity
- too many memories
- money owed to others (such as family loan for down payment) makes refinancing or buy-out impossible

Reasons Not to Sell

- stability for yourself and children
- inability to refinance or buy out spouse
- sufficient diversity of assets—i.e., in addition to house equity you also have liquid assets for emergencies and/or sufficient retirement funds given your age and employment
- ability to maintain house
- ability to make mortgage payments
- tax considerations (deductibility of mortgage payments and/or capital gains)

from mortgaging or selling the property without the other spouse knowing, but it also can create friction between divorced spouses who may have different priorities with respect to the upkeep and maintenance of the home.

If one spouse retains ownership, that spouse is entitled to make all decisions concerning the property, free from any interference from the other spouse. While this may not seem like a benefit initially, five, ten, or fifteen years later the benefit of having autonomy with respect to the home ownership becomes more tangible.

Ownership of the house is different, or can be different, than the responsibility for paying the mortgage. If both you and your spouse have signed the bank papers to be responsible for the mortgage, merely signing the *title* of the house over to one spouse does not relieve the other spouse of his or her responsibility to continue paying the *mortgage*. Refinancing the home mortgage in the sole name of the spouse keeping the house is the safest way to protect the spouse who won't be occupying the home. If refinancing is impossible or impractical, your lawyer can help you build language into the agreement to protect the spouse who has relinquished his or her interest in the house from having to pay the mortgage.

If You Decide to Sell:
Arrangements for Sale of Your Home

If you intend to sell your house, contact a neutral real estate agent who can give you trustworthy advice about preparing the property for a quick sale. Ask the Realtor to tell you the minimum number of repairs and alterations needed to make the house easier to sell. Keep records of your expenses for the fix-up, and keep track of who does all of the work. Don't do anything fancy or major to the house unless it is absolutely necessary, or unless you and your spouse unequivocally agree that the improvement will be financially worthwhile. For example, painting the hallway is inexpensive and easy to do on your own, and if it will help your house sell faster, do it. If you and your spouse can cooperate in this effort, then do it together. If you can't cooperate in doing this together, see if you can arrange to divide the tasks so that each of you can work on the house separately.

Even if your spouse won't participate, such tasks must still be accomplished. Perhaps you both can agree on hiring a painting company or maintenance person to do the work for you, and splitting the cost. Even if you have to do all of the work yourself, do it. A speedy sale for a higher price benefits both of you. It ultimately works against you to let a home deteriorate, or let a sale slip through your hands by refusing to fix a roof because your spouse won't help pay. Keep a list of everything you do, so that if your case needs to be tried you can tell the judge about it later, but try to remain practical and pragmatic for now. Continue to work toward a solution rather than create an impasse, irrespective of your spouse's behavior. Don't lose sight of the benefit you will bring to yourself by putting up with some inconvenience in the short term.

Timing of the Sale or Buy-Out of Equity
When Dividing Your House's Value

Evaluate your circumstances to determine when and how the equity in the house is best split, and whether that must be accomplished by a sale, a refinance, or a buy-out between spouses. Sometimes it can be done immediately, and in other situations a delay is preferable.

If one spouse wishes to keep the house, and there is a way to divide the equity and offset it against other assets, or refinance the house so that the spouse giving up the house is paid his or her share of the equity as soon as possible, then the spouse retaining the house would have complete ownership without ties to the vacating spouse. This is the cleanest way to handle this situation.

However, you may not be in the economic position to split your home equity in this manner, or may be ineligible or unable to afford a refinance. Therefore, the timing of how a spouse is paid his or her share of the house equity becomes a central issue.

If the division of equity will not happen immediately, there may be an obvious dividing point, such as when the children graduate from high school or college, the spouse retaining the house remarries, that spouse cohabits with someone, or any other life event that you determine in advance. Generally, when the first of these events occurs, the spouse who gave up ownership of the house or the right to occupy the house needs to be paid his or her equity, either through a refinance or a sale. Sometimes, the spouse to whom payment is owed is given an opportunity to buy the house if the spouse who retained the house wishes to sell it at that time.

Executing a Mortgage in Favor of Your Spouse

If you are not in a position to refinance the house or pay your spouse immediately, and there are not enough assets to offset your spouse's interest in the home, you might consider giving your spouse a mortgage on the home, or securing your spouse's interest in the home using an equitable interest notice.

If you have determined what your spouse will be paid for his or her interest in the home, and the terms of the agreement, your lawyer can prepare a mortgage document to secure the spouse's interest in the home in the land records. That way, even if you die, your spouse's interest is protected.

A negotiating point will be whether or not the mortgage secured against the home will bear interest. Sometimes, it makes financial sense to pay your spouse interest on the mortgage, which can accumulate if he or she has to wait a long period of time for the money rather than having to immediately sell or refinance the house. Understand, however, that even if the house value falls, you will still owe the amount of money set forth in the mortgage.

For example, let's say your home is worth $100,000 and there is an $80,000 mortgage on the home, leaving $20,000 in equity. You and your spouse have agreed to divide your assets fifty-fifty and you are going to keep the house, but you are unable to pay your spouse his or her $10,000 interest in the home. You agree to execute a mortgage in favor of your spouse that you will pay in a lump sum in ten years. This mortgage will be documented by your attorney, who will draft the proper papers, and record them on the land records. The mortgage to your spouse for his or her share of the equity is a new mortgage subsequent to any mortgages already owed.

The next question is whether this mortgage will bear interest for your spouse. Your spouse is waiting ten years to get $10,000. If she or he forced you to sell the house, he or she would get money immediately. Having to wait for the money may mean that your spouse is not able to buy another house or condominium immediately and has to make certain sacrifices. In such situations, having the mortgage pay interest is a desirable option.

If the market goes up, and in ten years the $100,000 house is worth $200,000, you are still obligated only to pay the $10,000 (plus interest, if negotiated) agreed upon in the original divorce agreement. Your spouse then gets $10,000 (plus interest, if negotiated) and you keep the $190,000 value (less any outstanding mortgages) of the house. If the value of the house skyrockets to $300,000, you would get to keep all of the extra equity by virtue of the house's appreciation, and you would only owe your spouse $10,000.

If, however, the housing market falls and your house is suddenly worth $70,000 when it comes time to pay this $10,000 mortgage, you must pay your spouse the $10,000 from the divorce agreement even though the value of the house is less than it was at the time of your divorce. This is also true even though the amount that you owe on the mortgages ($80,000 on the first mortgage and $10,000 on your spouse's mortgage) may be more than what you can expect to get for the house if you sell it. This is a risk that you take by not paying your spouse or dividing the asset immediately. Generally, real estate markets go up, but that isn't always the case.

A creative way of dividing the equity in the house is for spouses to record a *notice of equitable interest* against the land records, which gives the spouse relinquishing his or her ownership interest in the house a right to a certain percentage of the equity in the house when it is sold. So, if you agreed that the house would be sold in ten years and that each spouse would receive 50 percent of the net equity, if the house was worth $70,000 in ten years and the mortgage owed was still $70,000 in the example above, then your spouse would not receive any money, and you would not have to pay your spouse more than your house is worth at the time that the equitable interest becomes due.

Yet, if in the future the house is worth $300,000, and the mortgage has been reduced to $70,000, then your spouse would be entitled to share in one half of the $230,000 profit, even though he or she hasn't been cutting the lawn or making the mortgage payments.

Sometimes, in these circumstances, the spouse remaining in the house accrues a certain amount of credit for the fact that he or she has performed the maintenance and paid down the balance on the principal owed on the mortgage over time. You may also wish to make provisions with respect to repairs and maintenance on the house, having you and your spouse share expenses for big-ticket items such as the furnace, water heater, and roof. If both spouses will share in the appreciation of the house (or depreciation), they could both share in the maintenance costs.

These situations can get sticky emotionally and are not as straightforward as simply refinancing or selling the house at the time of the divorce, but they offer a creative solution to help you settle your case.

⚖

TAX CHECKLIST

- Decide who gets to use your children's dependency exemptions. By law, the custodial parent claims the exemptions, but you can use IRS Form 8332 to transfer the exemption(s) to the noncustodial parent if you agree to do so. For many families, allocation of the exemption to a noncustodial parent may save that parent money, making more money available for child support or spousal maintenance. For the parent who is transferring the exemption, it is safest if he or she signs the transfer year by year—after support payments have been made—rather than signing a permanent transfer.
- Determine whether you are eligible to file as head of household. A joint custody order can be structured so that one child resides primarily with one parent and another resides primarily with the other parent, thus entitling both parents to file as head of household.
- The primary custodial parent may be entitled to a child care credit.
- Either parent may claim medical and dental expenses that are above the designated percent of adjusted gross income.
- Determine what part of support payments are child support and which are alimony, because alimony is deducted by the payor and included in the taxable income of the payee, and child support is not deductible or taxable. If payments are designated as "unallocated child support and alimony," all payments are deductible by the payor and included in income for the payee.
- If alimony is reduced by more than $15,000 per year within the first three years of payment, the tax deduction enjoyed by the payor spouse may be subject to special IRS "recapture" rules, making excess alimony nondeductible.
- Know your tax basis for all assets, so that you can calculate how much capital gains tax would be owed in the event that these assets were sold. Transfers between spouses pursuant to a divorce are not taxable.

TAX CONSIDERATIONS

Before you sign any settlement papers, you must determine the tax impact of each decision you're making. A number of tax issues may apply to your situation, in addition to the capital gains tax on appreciation discussed above.

Transfer of Property Between Spouses

The transfer of property between you and your spouse as part of your divorce is not a taxable event as long as the transfer takes place within one year after the date of your divorce. That means that all of the settlement issues you're discussing in terms of who-gets-what won't have any immediate tax consequences.

The nontaxability of transfers between spouses also applies to stocks, bonds, mutual funds, and any other property that you owned jointly and that one of you will now own separately.

Capital gains taxes and transfer taxes (in the case of real estate or other titled assets like boats and cars) *will* apply if you later transfer that asset to a third party, either by sale or gift.

Bob and Jill jointly own a house that they purchased for $100,000, but which is now worth $175,000. They also own stocks worth $50,000 which they bought for $30,000. Bob transfers the house to Jill and Jill transfers the stocks to Bob. Both assets have appreciated in value, as indicated above. Neither of these transfers triggers any tax.

Bob then sells the stock (to a third party) two weeks later to pay off some debts. He will owe capital gains tax on the $20,000 appreciation of the stocks, typically about 33 percent.

Jill sells the house two months later to a third party, as well. Because the appreciation is $75,000, she won't owe capital gains tax because the first $250,000 of appreciation is exempt from capital gains, but she will owe any transfer taxes assessed by her county or town.

FAULT

WILL FAULT ISSUES IN THE DIVORCE IMPACT ASSET AND PROPERTY DIVISION EVEN IN "NO-FAULT" DIVORCE?

Even in "no-fault" divorce states, fault is one of the factors that the court may consider in dividing assets. That said, most courts will divide assets and property evenly between the parties unless there is some overriding reason why a fifty-fifty division would not be appropriate. Generally the division will not vary by more than 10 percent based on reasons why the marriage broke down, or punishment for the spouse who caused the marriage to break down. The judge is concerned with dividing assets fairly and according to the law. He or she is unlikely to be overly concerned about hurtful words, or even affairs, because such circumstances are common. An experienced judge has heard innumerable tragic stories. Only an unusual scenario captures the attention of most judges, a scenario that goes beyond an office affair or devastating argument.

The court's interest in fault has decreased dramatically in the past twenty years. Previously, one of the main reasons for an unequal property division was fault. The reason that the marriage broke down was attributed to one party and the punishment for that was a lesser share of the marital property awarded that spouse. That scenario has become less common over time.

By focusing on fault issues, you can lose your path toward your ultimate goal in the case. Trials and court procedures are not designed for vindication, revenge, or clearing one's name. They're designed to divide assets fairly between two spouses, taking into account your individual circumstances. As unfair as it seems, fault rarely constitutes a reason in the court's eyes for dividing assets unevenly. Accepting this now will save you much heartache later, as well as time and money.

IF FAULT RARELY AFFECTS ASSET AND PROPERTY DISTRIBUTION IN COURT, WHAT ROLE DOES FAULT PLAY IN THE DIVORCE?

Judges and courts aside, assignment of fault is a motivating factor in the reason spouses seek a divorce. Whether it's an affair, lack of respect, domestic violence, falling out of love, or more subtle issues, "fault" is an issue in almost every decision to divorce. Feelings of "I didn't break up the marriage, he/she did" are almost universal, and often the motivation behind destructive behavior during the legal process.

Many clients feel that they must explain the reasons they want a divorce to their spouse, including a list of past sins. Confessing mistakes and shortcomings often makes people feel better (e.g., less guilty), and it can help them forgive themselves for their perceived failures in the marriage. The temptation to confess bites early, but can continue throughout the case. By and large, the most popular "sin" confessed to is an affair.

Although admitting an affair may help you to feel less guilt, beware that it may be used against you in your divorce. It *can* be considered by most courts in dividing assets and determining spousal maintenance. Worse, it can add fuel to your spouse's already burning fire of hurt, rage, and revenge. Discussing an affair with your spouse can have many beneficial psychological outcomes, but your motivations and timing should be considered carefully.

If you're involved in an affair or other intimate-type relationship when you decide to divorce, put the relationship on hold until your case is finished. If the person with whom you're involved cares about you, he or she can wait until your divorce is finalized to continue your relationship. It is not worth having an illicit relationship become part of your case. The court process also can put undue pressure on a relationship that might feel healthier and serve you better if timed appropriately.

WHAT WILL BE HAPPENING BETWEEN MY SPOUSE AND ME DURING THIS TIME?

Friend or Foe

The waiting period between serving your spouse with divorce papers (or being served) and the time you reach settlement or decide to go to trial often feels like the longest leg of your journey. Most people find this period to be the decisive juncture in determining what their relationship will be with their spouse through the rest of the divorce process. You may not be ready or interested in being friends with your spouse, but you also want to prevent him or her from becoming an opponent in the divorce, if at all possible.

Some of the emotional issues that lead people down the path toward conflict stem from how each person feels about *how* the divorce was set in motion. If you have moved toward ending your marriage with grace thus far, it will be easier to resolve legal issues than if you have not taken your partner's feelings and needs into account. But even if you have, the confluence of angry and hurt feelings that are part and parcel of ending a long-term relationship provide a huge stumbling block to achieving a congenial divorce.

A common mistake is to focus only on your spouse's deficiencies and the qualities you dislike. This focus serves an important purpose; it helps you uncouple as you remind yourself over and over again that you are relieved to be rid of your spouse. But such feelings also become chains that bind you to your spouse by keeping him or her at the forefront of your thoughts. It is a fine line between love and hate, those powerful emotions that are both accompanied by a blinding preoccupation. As long as you hate, you do not have energy free to reinvest elsewhere, in a healing direction.

Seeing your spouse as all-bad is an attempt to rub soothing balm into injured pride. Spouses who are left for new partners are particularly vulnerable to this way of thinking. The negativity also absorbs time and energy that might otherwise be a dreaded reminder of the emptiness and loneliness most people feel at this stage of the divorce process. Such negativity is one way your mind works to cover up your ambivalence about the relationship ending, about starting over, and letting go. Negativity fuels desires to punish your spouse for the injustices he or she has wrought on you. And finally, seeing the world in such simple terms helps you to believe that you are a better person (or parent) than your spouse.

For all these reasons, it is understandable to feel yourself pulled toward exclusively negative opinions about your spouse. But there are ways to stop yourself from going down this slippery slope. List all your spouse's best qualities, then list those you like least. Try to find at least one positive for every few negatives. If your partner is stubborn and self-righteous, she might also be tenacious in her ideas. This tenacity might benefit your children, in the form of unwavering loyalty.

Look at your list of negatives and ask yourself: what do you gain by hanging on to all of them? If the answer includes some of the emotions discussed above, such as trying to save face or feeling less ambivalent about the divorce, first let yourself become fully aware of those feelings. Allow yourself to experience them but imagine doing so without trying to prove anything to your spouse.

Now list the negatives in descending order from most to least important to your divorced life, that is, to a life in which you do not know or care what is happening in your spouse's life if it does not affect your children. For example, your spouse's self-centeredness no longer will affect you. Nor will his sloppiness or his procrastination when it comes to paying bills.

Replace each negative near the top of your list with a positive attribute that is the mirror image of the negative trait. Perhaps being an irresponsible person contributes to your spouse's easygoing style with the children, a needed balance to your obsessive style. Listing good qualities as such reminds you, in the midst of your anger and hurt, that this person does have redeeming features, and those are reasons to be generous—if not forgiving—with each other.

NEGOTIATING WITH YOUR SPOUSE: SKILLS AND TIPS

One antidote for creating static, negative images of your spouse is to negotiate for what you want and need. If you are ready to look beyond your anger, then you can seek equitable solutions to your conflicts. To accomplish this, you must be ready to change the desired outcomes of your conflict. Roger Fisher and William Ury's book *Getting to Yes* teaches ways to negotiate win-win solutions to conflicts. They suggest that in order to create a mutual win-win position, "The first thing you are trying to win is a better way to negotiate."

Negotiating rather than fighting becomes a winning proposition on several levels:

- you develop skills that will serve you in this relationship and others after the legal process is over
- you get what you want in a positive atmosphere with less likelihood of later retaliation
- you want your spouse to feel he can get what he wants so that you do not push him toward an attorney interested in strong-arm tactics.

The basic methods for negotiation are similar to those discussed in Chapter 3 for resolving conflicts. Both are designed to create win-win outcomes based on mutual interests. The main tenets described include focusing on needs rather than positions. "I want to be an involved father with time spent each week with my children" is a need. "I want joint custody with equal time" is a position. You must be ready to look at both sides, using the art of paraphrasing and repeating what you have heard until both persons feel their "story" is understood. Problems must be described in neutral terms rather than in blaming language. "You are never on time to pick up the children on your day" is a blaming way of presenting the problem. An alternative way is: "On Tuesdays, I am supposed to leave for work just when you are due to pick up the children. When you are not on time, I am late for work and I get into trouble." This definition of a problem has a greater chance of being solved because it engenders less defensiveness.

Understanding negotiation leads to placing each conflict resolution opportunity into a broader context. Each conflict is a part of a whole negotiation strategy. The bigger picture requires a broader lens, like adding a panoramic lens to your camera to get a broader view. In addition to resolving individual conflicts, try looking at the whole picture.

Make a list of all the things you desire from the negotiations, and prioritize them from most to least important to you. Asterisk those items you could concede. It is important to give some things up without making a demand for something in return. You must have something to give that allows the other person to feel they're also getting what they need. The more generous you are, the more likely you are to gain concessions. Therefore, be clear from the beginning what you are prepared to give up as a gift. When the other person offers you something, express your appreciation, indicating that his or her gesture is valued. This increases the likelihood that such behavior will occur again. After every successful decision, write it down. Both spouses and their attorneys should have copies to make sure that everyone has the same understanding of the agreement that was reached. Too often people make progress in negotiations and then disagree later about what was actually said and meant, building resentment as each person accuses the other of stalling and wasting time. If you are the person most eager to divorce, you can circumvent your partner's stall tactics, conscious or not.

Another reason negotiations break down is because people take entrenched positions out of fear. For example, some mothers refuse to let the kids go away with their fathers because, believing their fathers offer more exciting weekends, they are afraid the children will want to spend less time with them. Discussing this, or ensuring that Mom has money reserved for special events with her children, alleviates the fear.

When negotiating, avoid handing down ultimatums. They rarely have the intended effect, and usually create deeper resentments. Contrary to popular opinion, do not pad your requests so that you wind up with what you really wanted from the beginning. This creates a sense of dishonesty that leads to fewer concessions, since guessing what is really important to each party becomes a central focus. Then assumptions and worst fears creep in. Be clear about what you want, and then know what you can give in on and what you can't.

If negotiations are breaking down, there are several effective remedies. If you both want the same outcomes, such as having the kids with you on Christmas Day, try adding some additional ideas to the negotiation rather than convincing the other you have the best reasons. One idea would be to arrange two events for Christmas Day, such as an early morning with one parent and a later dinner with the other, with each having its special charms. When you really want something your spouse is not giving in on, try sweetening the pie. If you already offered her the silver for the antique mirror you want, try offering the silver and the china for the mirror.

Other techniques include changing perspectives, so that you each argue for the other person's point. If both perspectives don't seem equally valuable to you, then they may not be equitable.

Another technique is to reach general decisions but save delineation of specifics for another session, when you are both fresher. For example, agree that you will divide your nonliquid assets between you, but do not decide which accounts or parts of the pension will go to each of you. Similarly, agree on a next step rather than an outcome—i.e., you will each talk to your employer about a change in work schedule, without deciding who will change their schedules and when. Yet another technique is to pose two or three options to a stalemated decision, and agree to try each for a specified amount of time. Often a trial run will help you decide an issue based on situations you did not anticipate.

Some agreements are built with contingency plans: if you get your raise at work, then you will increase your child support by $50. These plans depend on events that are likely but not assured. Negotiating one step at a time with built-in contingencies may take longer initially, but it reduces the likelihood of false starts and retracing steps later.

How Do I Manage My Anxiety During This Time?

As discussed earlier in this chapter, most states have a mandatory waiting period before people can be divorced, even if both parties have completely resolved all of their issues. This period is sometimes referred to as a "cooling-off" period, ostensibly designed so that people do not make hasty decisions to divorce. While you are waiting, a pervasive anxiety is natural. In its milder form, anxiety is a nonspecific, persistent feeling of uneasiness; a more intense version includes feelings of dread and fear. This period of the unknown is when most people turn off the trail of a rational divorce and begin bushwacking through unmarked territory. Such stumbling about can lead you to spend many wasted hours feeling lost, frightened, and looking for a way back to the familiar.

Use this period to plan rather than to plot. Fill it with the productive work that leads to negotiation. Make your lists of assets, property, debts, and future desires. While you are setting up and trying interim agreements with your spouse, take caution to specify the trial period. In many cases, postdivorce financial and child-related arrangements, yet to be discussed, are remarkably similar to the interim agreements couples set. Such agreements often lead to decisions by parents, and by the courts, that favor consistency and maintenance of current conditions, rendering it difficult to effect a major change. If you have agreed to pay $500 per month for alimony in the interim period, your claim that you cannot afford that amount will be difficult to prove subsequently.

One characteristic of the legal system that riddles this period with anxiety is that the legal process is slow, especially compared to individual desires to "get this over with as soon as possible." You will feel on some weeks that nothing is happening in your case. Check in with your spouse and your attorney (if you are using one). Perhaps there is some way you could help speed up the process—maybe documents are needed that you could amass more quickly—or perhaps there is nothing that can be done at this time and your spouse is working on his or her part. Knowing the status of your case and what to expect in terms of timing should help.

Manage the bulk of your anxiety through family and friends who are supportive, and turn to a mental health professional when your friends' reassurance is insufficient to keep you focused on your own life rather than on your spouse's. If you have a lawyer, use him or her only for legal questions. Call your lawyer to get help with the "whats" and "hows" of your divorce, but a phone conversation to report your spouse's bad behavior is an inappropriate use that will only cost you money. Anticipating your spouse's strategies in negotiations should be useful in helping you to practice backing up your choices with facts, examples, or alternatives. But try to spend your time planning, not worrying about "What if she won't let me have the kids often enough?" That kind of call to your lawyer evokes anger or frustration when the lawyer cannot fix your situation, and rarely leads to successful strategizing.

This time may be filled with a dawning awareness of the less glamorous aspects of divorce. Your quiet home now seems empty, lonely. You never realized how difficult it would be to get all three of your children to their activities without someone else to pick up Jamie at the middle school, be home when Mike calls for a ride, or get Susie to dance class, all within one hour of each other. This period often leads to requestioning the desirability of the divorce. Couples who are civil with each other in efforts to be cooperative may experience "mini-reconciliations." These brief interludes do not last for most couples, as they slip back into the patterns that led them to divorce in the first place. They do, however, provide temporary respite during the waiting process. When these reconciliations fail, people may emerge with renewed vigor to get the divorce over with, and become angry and frustrated with their lawyers and the legal process when they slow them down.

WHAT IF I HAVE SEX WITH MY SPOUSE?

One natural response to the anxiety of this period is to have sexual relations with your spouse, especially if you are both still living in the same house. Having sex with your spouse is comforting because it is familiar, discharges anxiety, and may be one of the more satisfying aspects of your relationship. However, continuing the sexual relationship sets you up to feel disappointed once again, as it proves to be only a fleeting moment of contentment. It may even provide another opening to feel belittled or used by your spouse. Engaging in sexual relations can also prolong the psychological and emotional separation process that is taking place during the legal divorce. And it can give your children a mixed message about what is about to happen in their lives, and what the future may hold. They will get their hopes up that the divorce is not going to happen, and when the situation reverts back, you can expect them to feel confused and angry at you.

WHAT IF I WANT TO DATE SOMEONE NEW?

In this era of no-fault divorce, judges rarely focus on transgressions such as dating. Unfortunately, sexism still reigns supreme in some courtrooms, and standards are tougher in this regard for women. Mothers are expected to put their children's needs above their own. Dating someone else seriously, especially when a sexual relationship is involved, is still viewed as a distraction from mothers' primary responsibility to their children. Fathers may not be viewed as negatively for dating someone else, but if you are a father who is in arrears for child support and seeing someone else, beware of the message you are sending to the judge. The new relationship may not be viewed as a distinct issue from the divorce.

Having sex with other people during divorce is often raised by spouses as an example of why the other parent is not fit to be a sole custodian, have liberal access, or spend overnights with the children. Unmarried sex is still viewed as controversial in many relationships and this view is reflected in the legal system. The amount of emphasis placed on sexual relations differs across the country based on the values and mores of the area, the court, and the particular judge. Having sex when minor children are present in the home is still viewed in many districts as constituting an unwholesome living environment.

But it is not the judge who is going to give you the hardest time about dating in most cases. It is your spouse. No matter how your spouse has behaved previously, dating during the divorce process can be a hazardous venture. Many spouses are amazed at the jealousy their partners exhibit as soon as they find out about a new relationship. A double standard emerges in which your spouse explains her behavior based on what's her due because of past hurts. You, on the other hand, should stay home, and lament her new relationship. Once you begin to enjoy a new relationship, your spouse may resent it, and begin to give you a very difficult time in the divorce.

Socializing with persons of the opposite sex can do wonders to improve your self-image. Do not stay out overnight, especially if you have children. If you have children, make sure that they have a proper babysitter, and that you do not go out too often. If you have someone stay over, do so when the children are out of the house. Regardless of your values, it is best to refrain from sexual relations until the divorce is completed. Remember that you are under your spouse's and the court's microscope regarding parenting arrangements, and your spouse could at any time initiate a custody proceeding if he or she perceives that you are enjoying yourself too much, and spending too little time with the children.

As rules of thumb, if you are considering entering a new relationship while in the midst of a divorce, here are some factors that will influence the importance that relationship may play in the divorce:

How long have you been separated? How long have you known the person you are now dating? Is your spouse involved with someone too? Is he or she likely to give you a harder time as a result of the new relationship? Do you have children and what ages are they? Children who are about five or six years of age and those entering adolescence are particularly vulnerable to feeling competitive with the new partner. In all instances, proceed cautiously and with discretion.

From an emotional perspective, dating seriously while you are in the throes of a legal divorce is a complex business. There are several reasons why you must be vigilant about your new relationships during this time. First, this is a time of high tension and emotional vulnerability. You and your spouse are undergoing a time of stress and anxiety wherein emotions are irrational, and sometimes simply crazy. Partners are given to jealousy that sometimes blows into full rages. Even if your partner is dating, he or she is still likely to be emotionally connected to you. Your partner can begin to make the legal process lengthy and difficult, or may wish to try to control you in some other form via the interim financial arrangements.

Second, this is a time when you should be preparing for the successful end of your divorce and adjustment to your life afterward. Your focus at this time should be on adjusting to this new status, and helping your children with the multiple transitions inherent in divorce. It is a time when you will be thinking about how you are going to be financially responsible. This is your time to recover from the emotional hurt and pain that you have sustained to this point. It may be a time when you experience some depression and grief. These adaptations take energy. It is energy best put into concluding your divorce rather than establishing your new life, which will be waiting for you when you are finished.

Third, after years of lacking love and consideration from your partner, the experience of rejection, neglect, and abandonment that you may have felt in your relationship can lead you into a "rebound" relationship. You are at highest risk of choosing someone like your spouse in ways that have not been good for you. Often people who date at this period of time enter into a dating relationship with the emotional mind-set of the time when they were first dating and courting their spouse. People report feeling giddy and excited, as they had prior to the marriage. Remember that you are older and wiser now, and your requirements in a relationship are different.

Give yourself time to know who is emerging from the ended marriage. You have a better chance then of entering into a happy and healthy relationship that can develop into a deeper and more mature one over time. Transitional relationships can have shaky foundations, yet you are probably thrilled with the attention and interest that your new love shows you. Enjoy a relationship that begins in friendship and shows care for what you need at this time. Then you won't let yourself get caught up in the excitement of the moment at the expense of your emotional well-being later on. Be patient; there will be time to start new relationships after your divorce is final.

Ralph and his wife had been married for eighteen years. Linda had kept a superbly clean house, had helped Ralph with the bookkeeping for his building business, and had seen to it that both of them stayed on the straight and narrow. Ralph had become disenchanted with Linda and filed for divorce. Upon meeting a woman who was to him exciting, fun, more relaxed and flexible than his wife had ever been, Ralph began to date this woman during the time of the separation. Initially elated with this new relationship, he very quickly found that his new love had very little regard for money matters, seemed to be more interested in going out for dinner than having a meal at home, and housekeeping was the last thing on her mind. When it came time for the final divorce, Ralph began to withdraw from his new relationship. He began to think more clearly about the qualities that he would like in a partner at this stage of his life. Shortly after the divorce he met another woman with whom he was more compatible, who seemed to have a better balance in her view of the necessities of keeping a home and business and a relationship working well. Taking this new relationship slower than his first postseparation relationship, Ralph remarried twenty-two months after the divorce.

Carol entered into a series of brief relationships during the course of the mandatory waiting period. In these relationships, she found herself acting in ways that made her dislike herself. She complained that she would respond to these new men in the same way she had responded to her husband during the course of her marriage. Carol, so fearful of losing these relationships, would complain endlessly about how difficult her life was at this time: looking after the kids alone, having to be solely responsible for the household, and the lack of emotional support. When not complaining, Carol would endlessly try to please each of her new dates. She didn't know how to ask directly for her needs to be met in these relationships. She tried to take on the interests and the hobbies of each boyfriend, regardless of whether or not she enjoyed these pursuits. The seesaw of complaining and compliance made Carol seem, even to herself, emotionally childish, and she began to doubt whether she would ever be able to have a relationship that was fulfilling and meaningful.

The bottom line: postpone serious involvement with someone new until you are certain that you are past both the legal and emotional divorce recovery time!

WHAT DO I DO IF I WANT TO HAVE A CALMER, FRIENDLIER DIVORCE BUT MY LAWYER HAS ADVISED ME TO BE TOUGHER?

You need to determine why your lawyer feels you should be handling your case in a way that feels wrong to you. Ask if he or she feels you are being too passive, willing to accept much less than a court would deem appropriate? Are you being bullied by an abusive spouse into accepting an inappropriate custody and visitation arrangement? The lawyer should be able to outline for you the parameters of the likely outcomes for your case, and together you can match your goals to what the law deems fair. By the same token, after you've discussed the likely outcomes with your lawyer, if you decide for your own reasons to accept a lesser settlement, or to capitulate to a pushy spouse, then it's your lawyer's job to follow your wishes.

The most important thing to do for yourself during divorce is to maintain control over your case. You can do that by implementing the planning strategies in this book, and by determining your priorities. Your attorney works for you. He or she has expertise, but that is useful to the extent that it is applied toward making you feel more comfortable about the direction your divorce is taking and helping you to achieve the goals you've set for your case—not the other way around. Many clients seem afraid of their attorneys. Others are so afraid they will make a fatal error in negotiation that they don't dare redirect a lawyer who seems to be heading them in a direction they do not wish to go.

If you have doubts about the direction your divorce is taking, talk over your concerns with your lawyer immediately. If you are not satisfied with the conversation, or if you are afraid to have it, then switch lawyers before more time goes by.

Bonnie wanted to participate in a free alternative dispute resolution program being offered to divorcing spouses with young children. Both Bonnie and her husband Paul expressed their interest, and made plans to enroll in the program. Bonnie called back to cancel, saying her attorney advised her not to participate, playing on her fears that it would result in a settlement less beneficial to her than one he could negotiate. Bonnie could not explain why her attorney felt this way, she just kept insisting that she had to go along with her attorney. Eventually, her divorce became a prolonged legal battle that seemed to emanate from the lawyer's agenda.

PERSONAL ASSESSMENT

Have I set realistic, sensible goals? Have I accounted for our income, assets, and debts and thought about which division best suits my needs? Have I ranked each asset in terms of its importance to me? If I keep my own priorities in mind, it will be easier to avoid becoming trapped in arguments and self-pity when negotiations become difficult.

Have I tried to consider what is a fair resolution of this divorce from my spouse's perspective? If what I expect from the divorce and what I'm prepared to offer to my spouse are out of balance, then I cannot expect my spouse to work with me to achieve a peaceful settlement. If I can understand my spouse's motivations as well as my own, we can work together for resolution.

Have I considered the emotional and financial costs to me if we cannot settle our case? If I cannot have everything that I want from the settlement, is what is being offered sufficient for my needs? If I am able to weigh all of the costs and benefits of accepting or rejecting a settlement that represents a compromise of my goals, I will make the best decision under the circumstances.

Have I learned to negotiate fairly? Am I prepared to give up things that mean more to my spouse than to me without expecting anything in return? If I am committed to negotiating in good faith and am willing to compromise on less important points, I will foster an atmosphere in which we have the best chance of reaching an agreement.

Have I conducted my new life with decorum and sensitivity? Have I let my anxiety propel me into behaving thoughtlessly or impetuously? I have much to think about during this time, and much planning to do, and my emotions must not derail me from what needs to be done.

5.

Evidence and Pretrial Procedures: You Can Never Be Too Prepared

We have emphasized the financial and emotional benefits of working out your divorce amicably. Sometimes it is impossible to resolve things without court intervention, despite your best intentions. If the breakdown in the negotiation process is a result of your spouse's refusal to cooperate, and if you have tried everything you can think of to make the situation more amiable to no avail, then you need to shift into a protective mode. In the event your case proceeds to trial, you will need as much information as you can get. If you are able to resolve your case before you get to trial, it will be because you were prepared. Divorce never feels fair, but you need to optimize your chances of a fair result, irrespective of the path that brought you to this end on your journey.

The next step toward being prepared is putting all of the evidence together which you will need to make intelligent, informed decisions. Some of this evidence will be easy to obtain, and some will require investigation or even court intervention. Once you have the whole financial picture, you are ready to proceed to the next step, the pretrial settlement conference, which is the court's last attempt to assist you in settling your case before trial. It is at this stage that many seemingly adversarial divorce cases are resolved because most (if not all) of your questions about income and assets have been answered, and with the help of competent legal advisors, the court settlement officers, or judge acting as a settlement officer, a reasonable recommendation for resolution can be made. By this point in the process, most people settle prior to trial.

PUTTING THE EVIDENCE TOGETHER

No matter how amicable your divorce, it's still important to assemble financial documents as soon, and as thoroughly, as possible, as discussed in Chapter 2. The pretrial waiting period is a final chance to collect the information required to complete your divorce.

It may be tempting to procrastinate in amassing information, because this brings you closer to divorce. But it is best to begin early, because though there is information you can assemble on your own, there will also be documents you and/or your lawyer will need to get from other sources, which can take time to acquire. In the event that your divorce turns adversarial, you'll also be able to start thinking about additional evidence you wouldn't otherwise need, such as testimony, photographs, and physical evidence.

Some of the necessary information may need to come from your spouse. His or her year-to-date earnings, pension statements, or individual bank accounts are some examples of documents that your spouse will have to provide, since you won't have access to them unless your spouse shares them voluntarily.

The simplest way for you and your lawyer to get these documents is to make a list of what you want and to ask for them. If you and your spouse (and any attorneys involved) are cooperative, the information exchange occurs smoothly and quickly. This is the simplest, least expensive way to accomplish necessary financial disclosures. When you cannot obtain the information that you need, you will utilize legal procedures known as "discovery." You can do discovery without a lawyer, but if your case becomes adversarial, you will probably wish to seek legal counsel.

DISCOVERY: RELEASES, INTERROGATORIES, DEPOSITIONS, AND SUBPOENAS

Discovery is a legal method to obtain information about your case from your spouse or other sources. Discovery mechanisms generally fall into four categories: releases, interrogatories, depostions, and subpoenas.

Releases

In some cases, neither you nor your spouse will be in possession of strategic documents. For example, you may have misplaced tax returns, lost bank statements, or thrown away your pay stubs and pension account statements. If it's simply a question of copying documents, you can sign a release to have the document copies sent to you or your attorney. For tax returns, the IRS has a standard form release that allows them to send copies of tax returns to you for a fee. Most banks will also send copies of records that have been misplaced. Banks retain records for a long period of time, but for a fee (ask in advance, the fee is not always small) they will provide your records.

Interrogatories

Interrogatories are written questions to which your spouse must provide answers in writing, and under oath. They are often accompanied by "a request for documents," which is a list of requests for copies of documents to be provided along with the interrogatory responses. Interrogatories may be of any length and there are relatively few rules limiting the content of the questions. Generally, the legal standard is that you may ask any question that would lead to potentially admissible information. Admissible information is information that the court would use in the event of a trial.

Because a divorce case pertains to your entire married life, and in some states it also concerns financial transactions prior to your marriage, interrogatories can be very open-ended. Questions can be asked concerning almost any topic, ranging from finances to children's report cards to sexual relations. If you are looking over an interrogatory package that your lawyer has sent you for response, and you see questions that don't look appropriate, consult your lawyer immediately, but be forewarned that almost every subject is fair game.

Depositions

Depositions are sworn testimony taken under oath in an informal setting, such as the lawyer's office, in the presence of a court stenographer. The stenographer records the testimony word for word and prints a transcript of it. This transcript can be used subsequently at trial in the event that the witness, presumably your spouse in this case, gives a different answer at the trial, or for some reason is unavailable to testify. Like interrogatories, you can ask any question pertaining to the marriage. That leaves the field wide open.

Depositions are wonderful tools for preparing cases for trial. Imagine being able to ask your spouse in advance what arguments he or she intends to use, witnesses he or she intends to call, and what he or she is going to say about you on the stand. Depositions settle more cases than almost any other vehicle available to you. See page 328 of the Appendix for a set of sample deposition questions.

The drawback to depositions is that they are expensive and time consuming. You must decide upon which questions to ask your spouse, and your lawyer will also make a list of questions to ask. You and your lawyer will need to discuss these questions ahead of time and make sure you have all the bases covered; your lawyer is then present at the deposition. This adds up to a great deal of legal time, so ask for a cost estimate from your lawyer in advance. You also must pay for the court reporter, which is frequently quite expensive. Ask your lawyer to approximate how much the court reporter's fees will be for a deposition so that you may budget accordingly.

Subpoenas

A subpoena is a legal document that is issued by the court or your lawyer, requesting that certain witnesses or documents be made available on a certain date. Subpoenas generally must be served by a sheriff in advance of the court hearing, deposition or other proceeding at which the witness's presence is being requested. Therefore, determine with your lawyer in advance what information you need and from whom.

Subpoenas are used to obtain information from independent sources, like an employer, when your spouse refuses to turn over information voluntarily. The most common use for a subpoena is for wage and pension records. If you believe your spouse has lied (or made a mistake) about his or her wages, get a copy of the wage documents from the employer. One subpoena, which typically costs $50 to $100, can be served on the employer for the past two to three years of records and can cover income, pension records, and health insurance plans. The second most common use for a subpoena is to obtain bank records. If an account is solely in your spouse's name, and is not provided as part of a voluntary exchange of documents, you can obtain the missing statements with a subpoena. You can also use a subpoena to double-check records received from your spouse that look suspicious—for example, a dishonest spouse with a container of correction fluid and access to a copy machine can misrepresent balances or withdrawals.

How to Maximize Discovery's Usefulness

Proceed with discovery in logical order and work for cooperation first. Start early enough to have time to do discovery step by step. Start by asking for a voluntary exchange of documents and releases. If your spouse is uncooperative then use subpoenas or interrogatories. See if you uncover suspicious information that seems worth investigating further. If so, then take the next step to find hidden income or assets. Use increasingly aggressive methods sparingly, only as needed. Few cases actually warrant a full-blown investigation. On the other hand, if you skimp on your discovery, you may feel as though you did not get a fair shake, and that is a decision you will be living with for the rest of your life.

Despite its cost, wisely used discovery can be well worth the time and money it takes. Although time-consuming, it can be accomplished during the mandatory waiting period. Most cases require only a few subpoenas, which can be a very cost-effective way of resolving financial disputes.

Most people maintain their money in only a few places. If the bank records that you and your spouse have are incomplete or not fully disclosed, you can issue a subpoena to the bank or brokerage house that holds the account. In such instances, using simple discovery techniques (e.g., interrogatories) can be cost-effective and efficient.

Extensive discovery, on the other hand, is expensive. If you're taking depositions, your costs quickly add up when you account for lawyer time and court reporter fees. Issuing twenty or thirty subpoenas to financial institutions tends to be wasteful and expensive. It isn't worthwhile to spend $1,000 to find only $1,000. You and your lawyer can work together to quantify what you suspect is missing. Then you can make decisions about what is worthwhile to pursue.

Jeannette, absolutely, positively did not trust her husband. She felt he was lying about everything. For years she'd believed every word he said, and then one day she found out he was having an affair. After that, her trust in him evaporated. Although her husband was a police officer who earned $50,000 a year, she was convinced that he had money hidden. Because she was so suspicious, and because police officers often have overtime pay that can be hard to accurately calculate, as well as substantial pensions, we issued a subpoena to his employer. We received the income and pension records from the employer. Sure enough, the husband had made a mistake (intentional or not) on his financial affidavit and had not included some overtime income. He had also underestimated his pension benefits. It was only about $50 per week in income and $2,500 from his pension, and his lawyer, embarrassed at his client's mistake, quickly revised his financial statement. This cost about $50.

Jeannette remained convinced that her husband had thousands of dollars stashed. She could not point to any illegal income or activity to confirm her suspicions. The couple had two children who were teenagers, a mortgage, and car payments. Jeannette didn't work outside of the home, and had not worked in over six years. Although it was unlikely that a police officer earning $50,000 per year had much money left over after paying for children's expenses, a mortgage, two cars, and payroll taxes, she insisted on a full asset search. She hired an asset locator firm to search bank account and stock records both nationally and offshore. The total bill for the investigator alone totaled over $5,000. The investigator found nothing that wasn't already disclosed. Jeannette let her suspicions run away with her common sense, and it ended up costing her a great deal of money—money that would have been better spent on her children or her home.

INCOME INVENTORY

Income can include money beyond the typical paycheck. Make sure you've included each of these sources:

- Salary
- Bonuses
- Commissions
- Overtime and extra duty
- Dividends (taxable and nontaxable)
- Interest (taxable and nontaxable)
- Royalties
- Pension/retirement payments
- Social Security payments
- Disability income
- Unemployment compensation
- Reimbursed business expenses

Sometimes, your financial picture is more complicated than simply reviewing documents provided and deposition testimony. Perhaps the most confusing of these more complicated issues is *finding hidden income.*

HIDDEN INCOME

Ethical Problems If It's Your Hidden Income

On the financial statement you submit to the court, you are required to make a full disclosure, under oath, about your income, assets, and liabilities. If you are untruthful, you take the risk of having your case reopened for fraud. Domestic cases are fraught with lies, deceit, and attempts to hide assets. If a judge perceives that you've engaged in any of these, plan on being punished for it. Occasionally a judge will refer a case to the prosecutor's office to be prosecuted for perjury, in addition to appropriate financial sanctions in the divorce case. Hiding assets is tricky, and not worth the potential punishment on discovery.

Finding Your Spouse's Hidden Assets

Irrespective of the risk, hiding assets is not an infrequent event. Fortunately, finding most hidden assets is reasonably easy. It's a matter of being thorough and persistent. Almost every source of income and asset has a paper trail, or other evidence of its existence. Private investigators now have databases to search even off-shore bank accounts and stock holdings. You have access to a great deal of personal information about your spouse, so if you have the incentive and time to spend doing a little detective work on your own, you can save a bundle on private detective fees.

Income

All wages and income that have been paid by an employer are required to be reported to employees and the IRS via W-2 and 1099 forms. Therefore, the employer will have records of wage information, which also appear on tax returns.

Sometimes people are paid "under the table" or "off the books." This kind of wage money is harder to trace because such practices are illegal, and hence secretive. Employers who practice this illegal bookkeeping will be unlikely to cooperate in requests to provide accurate wage information. Unless you think there is much money of this type involved, it may not be worth tracking down since it will be so difficult and costly to prove.

Many clients claim that their spouse is not disclosing all of his or her income to the IRS, or to the court. One scenario is a self-employed spouse who does not declare all of the income of his or her business on a tax return. This scenario is frequent among waitresses, who receive large portions of income in tips. In these instances, the tax return does not tell the whole story, and you may need to search out hidden assets.

The first place to start is with your lifestyle. If you are going on lavish vacations, eating at expensive restaurants, and driving luxury cars, consider

☖

FINDING HIDDEN INCOME

❑ Look for reimbursed business expenses most people pay out of their own pockets:
  • company car
  • meals and entertainment
  • business trips to exotic locales
  • club dues
  • tuition reimbursement
❑ To find information about a closely held business, contact a disgruntled current or former employee
❑ Check for excessive deductions from income: federal and state income taxes, Social Security
❑ Check prepayment of debts: estimated tax payments, rent, insurance premiums, charge accounts, etc.
❑ Check for prepayment of expenses: a year's worth of supplies, purchase of fancy equipment, etc.

how much money these things cost. The $30,000 that your spouse is claiming as the income from the florist shop is not sufficient to support the lifestyle you have been living. The more details you can put together about your lifestyle situation, the more helpful you can be to your attorney. How much does the car cost every month? How much did your last vacation cost? Or, at least, how long were you gone and where did you go? Does your spouse keep cash around the house? Does there always seem to be money for what your spouse wants to do? These are all clues as to actual income, as opposed to what may be reflected on a tax return.

An even more obvious way is to look through your checkbook register. If your spouse is claiming $30,000 in income, but $60,000 passed through your checking account every year, that is the first and most obvious evidence. You might also search in your safe deposit box. Your spouse may even admit extra cash to you or talk about undeclared income. If this occurs, be sure to take notes!

Tax returns

Copies of your tax returns should be available from your accountant, or you can get them directly from the IRS by sending a copy of IRS form 4506 with a check for $23 per tax return to the address listed on the form (where you send your request depends on your state of residence). You can also access the IRS online at http://www.irs.ustreas.gov/prod/cover.html.

Registrations and official records

Almost every kind of asset has some sort of ownership record. The secretary of state in each state maintains records of corporations and partnership registrations. Professional associations in each state keep track of all professional licenses, and court clerks' offices keep a registry of lawsuits. Every car, boat, house trailer, and camper has a title and registration. In the case of a car, house trailer, or camper, the title is registered with your state's department of motor vehicles. Boats are registered with your state's department of motor vehicles, and oceangoing vessels with the U.S. Coast Guard. Houses and condominiums are registered with the town clerk in the town hall in the city in which the property is located. The town clerk's office, assessor, or tax collector maintains these deeds. You can request a certified copy of a deed at the recorder's office. Sometimes they will honor these requests via mail. The copying fee is nominal. Typically, you can check these records even if they are not in your name.

For each asset, you can search the source directly; the Internet is also a useful resource. Lexis and Westlaw legal research companies have extensive online public-records databases. An example of a comprehensive Internet site that permits you to search various record databases is http://www.choicepointinc.com, and new sites become available every day. Other useful Web sites are listed in the Resources section, beginning on page 333.

Pension, profit-sharing, 401k, and stock option records

Pension, profit-sharing, 401k, and stock option records can be accessed through the providing entity. Typically, this is an employer or brokerage firm. If you do not know what that entity is for your spouse, you can find out by using interrogatories or a deposition, but in most cases, a simple request from your spouse's attorney should suffice.

Social Security

Social Security records can be accessed through your local Social Security office. A release from your spouse or a subpoena is necessary to obtain such records. The process can take time, so if you need such records, start on this project early!

Credit reports

Your spouse's credit report is a great source of information. Oftentimes it will contain addresses given by your spouse, employment and wage information, and open or available credit, as well as credit-worthiness. You will need either a signed authorization from your spouse or a subpoena to get a copy of your spouse's report, since this information is confidential. To obtain a copy if your spouse is uncooperative, you or your lawyer can file a motion requesting authorization, but you will need to prove to the court why it is important for your case. For example, if your spouse is claiming that he or she cannot refinance the house because of bad credit, then he or she can be required to prove that this claim is true by providing a copy of a credit report. Your spouse may have given another address as part of a credit application. This address will show up on the credit report.

Loan and credit applications

Most people present themselves in the most favorable light possible when applying for loans, mortgages, and credit cards. If you believe your spouse has not been truthful about his or her income, get a copy (you may need a subpoena) of a recent loan application and compare what your spouse now reports as earnings with the loan application. This information is typically provided with a statement that the information given on the loan is true and correct, and sometimes it's even provided under oath, such as for a mortgage application. This information can be used to establish your spouse's income at trial if your spouse is not being honest about his or her earnings. It can also be used to challenge your mate's credibility if the credit application states one amount and the financial statement submitted by your spouse to the court states another figure.

Financial institutions keep copies of loan applications for several years. The more recent the loan application, the greater the likelihood that the institution from whom you are seeking information has a copy of the appli-

will need a signed authorization from your spouse or a sub-
t this information, as it is confidential.

PERSONAL AND FAULT ISSUES

Suspicion about money hiding sometimes carries over into suspicions about other aspects of your spouse's behavior. Unlike finances, proving fault issues or dishonesty in the relationship may not have concrete implications for the divorce. It may confirm or cause you to reevaluate your opinion of your spouse, but although conducting illicit searches can be emotionally satisfying, they may also be only minimally productive legally. Consider carefully whether you really need to know what you are trying to learn about your spouse. If you decide to proceed with an investigation, personally or through a private detective, remember that lying down with dogs can give you fleas. Besides, as discussed above, fault is typically of secondary importance to the court. Spending money on a private investigator to establish fault issues is usually a poor investment. If you must proceed, here are some tips:

If you think that your spouse is having an affair, or has a secret business partner, the first place to look is your old phone bills. Are there numbers you don't recognize? You can determine to whom the phone numbers belong through an Internet search. One such Web site is located at: http://www.infospace.com.

If you feel that it is absolutely necessary, you can follow your spouse in the car, call at odd times at work, or ask your friends to help you out. Obviously, do not attempt such tracking if you think your spouse could become violent. Consider the ramifications in any case, because if you are wrong and your spouse finds out what you are doing, you will be on the defensive. If you or your attorney feel that you need to accumulate this evidence, however, consider doing the sleuthing yourself. You may be able to see with your own eyes what you would pay a hefty fee to a private detective to see. Obviously, don't do anything illegal or dangerous.

When Should I Think About Hiring a Professional Detective?

When your financial picture or personal situation is complicated (i.e., you know that your spouse makes a great deal of money but you have no savings to show for it, or a large bank account has "disappeared" and you can't find any evidence of where the money went using the techniques outlined above), you may want to hire a private detective or asset searcher who can run a computer check on your spouse's Social Security number, name, and date of birth to determine if he or she has bank accounts in this country or abroad. Such procedures are expensive, however, costing upwards of $750 for each search. Searching for any amount under $5,000 is probably not worth it. The bottom line should be whether uncovering additional money is critical to your standard of living, rather than satisfying a psychological determination to trap your spouse.

Reveal Any Potentially Damaging Secrets to Your Lawyer

If you are dating someone, if you have had an affair, if you have had a drug or alcohol problem, or if there is anything else that might be embarrassing or has the potential to undermine your case, tell your lawyer about it. All discussions with your lawyer are confidential. If you ask your lawyer not to reveal the information to anyone else, your lawyer will not disclose it. Even if you feel some facts are unfavorable to you, it is better to put them on the table with your lawyer and deal with them. It would not be possible for your lawyer to address a situation adequately at the time of a trial if he or she has not been able to prepare for it.

Consider the following situation: Jeanie was trying to get custody of her son, who she claimed had been kidnapped by her ex-husband Robbie. She seemed very straightforward and earnest, and her lawyer prepared the necessary papers to attempt to get the child back. At the hearing, which was held several weeks later, her lawyer learned for the first time under direct examination by the opposing attorney that Jeanie was a pornographic movie star—and she'd initially given the child to Robbie voluntarily to care for while she got her life in order. Unfortunately, she had not shared this information in advance. Her lawyer was unable to describe the events in a favorable light. Jeanie took a huge chance that her job and lapse in judgment by giving up the child would not come up in questioning, and that if they did, the judge would not care. As it turned out, the judge was very conservative. He questioned her moral character, and was upset that she had lied to the court about what she did for a living and the circumstances under which the child had ended up with the ex-husband. The judge not only took custody away from Jeanie, but he suspended her visitation completely pending further investigation by the court.

Not all hearings are quite so dramatic, but it's better that your lawyer knows in advance about a situation that you may find potentially embarrassing.

Why People Are Tempted to Sugarcoat Their Financial Situation or Behavior

It is a human impulse to save face. We often sugarcoat our behavior because we see ourselves in a positive light and see others with whom we are angry in a more negative light. Skewed attributions help us preserve our self-esteem and justify our behavior. Similarly, people often try to make themselves seem poorer and their spouses richer during adversarial divorces in order to get all they can out of the divorce. Sometimes this is done to protect themselves in the event of hard times, the way squirrels bury acorns to have enough to eat in colder months. Sometimes it is done out of a desire to punish their spouses. When spouses do the sugarcoating, it is hard to believe that they actually believe the spin they put on the situation. But they might! People are wonderful at fooling themselves into believing what they want to believe, and it takes a lot of honesty to accurately assess a situation from another's viewpoint. That is especially hard to do during times of stress, such as a divorce.

WHAT ARE THE STANDARD PRETRIAL PROCEDURES?

Many states have pretrial processes that encourage settlement. Conferences or mediations are scheduled by the court when the case is ready for trial. This stage is your last chance to settle your case before trial. You may opt to negotiate on your own prior to the court's mandatory pretrial procedures, but once you arrive at the pretrial stage in the court process, the court may encourage or order further mediation to be followed by a court-ordered settlement conference.

Pretrial Mediations

Increasingly, mediations are being encouraged by the court. It is a generally held notion that family courts are a poor way of solving family-oriented problems. The adversarial system is not conducive to a family functioning peacefully after litigation, and irrespective of your feelings now, there are many years of confirmations, bar mitzvahs, graduations, weddings, and family gatherings at which both your spouse and you will need to be present. When things can be mediated and settled, that is always a good route to follow. If your court encourages mediation, participate fully. You have little to lose, and much to gain by settling before trial.

Don't be too quick to break off mediation in the final stages of pretrial negotiation. This is one of the most emotionally volatile times in your divorce life, and it is tempting when you feel you have no power left with your spouse or the legal system to break off mediation and negotiation to hold out for what you want. This rarely pays off, as you often wind up settling the day before the trial for a similar result, but with more legal fees and a whopping headache and heartache. When you are about to give up, push through one more time, resolving to give up something to break the impasse.

COURT-SPONSORED SETTLEMENT CONFERENCES

In most jurisdictions, before scheduling a trial, the court will order a settlement conference. These settlement conferences are the court's last attempt to help you settle the matter before trial, and they are mandatory. They may be called pretrials, mediations, special masters' sessions, alternative dispute resolutions, or mandatory settlement conferences, and are typically scheduled to last between a half hour and a day.

The court may or may not furnish a settlement officer. For example, in Connecticut the court furnishes an officer from the Family Relations Office, and if you are unable to settle your case using the Family Relations Office, the court will supply a judge to act as a settlement officer. If you have a contested custody matter, you may also participate in a settlement conference using an attorney-therapist team. In California, volunteer programs through the bar association supply lawyers to assist in settlement conferences. Other states' programs team a lawyer and mental health professional to make recommendations. Typically, clients don't participate directly in this process but wait in the hallway to discuss, accept, or reject the recommendations made by the officers. You may only have a few minutes to talk with your lawyer about the recommendations before being required to respond. At this stage, if not before, the benefits of private mediations discussed in Chapter 3 become apparent.

You have the option of rejecting recommendations made, but it is often counterproductive to do so when an experienced officer of the court tells you your likely outcomes in the event of a trial.

Once your case has been negotiated and, hopefully, settled, you can ask the court for a date upon which you can do an uncontested divorce hearing where you will present the agreement for the judge to approve. In some districts, you can divorce immediately upon agreement. If you do not settle your case at this stage, a trial is scheduled.

HOW TO USE PRETRIAL PROCESS

If you do not settle at the court-ordered settlement conference, you "advance" to the pretrial stage. During the pretrial process, discuss the pros and cons of all possible outcomes with your lawyer. Your lawyer should be able to give you a worst possible and best possible scenario, and a range of expected outcomes in-between the two extremes. Your lawyer should also be able to tell you where any particular offer on the table falls in this continuum. Of course your lawyer doesn't know for certain what would happen at a trial, but any experienced lawyer can give you an educated guess. Once in a while a case will have a factual scenario that is so unusual that it is impossible to predict a range of outcomes.

Sometimes you will have the unhappy choice of the settlement offer being unacceptably low for you to take, but it simply is not worth the economic or emotional toll to go to trial. It will take some tough thinking on your part to determine whether or not you wish to proceed with a trial. While the settlement may not be fair, it may be better than what even a more favorable outcome would be for you after a trial. You need to consider all of the costs, emotional, financial, and legal, before you decide to turn down a settlement offer.

For example, suppose your lawyer thinks that you should receive at least $20,000 from the settlement on the house. The offer on the table is $15,000, but your lawyer estimates that it will cost you $7,000 to try the case, and that if you try the case you should end up with between $17,000 and $25,000. In this scenario it may not make sense to make the additional $7,000 investment, because you would have to come out with more than $22,000 in order to "break even" with the offer that's on the table. It therefore makes sense to take an offer that seems unfair, but that is ultimately more cost-effective.

Sometimes when a scenario like this happens you may feel your lawyer is representing the compromise rather than yourself—the client. This is always a tough situation for a client and for an attorney. It's easy for the attorney to see the dollars and cents aspect of the case, but you may be feeling that the lawyer should be advocating for what's optimal for you. Yet the lawyer is advocating that you take a settlement that you both agree is unfair. If you truly don't think that your lawyer is looking out for your best interests, you need to get a second opinion or a different lawyer. If your lawyer feels that you are in a situation that has become a choice between two unfavorable options, your lawyer should be straightforward with you about that.

Accepting an Unfair Settlement

It is especially painful when you know that the offer on the table is unfair, and realize your spouse is more willing than you to sacrifice family peace or the children's interests, certain you will not fight much longer. This is one of the most emotionally charged situations for all involved, because the client gets angry at his or her attorney and the system for its inherent unfairness. The system can protect you from the extremes of abuse, but it cannot always protect you from a selfish and manipulative spouse. Nor can a lawyer deflect such behavior. In these situations, realize that you chose to marry and/or have children with the person who could act this way. No one can fix that for you. Get out of the relationship and rebuild your life the best you can. If you seek justice in family court, you will be dismayed. The outcome is usually as fair as *both* people involved.

In order to negotiate a settlement favorable for you, inform your lawyer of all relevant and pending issues, even if they seem small. A common example of this is the question of who will be permitted to claim certain tax exemptions once the divorce is finalized. You may view this as a small issue, but if it remains unresolved and problems erupt with tax returns it could be the source of more stress and strife later on. It's better to deal with even the small items, so that the agreement you negotiate is a total resolution of all the outstanding issues. Your lawyer will tell you if he/she thinks that an issue is too small to bother with, for example fighting over the stainless steel flatware.

WHEN AND WHY SHOULD I GO TO TRIAL?

Before you even think of preparing for a trial make sure that you have exhausted all mediation and settlement negotiation possibilities. There are two costs in a trial: economic and psychological.

The economics of a trial are clear. Unless you are fighting about more than $15,000, a trial could not possibly make any economic sense whatsoever. It makes more sense to keep the money in your family, even if that means paying more money to your mate than you'd like to pay, rather than paying more money to the lawyers to prepare for and hold a trial. The amount of trial preparation that goes into a case is enormous, even for the smallest trial. Trials don't create money, and they don't give you more hours in a day to spend with your children. The fees you'll spend for your lawyer, your spouse's lawyer, expert witness fees, psychologists, and anyone else who has to be paid as part of the process comes out of your joint pocketbook. Although a judge may allocate the fees to one or the other to pay, that still leaves less total money to divide up.

One reason the fee situation is as expensive as it is, is because a lawyer can't take a chance of ruining someone's life by doing a poor job in a trial. Your lawyer will want to make sure you have the best representation possible, for the best chance at a favorable outcome. As a result, your lawyer will probably overprepare. In the end, you may not feel the preparation cost was worth it, especially if you settle the case just hours before the trial is scheduled to start.

In psychological terms, it is never worthwhile to go to trial except in the most extreme circumstances. The amount of emotional damage that occurs between two spouses during a trial is immeasurable. Imagine how you will feel after you have said every unfavorable thing you can think of about your spouse, and your mate has said every unfavorable thing that he or she can think of about you. And your spouse has probably exaggerated, misinterpreted, or made some things up (at least in your opinion!) about you. Now imagine sitting next to this person at your child's wedding. Imagine running into that individual at the grocery store. Imagine trying to call a former mutual friend. It won't be easy to live in the same community after a trial, and it will be even harder to effectively co-parent your children. When you're thinking about whether to take your case to trial, don't just count the dollars and cents. You need to consider the emotional price as well.

Before you proceed to a trial, apply the five-year rule. Will what you are fighting over matter five years from now? If it will not, then find a way to settle.

When You Can't Avoid a Trial

If you simply can't abide by the most recent negotiations and offers that are on the table, then a trial is your remaining option. Inappropriate or nonexistent settlement offers are legitimate reasons to try your case. However, needing to tell your story, seeking justice, or getting revenge by venting every perceived misdeed perpetrated by your mate during your marriage are *not* legitimate reasons.

Sometimes clients and lawyers are not on the same wavelength concerning what will be important at a trial. While the client may be feeling a great deal of stress, grief, loss, and anger over the situation, the lawyer views this essentially as a business deal. The lawyer needs to view it that way—that's why you are paying him/her: for expertise, experience, and objectivity.

While for the divorcing parties a trial is both an economic and psychological decision, judges are mostly concerned with providing a reasonably fair allocation of income and assets based on the laws of your state. They are not concerned with unraveling every transaction between you and your spouse. Fault issues like endless arguments and hurtful words may be at the forefront of your mind, but they will seem minor to the judge. Don't make the decision to try your case on moral grounds alone. This is essentially a business transaction, even if it doesn't feel that way, and you need to decide how you can finalize your case in the least expensive way possible. Don't let your emotions get in the way of a good, solid business decision.

EFFECTING A SETTLEMENT

As you are headed for trial, take a final breath and ask yourself whether you have done all you can to avoid the continuation of conflict. By now, if you are still disputing a settlement, you have probably decided that it is really your spouse who does not want to settle, and who is doing everything possible to prevent your getting your fair share. True or not, you still have the power to end the dispute. One can always turn the other cheek in a fight. Even in war, it takes two to tango. The sixties' slogan is apropos here: what if they had a war and nobody came?

Taking stock of your situation one final time, and determining whether settlement is possible, evaluate . . .

- Am I still consumed with hurt and rage that I wish to visit on my ex-spouse?

- Do I still want my mate to come to her senses and call the whole thing off?

- Have I acknowledged my share of what went wrong in the marriage, even if my spouse had the affair or became the alcoholic? What did I do, or what did I overlook?

- Am I ready to become more self-sufficient economically? If I have small children, do I have a reasonable plan for how I can be with them as much as I need to and participate in the family moneymaking as soon as I am able?

- Do I have a lawyer who advises me to make compromises, to keep my family interests at the center of the divorce, and to settle issues whenever possible? Or do I have a lawyer who encourages me openly or indirectly to fight?

- Do I need to keep fighting or do my children and I have the basis for a healthy postdivorce life? Maybe my ex-spouse will spend more time with the child than I want her to, but will that really harm my child, or will it be an irritation my child will have to stand up to when at an appropriate age to do so?

- Am I acting out of fear of the unknown; are my fears rational or irrational?

- Have I worked out ways of separating from my spouse physically and psychologically? Do we have plans that limit contact to the extent I feel comfortable; could limiting contact further help us reach settlement?

- If we're stuck on economic issues, is there another way to look at them? Could we make an interim agreement that has a definite endpoint that will give us both time to adjust? Maybe it is less fair for one of us for five years, and then tips the other way. Maybe our negotiations leave things too open-ended for too long.

- Are we communicating in a way that serves the divorce? Am I badgering him? Is she provoking me? Could we get help communicating rather than negotiating?

- Am I still focused on the past? What could I do to look more happily toward the future? How will the settlement proposals support my goals for the future?

• Do I have proposals on the table that I can live with? Are they really impossible or merely unfair? If unfair, how much fairer would they need to be before I can live with them?

After answering these questions, you will have a sense of whether you are ready to settle or in what areas you need to do more work. Your inability to find an acceptable settlement could be personal, or it could be between partners, or it might require more assurances where your children are concerned. In this imperfect world, weigh the value of stretching out the divorce versus living with this amount of imperfection. If you are satisfied that you have not settled your divorce for solid reasons—that you or your child's safety, mental health, or long-term economic stability are at issue—then you need to switch into the mind-set of preparing for trial.

PERSONAL ASSESSMENT

Have I exercised all of the reasonable, productive alternatives for determining the total amount of our assets and income? Have I done my research thoroughly, so that I have a valid understanding of our financial situation? If I do a thorough job of investigation and reviewing the available information, I will feel confident to choose a settlement offer that is acceptable. Taking responsibility for my own protection through educating myself is a positive step toward my future financial independence.

Have I exhausted all available mediation and settlement opportunities? I am confident that I can protect my own financial and economic well-being through my ability to evaluate settlement opportunities carefully, even when my feelings are hurt or I long for revenge.

Have I acknowledged my share of what went wrong in the marriage, even if I feel it's mostly my spouse's actions that have caused us to divorce? Being able to recognize that each of us has contributed to the situation will help me to have a balanced perspective for settlement.

Have I made the right choices for myself in terms of advisors, goals toward economic self-sufficiency, and emotional independence? Learning to separate my finances and emotions before the divorce is finalized will help me negotiate a fair resolution based on facts, not feelings.

Have I honestly evaluated whether the proposals that have been made are reasonable? If I do not believe them to be reasonable, do they provide for me sufficiently so that I am able to accomplish most of my goals? Learning to accept a settlement that is imperfect may be the best way to resolve my divorce in the long run, even if it is disappointing in the short term.

6.

Trials: Taking the Long, Hard Route

All divorces require court approval to be final and legally binding. These final agreements are put in writing and signed by the judge. This is called an "uncontested divorce" despite the fact that there may have been many conflicts and disputes during the process. Only about 5 percent of divorcing spouses reach the trial stage of divorce. Since trials are costly financially and emotionally, most people, including judges and lawyers, make every effort to settle their disputes without reaching this stage. Trials are last-resort options when your well-being or your children's hangs in the balance.

However, be cautioned. Do not delude yourself. Many people want a judge to decide because they hope to gain an advantage in the case. For them, trials are about "winning," not justice.

COURT INTERVENTION

The amount of court intervention your case requires depends upon the number of issues that need to be resolved. If you can settle some of the support, custody, or property issues, you can present those as an agreement and limit your trial to evidence only on the issues you weren't able to resolve.

Once the court has been called upon to resolve a divorce, the court's role changes from one of simple review of an agreement to a forum for adversarial conflict resolution. The adversarial system doesn't serve families and children well, sustaining conflict by enabling people to testify against one another in hopes of gaining money, property, or child custody rights. Once divorcing spouses have entered the court arena, the chance for a meeting of the minds is greatly diminished. After a bitter trial, you may have a difficult time working through the inevitable loose ends: such as exchanging parenting schedules or sitting down together at a parent/teacher conference at your child's school. Going to court may be the only reasonable choice after you've exhausted negotiations with your spouse in every available forum, but it's best used as a last resort.

If you are headed to trial, and you have been representing yourself, you will want to consider hiring a lawyer to represent you in court. If your spouse has an attorney, it is in your best interests to hire your own representative. At the very least, you should seek out the assistance of a lawyer in planning your strategy and assembling your evidence so that you present a concise, well-organized case to the judge.

What Is the Procedure in a Trial?

If you are representing yourself without an attorney, you will need to know the step-by-step procedures for a trial. If you'd like to observe an actual trial, most divorce courts are open to the public, and you can quietly slip into a courtroom to observe. You can also consult a trial practice book.

If you are represented by an attorney, the attorney will guide you through the procedures that must be followed, but as with any trip, a map of where you are going is helpful. This chapter includes a brief explanation of how things work.

When you enter the courtroom, the judge presides behind the center podium. A court reporter sits between the judge and the litigants. You will take your place at the table facing the judge on one side of the room, and your spouse will do the same across the room. Typically, there is no jury. A court officer sits toward the front of the room as well. He or she will swear in witnesses and announce the judge's comings and goings.

The plaintiff's side gets to present first. If you are represented by an attorney, the attorney will decide the order of witnesses and will pose all of the questions. If you are representing yourself, you will make those decisions. The plaintiff gets the opportunity to present his or her whole case before the defendant gets a chance to present his or her side of the story. As the plaintiff calls each witness, the defendant (or the defendant's attorney) asks questions of each witness after the plaintiff is done. Then the next witness is called. This procedure continues until the plaintiff has finished his or her side of the case. Then the plaintiff "rests the case," which is the official phrase that tells the judge it's the defendant's turn.

The defendant then gets to present his or her side of the case. Ideally, the defendant will not repeat obvious, undisputed facts that were presented in the plaintiff's case. Facts like "When and where were you married?" and "How old are your children?" need not be repeated. The defendant's case should focus on introducing that individual and advocating the defendant's perspective through testimony and evidence. The same procedure for cross-examination as described above is used during the defendant's part of the case.

In high-conflict cases involving children, the court may appoint an attorney or other advocate, known as a guardian *ad litem*, to represent the minor children. This attorney/guardian will present the case from the children's point of view after the defendant is finished and "rests."

When presenting evidence, it's easy to get caught up in the minute details of the marriage, and to offer hours and hours of testimony that are not relevant for the judge. There's a fine line among important details, and those that just slow down the proceedings. The judge will not want testimony about a picnic in 1986 during which your spouse called you a "bitch" in front of friends and neighbors. On the other hand, present all important incidents and provide sufficient detail. Use the most concise way to get your point across. This advice is important whether you're represented by a lawyer or representing yourself. Every lawyer has a story about having a judge fall asleep during a trial—don't let it be yours!

WHAT COUNTS AS EVIDENCE?

Evidence is testimony, documents, physical evidence, and nearly anything else that provides information to help prove the truth (or untruth) of a fact that's been alleged by either side. Most people think of "evidence" as murder weapons and experts who testify; evidence also can be less dramatic and sophisticated. All of the documents that you collected in Chapters 2 and 5 are evidence. Everything labeled as "discovery" is evidence. In addition to these materials, everything you and your spouse say on the stand is evidence.

A finer point, but an important one, is that *arguments* made by lawyers (or by you, if you're serving as your own lawyer) are not evidence. They are persuasive statements that will attempt to summarize the evidence in a way that's favorable to your case. Arguments don't introduce new facts. That's the difference between evidence and arguments. Evidence introduces new facts, and arguments interpret those facts. That's why it's important to make all of your points through testimony. For example, if you "forget" to say something on the stand, your lawyer cannot say it for you.

Various kinds of evidence will be accepted by the court. There are many complicated legal rules, but a few basic concepts will help you to understand how and why a judge will accept or reject evidence at a trial. Knowing this in advance will help you prepare your case with your lawyer. If you are representing yourself, you will need more detailed information about the rules of evidence in your state's court system. You can find this at a law library, or for some jurisdictions, on the Internet.

Hearsay

Hearsay is a statement that is made by someone who is not in court to testify, and it is generally not accepted as evidence. You cannot repeat something that someone said outside of the courtroom while you're in court, unless that person is also in court to testify. If you want to testify that your neighbor said to you that your spouse is not a good parent, you cannot repeat this to the judge unless your neighbor is in court to verify that this is indeed what he or she said. Statements such as "the doctor told me that . . ." or "the neighbor said . . ." are not admissible unless either the doctor or the neighbor are in court, present, and able to testify. On the other hand, if you want to testify that your spouse made a hurtful comment to you three months before the case started, this is permissible provided your spouse is in court to testify.

Typically, you cannot use letters in court. They are hearsay because

CHILDREN AS WITNESSES

Courts are divided as to whether or not they permit you to repeat what your children have said. Some courts have determined that it is more important that the child not be called into court to testify than it is to follow this evidence rule, and they permit testimony. Other courts appoint attorneys or guardians *ad litem* to testify on behalf of the child. Very few courts will permit a child to testify, as most judges believe it should be avoided at all costs.

It is tempting to want your child to testify especially after all the comments the child has made about your ex and his or her home. Yet you should consider that children often shift their allegiances depending on whom they are talking to, and children will feed parents what they think the parents want to hear. This is how they express their support and love, especially if they are rewarded by your concern about them. Putting your child on the stand requires a public stance that can be devastating to the child, and can tear away at the child's relationship to one or both parents.

they were written outside of court, even though the letter may be signed. If you want to use a letter in court, the letter writer will usually need to be in court to testify.

Documents

While all documents are technically considered to be hearsay, there are special exceptions for certain types of documents. Certified public records, certified business records, and easily verified information are usually exempt from hearsay objections. Examples of these types of documents include copies of deeds recorded on the land records and signed by a clerk; court judgments signed by the court clerk indicating that they are true copies of the original; and employment and wage information signed by the employer's record keepers.

Sometimes, for the sake of expediting a trial, the lawyers will agree to waive the hearsay objections for certain documents or testimony. Such an agreement (sometimes called "pre-marking exhibits") must be made prior to the start of the trial or before the introduction of that evidence. *Perry Mason* fans will be disappointed to learn that there is rarely surprise evidence in family court proceedings, but on a practical level it makes sense. If everyone agrees that tax returns are accurate and relevant, there's no need to bring the accountant in to testify about how they were prepared. A good example of a hearsay objection that is often waived by agreement is a written appraiser's report. Assuming that everyone involved with the case has had an opportunity to review the report, the appraiser has a good reputation, and the value placed on the asset is within the expected range, then the lawyers may agree that the report come into evidence without a hearsay objection.

Best Evidence Rule

You must produce the original of a document if it is available. If it is not available, then a copy will suffice.

If an eyewitness is available to testify about an event, you need to bring that witness into court to testify, as opposed to someone who heard about the incident afterward.

Always "go to the source" for your evidence, and you should have no problem satisfying the Best Evidence requirement.

Getting Evidence Accepted by the Court

During a witness's testimony, documents such as those described above are introduced into evidence to substantiate a point the witness is making. The witness will identify the document, and say why it's pertinent. The other lawyer has an opportunity to object to the document, and then the judge decides if the document becomes evidence in the case or not. Typically, most financial documents are accepted as evidence without a problem. Controversial documents, such as unsigned love letters used to prove that one spouse was having an affair, can trigger more objections and may or may not be accepted into evidence at the trial. The evidence is important to the judge insofar as it helps him or her understand how assets accumulated or were dissipated in your marriage, how to divide those remaining assets in a way that's fair, and what's best for your children.

WHAT DOCUMENTS ARE NEEDED BY THE COURT?

You and your lawyer will make a list in advance of all of the documents that you have, and those that will be needed at trial. If your financial issues are unresolved, typical documents used at trial are:

- your five most recent tax returns
- six months to a year's worth of payroll records or pay stubs for you and your spouse
- any other income records, including independent contractor work, interest and dividends, commissions, bonuses, and earned but not-yet-paid commissions and bonuses
- your most recent bank statements, stock statements, and credit card statements as well as your spouse's
- any bank, stock, or credit card statements that show a discrepancy or questionable item, such as an unauthorized withdrawal or charge
- loan applications and financial statements prepared by you and/or your spouse
- pension, IRA, and 401k statements
- real estate records, especially house closing statements and appraisals
- financial records for any businesses or partnership ventures you or your spouse own by yourselves or with partners
- copies of any documents that show that money is owed by you or your spouse, or to you or your spouse
- documents showing assets that belong to you via inheritances or trust income. Wills and trusts of persons not yet deceased are typically not pertinent. The court is interested only in money that you have, or that you have a legal right to but just haven't received yet. For example, a person may have died, leaving you money in his will, but you haven't received it yet (as opposed to being named as a beneficiary in the will of someone who is still alive).

- life insurance statements showing life insurance polices, and any cash value on those policies
- records of any gifts you or your spouse have made (over $100 or so) in the last five years
- records of the sale of any real property or personal property over $350
- a list of personal property that is in dispute
- other documents that tend to prove the allegations you're making in your case

Provided you've followed the admissibility guidelines above, these documents should be admissible as evidence. Because these documents are used in practically every case, it makes sense to share copies with the opposing side in advance (if you have not already done so through discovery, Chapter 5) to see if you can agree that the documents will be admitted and mark them as exhibits in advance of the trial. If there is an issue about the accuracy of any document, be prepared to prove that the contents are true.

Some of these same documents may be needed if your trial is focused on child custody issues, since living arrangements and financial issues (especially child support, and to a lesser extent alimony) may be tied to decisions about the child's living conditions. This will be discussed further in Chapter 9.

How Can I Do Much of the Work Myself and Save the Lawyer's Fees?

You can save yourself money and aggravation if you help your lawyer prepare for the trial. Only you will truly know if the lawyer has everything required, for who is more familiar with your circumstances than you?

There are a number of ways you can help your lawyer prepare your case, especially in determining what types of witnesses will be most beneficial, and in deciding and assembling the documents that will be needed. Both of these tasks are time consuming, so if you can do them yourself, or at least assist your lawyer, you can save money in addition to feeling as if

⚖

FOR *PRO SE* LITIGANTS

To increase the likelihood that your documents will be accepted as evidence:

- find a copy of your state's rules of evidence. Good sources are your local library, law library, or the Internet
- make sure you are using an original or a certified copy of an original
- make sure it is signed and its accuracy is certified by its preparer (i.e., wage records, tax returns)
- if you are required to disclose a document to the other side before the trial—e.g., in a subpoena or other discovery request—make sure you have done so
- if the document is hearsay (see page 157), determine if there are exceptions to the hearsay rule that may allow the document's admissibility anyway. You may need a lawyer to assist with this determination
- Even if your document violates a rule of evidence and should be inadmissible, in order for a document to be excluded from evidence, the opposing side must object to it. Sometimes the opposing side will forget to object, or they just won't bother. The worst that can happen is that the other side objects and the document is not admitted, but you don't know until you try. Caveat: there's a difference between assertively attempting to get important documents into evidence and aggressively alienating the judge with endless, repetitive requests
- Practical hint: come to court with photocopies of the document for the opposing side, for the witness to use, and for you to use, as the judge will end up with the original if it is accepted into evidence

you have more control over your case—and your life. Obviously, if you're representing yourself, this entire task falls on your shoulders.

WHAT KINDS OF WITNESSES SHOULD I CONSIDER?

Fact witnesses are people who can testify about the facts of the case, such as the length of the marriage, the finances, and why the marriage

broke down. They testify about things that happened. Most ⟨...⟩
fact witnesses. You are a fact witness. Your neighbor who sa⟨...⟩
throw a barbecue spatula at your head is a fact witness. Your employer's
payroll clerk is a fact witness.

Your Testimony

You are the most important and best witness in your case. You will testify about the length of the marriage, how assets accumulated, and why and how the marriage broke down. You will testify about your children, and what their lives are like from day to day. You will testify about virtually everything that has anything to do with your case. Your testimony will be very important to the judge. How you look, what you wear, how you talk, and how you present yourself to the judge are all important issues. It's imperative that the judge believes you, and sympathizes with you. If you are using an attorney, your lawyer will work with you to make the best presentation possible. If you are not represented by an attorney you should seriously reconsider settling your case before the trial. You also should at least consult with one about trial preparation.

You can present well only if you are prepared, if you understand the court's priorities, and if you understand the theory of your case, which is the underlying theme that you or your lawyer hope to emphasize in your trial. It could be you as dutiful, wronged spouse or you as devoted parent unable to make ends meet while your spouse gambles. Develop your theory fully and organize your case based on your theory, so you provide a consistent picture of your situation.

By the time you get to this point, your lawyer will have requested that you prepare a full written marital history as described on page 164 as well as a list of your goals for trial. Putting these two things together will give you a good idea of the theory of your case, and which parts of your testimony are clearly needed. Then you must reconcile your theory with the priorities of the court. Focus your theory around what the judge will want to know. For example, the judge will want to know about your health, your ability to continue working, and what you expect to be earning; the judge will want the same information from your spouse. The court will also need

⚖

WRITTEN MARITAL HISTORY

It's helpful to write out a marital history, both for yourself, and for your lawyer. Doing so helps you clarify the main issues in your case in your own mind, and will help you focus on what's important. Include:

- A chronology of important events in your relationship, beginning with when you met. This chronology should include a time line that illustrates significant events in the relationship and events in your families, such as the death of a close relative, starting a new job, birth of a child, or receipt of an inheritance.
- A list detailing any forgone opportunities that you (or your spouse) have lost (family, economic, and career) because of your relationship. Example: You had to quit a good job because of your spouse's job transfer and your career never regained its prior momentum.
- A chronology of your contributions to the marriage, monetary and otherwise, and the contributions of your family members. Also make a chronology of the contributions of your spouse and his or her family.
- A list of all of the things which your spouse (and you) have done recently that you feel are inappropriate or hurtful, and which may need to be addressed. Be very honest, especially in the description of your own behaviors. If there are significant things that have happened in the past, such as domestic violence or affairs, include those things as well.
- A list of your short-term and long-term priorities, in order of importance regarding custody of the children, property settlement, use and possession of your car, child support, alimony, and special requirements such as restraining orders.

to know if either you or your spouse contributed a larger amount of money than the other to the marriage, and how you and your spouse contributed in nonfinancial ways. If you feel that it's not appropriate that either you or your spouse works, perhaps because your children are young, or for other reasons, the judge will also need to know about that.

If the reasons that the marriage broke down may influence alimony or property division in your case (each state's law is different), you will have to describe these reasons clearly and succinctly. That is not to say that you should do this in an unemotional fashion; however, you need to be focused and to the point.

After preparing for this day for so long, you will feel very nervous, even queasy on the day(s) of trial. Preparation helps reduce anxiety. Have your story clear, know what is important, and practice separating out the emotion you feel from the facts you wish to convey. Tell the judge about the situation, not how you have been wronged. The story will speak for itself. Practice in the mirror the night before if it helps you to feel prepared. Have a friend or family member ask you questions you think the judge might ask. In court, have a trusted supporter sitting in the courtroom, and keep your eyes on that person. Try not to look at your ex-spouse.

Other Fact Witnesses

In addition to your own testimony, you will have to decide whom you would like to assist you with your case. Get together a list of the names, addresses, and telephone numbers of each possible witness along with a short summary of what information the witness would contribute. Speak with them to find out if they are willing to come to court to testify if necessary, and ask the witnesses if they would speak with your lawyer in advance of the case.

When custody matters are at issue, you may need witnesses as personal references for what kind of a parent you are, how you discipline or treat your children on a day-to-day basis, whether or not you attended parent/teacher conferences, and other parenting issues. Witnesses may include the children's teachers, doctors, therapists, the parents of playmates, or your neighbors. Typically the best custody witnesses are people to whom you are not related, and with whom you do not have a particular friendship. A good example is the teacher who saw you driving your child to nursery school every single day and observed you interacting with your child. If a private investigator has been involved, he or she may also be a fact witness. Typical evidence introduced through an investigator includes your spouse's driving record, criminal record, and related damaging evidence.

Unless your character has been called into serious question, character witnesses such as those seen on TV trials won't be necessary. The judge will assume that your friends will say nice things about you.

Typically, the lawyer will call witnesses in advance of the trial and let them know what they can expect to be asked on the stand. The lawyer may even practice asking and answering the questions with the witness, which helps evaluate whether your proposed witness would be helpful in court.

Expert Witnesses and Valuations

If you have had an expert appraise your home, review your income figures, perform a custody evaluation, a business valuation, or analyze other types of evidence, but you are unable to reach an agreement on these matters with your spouse, the expert witness may need to be called to testify in court. This testimony will aid the judge in making a decision about the matters in dispute.

The expert must be disclosed to the opposing side, meaning that his or her name, address, business telephone number, as well as a summary of the person's conclusions must be provided in advance of the trial. If the expert has prepared a report, such as an appraisal or written evaluation, that must also be provided. If the opposing side wishes to depose the expert, he or she may do so.

If you must have an expert testify in court, the expert's fees are your responsibility unless the court orders otherwise.

WHAT KINDS OF DISCOVERY CAN BE USED AT TRIAL AS EVIDENCE?

In addition to documents and live witnesses, you can also use depositions and prior testimony as evidence in trial.

Depositions and Prior Testimony

Depositions are sworn testimony taken under oath prior to a trial or hearing as more fully discussed in Chapter 5. Because the testimony at a deposition is obtained under oath, recorded by a court-authorized professional, and all parties have had an opportunity to be present for testimony, a deposition can later be used in court under certain circumstances:

• If you depose a witness who testifies in court with answers that are different than those given in the deposition, you can use the deposition in court to show that the witness's testimony is contradictory. Your goal is to indicate to the court that the witness is either lying now, or has lied previously under oath.

• If you depose a witness who is not available at the time of the trial (i.e., out of state, in the hospital, deceased), the deposition can be entered into evidence in lieu of that person's testimony.

How Do I Prepare for the Financial Part of the Trial?

Once all of your documents are in order, the financial issues that are still in dispute should be fairly obvious. You can work with your attorney to organize the documents according to the issues they represent. If you are not represented by an attorney, you can organize the documents yourself.

For example, if you are claiming your spouse hid money in an account, likely documents that would support that claim would be the bank or stock account records that reflect the money, deposit slips showing deposits into those accounts, pay stubs showing automatic deposits to that account, and perhaps loan documents showing that account as an asset. Together those different documents prove the same point.

Each of the points you intend to cover should be organized in terms of importance. The most important should be covered early in the trial. The presentation will also have to make sense chronologically. If you jump around too much in time, the court is likely to get confused.

Make an outline, or assist your attorney in making an outline, of the points that you intend to make in the trial. You will not be permitted to

from your outline during the trial, but the act of outlining
  to cover increases the likelihood that you will include all of
the crucial points. You may refer to your notes or documents during your
testimony with permission of the court, but keep in mind that opposing
counsel may also look at any document you use to refresh your memory
during the trial.

Also make an outline of issues you anticipate your spouse's case will
cover. Be prepared to answer questions about those issues. For example, if
your spouse has repeatedly accused you of overspending, assume that this
will be one of the major arguments used in the case against you, and be prepared to justify your expenditures.

IF I DID SOMETHING ALONG THE WAY THAT MAY HURT MY CASE, SHOULD I LIE ABOUT IT?

Your credibility is the most important element of your case. Deceit is
rampant in divorce cases, and judges have little patience for such behavior.
If there is a weak point in your case, meet the problem head-on. All people
make mistakes, and you can describe an incident as a lapse of judgment
under trying conditions. If you are sincere and convincing, it will damage
your case less than lying will.

The importance of truthfulness holds true when the issue is infidelity
within the marriage. It is best to admit to obvious affairs and deal with the
problem on the stand to take the punch out of your spouse's argument
about an affair. That's not to say that complete confession during the negotiation phase is optimal. Certainly, each case is different, but telling the
truth to a judge in a straightforward and brief fashion at a trial can be much
less damaging than ignoring the scenario and waiting for it to be raised by
your spouse's attorney, or having your spouse parade a series of witnesses or
photographs through the court after you have not been truthful about a
new relationship.

*Bud and Janice went to trial for divorce. Bud had been unhappy in his mar-
riage for many years but had not had an affair. During the final months before
separating, Bud fell in love with Samantha, a coworker, and became sexually in-*

volved with her. He never told Janice about the relationship or
marry, but he was pretty sure she suspected something since he
consider counseling or reconciliation. At the trial, he readily adm
volved before Janice could accuse him, discussing his loneliness and the happiness
that Samantha brought into his life. He depicted the new relationship as unfor-
tunate (because it started before his marriage ended) but loving and positive, and
expressed the importance to him that Janice not suffer needlessly for it. Despite the
high degree of animosity between the couple, the judge believed Bud's account and
rendered the affair as inconsequential compared to the other issues in the divorce.

If you lie during your trial, and (for instance) your spouse has a photograph or document that proves your statement is untrue, the lie becomes a
credibility issue that affects your entire case. If you are tempted to lie about
a situation in your case, speak with your lawyer instead so that you can decide together the best way to handle the situation. No reputable lawyer will
permit you to lie or will condone any suggestion to lie on the stand.

Lying under oath is perjury. Perjury is a crime. Many judges refer perjury in divorce cases to the prosecutor's office. Judges may also refer matters
involving drugs, false tax returns, or other crimes. If these are issues in your
case, strongly consider settling with your spouse out of court rather than
taking the chance of facing criminal prosecution as well as your divorce
case.

WHAT IF MY SPOUSE IS LYING?

If you know that your spouse is lying, inform your lawyer. You are not
permitted to talk during the trial while someone else is testifying, so write
down anything that your spouse (or anyone else) says that is not true. If it's
urgent, slide the paper over to your lawyer so he or she can read it immediately. If it can wait, talk to your lawyer during a court break. If you are not
using a lawyer, wait until it is your turn to speak before bringing the lie to
the court's attention. Never allow yourself to have an emotional outburst
while court is in session.

Immediately think about what you or someone else knows that will
prove that your spouse is lying. If there is a document already in evidence

that will show that your spouse is lying, then so much the better. You or your lawyer can bring it to the attention of the court as part of your presentation.

Sometimes the lie is about such a small issue that it isn't worth bringing up to the court or the judge. Sometimes what you perceive as a "lie" is just a different interpretation of the facts. On the other hand, if your spouse says, "I never took money out of the account" and you have canceled checks from the account showing your mate withdrew $2,000 two days before filing divorce papers, this needs to come to the court's attention. It is important to decide what is worthwhile to pursue, and what is best let go.

How Should I React When My Spouse Lies?

Because so much is on the line at trial, when your spouse lies it inflames your sense of injustice. This person is taking you and your life apart, and then lying, putting money above a relationship with you or your children. It reminds you of all the unfairness in the relationship, all the broken promises and smashed dreams. You are especially angry if you know that your spouse is capable of being a more decent person when less self-interested. It is infuriating to have someone get away with an injustice in the forum that is supposed to protect people and see through deceit. You long for the court to recognize your spouse's manipulations; can't somebody realize what your spouse is doing when it is so obvious?! Whether or not the court can fathom the lie, such behavior will likely resurface many times again. You must accept that others may not be able to view your ex as you do, and that you may never get justice. Remind yourself this is why you are divorcing. It is more important to minimize future interactions with this person than to prove something here. Let it reinforce that you are fighting to separate your lives, not to punish each other.

WHAT AM I LIKELY TO BE FEELING DURING THE TRIAL?

There are often wild emotional displays during the trial process. Spouses act increasingly outrageous, upping the ante associated with settlement until realistic strategies have been replaced by tantrums, aggressions, and shutting down reminiscent of the movie *The War of the Roses*. Both spouses feel the other is a stranger and a caricature of his or her worst qualities. Many times people barely recognize themselves, let alone their spouse. People will say they want to stop the fighting, yet they can't get off the wild flight they are on. It seems to pick up speed until they are acting on automatic pilot. There is a commonly described "out-of-body" sensation that goes along with a traumatic experience. It is as if you are outside of your own body and life, watching yourself act and react, yet feeling powerless to control yourself.

If you are in this position, it helps to look at some of the underlying motivations for such behavior.

"My Own Behavior Is Dreadful, but I Am Afraid Not to Keep Fighting"

Jennie entered her therapist's office and said, "I know I'm being a total wretch, and I can't stand myself. I look in the mirror sometimes and think, 'Who are you?' I know I am fighting about every little thing, making it impossible not to drag this all out in trial. I have been prepping all of our friends and any one I can to take my side. I feel like a politician banging on doors saying 'vote for me.' " The real problem for Jennie was that she couldn't trust her husband Ben not to lie and change his story. She was afraid that if she acted civilly he would use her behavior to get more money and more time with the kids, and to leave her with nothing. She knew he was angry because she'd initiated the divorce, and she was not sure how far he'd go to punish her. Since she also felt guilty about the situation, she believed she had to defend herself, including justifying all of her actions.

However, Ben was feeling very similarly. The more Jennie acted crazy and furious, the more he thought that if she was willing to get a divorce so suddenly, who knew what else she was capable of? The lack of trust that accompanies many divorces spirals into believing that everything your spouse is doing is aimed at making you angry or hurting you. Often the other person sees the same picture very differently. Both spouses are locked into a blaming cycle that escalates, using the legal system as the battleground.

The fear of losing one's property or children becomes a central motivator to fight back, the way an animal strikes out blindly when it senses its personal or familial security is threatened. As the conflict increases, each person becomes more certain that the other cannot be trusted, and, therefore, they must turn to an outside party to police their interactions. The legal system is brought in for its protective functions. However, this view of the legal system stems from its functions in a criminal situation. In the civil realm, the court has few protections that it can enforce. It may be able to stop spouses from being violent or stealing property from each other. But it is a slow and cumbersome process, and often it does too little too late to be of assistance. The threat of the court's authority keeps people afraid. They fear that their spouses will somehow prevail, they will succeed in unleashing their wrath legally, and the power of the court will be used to condone it.

If it is early enough in the conflict, you can stop this cycle by refusing to engage. Don't fight back. Hold your ground but do what you can not to inflame your spouse. Make small concessions, and bend over backward not to fight. It means turning the other cheek and letting the other person have his or her way, but having the fighting stop will work to your advantage later. If you are already fighting over issues you cannot accede, like sole custody of your child, then you must use the legal process. If you decide to hire a lawyer, be sure to work with an attorney who understands your important bottom lines and what is worth fighting for, rather than an attorney who's interested in supporting the fight. Sometimes an attorney is well-meaning, and encourages you to fight because he or she agrees you have been wronged. Such support does not always work to your advantage, despite the best of intentions. Your attorney should help you decide what *not* to fight about, as well.

My Spouse's View of Me Doesn't Fit with My Own Perceptions

Nothing is more frustrating than having your ex go all over town saying things about you that you believe are not true. Worse, they are often things that are the opposite of how you view yourself.

Mike's wife viewed every effort he made to be involved in his son Tommy's life as controlling. So when Mike wanted to come to all his son's tennis matches, his wife told Tommy that his dad just wanted to use the games as a way to see her, and that he wanted the boy to win games for his own gratification. Mike was furious because he wound up fighting with his son every time he attended one of his matches. He wanted Tommy to win, but that's not why he loved being at the games. He felt that there was so little he could share day-to-day with Tommy, since he didn't live with him anymore, and the games gave him something to talk about and a way to show his desire to be a steadfast presence in his son's life.

People often get caught up in going to trial to prove that their spouse's view of them is wrong. This is a losing proposition, because you can't change someone's mind just because you want to; that person has to have the desire to be open to a new interpretation. Often he or she does not. The court process is not going to change anyone's opinion either. People who reach trial often say the exact same things about each other, using words like controlling, nasty, and lying. Some people diagnose each other, giving their spouse psychological labels that they only partially understand: borderline, antisocial, sex-addicted, or narcissistic. Often someone is accused of being controlling and intimidating, and the other spouse is labeled as inconsistent and emotionally unstable. You can easily see how these two personality styles could influence the other, bringing out the worst.

In Dr. Pruett's research (referred to on page 346), couples who reported at least some conflict in their divorce said that their spouse used the legal system to get back at them in some way, while they *never* used the system to retaliate against their spouse. Usually there is some kernel of objective truth in how spouses describe each other. Maybe he *is* more forceful than she is, or she *does* cry easily. But it is the *extent* of the trait that is blown out of proportion, as spouses' natural tendencies get polarized in relationship to one another.

In any case, you cannot change someone's negative view of you by fighting about it. You can only try and change that view by changing your own behavior. Refuse to engage at that level. Even so, understand that your spouse may never see you the way you see yourself. It is important not to accept your spouse's view of you, but to ask yourself if others see you simi-

larly. Maybe even ask people close to you. Perhaps you can find the kernel
of truth in your ex's view, and use the divorce as an opportunity to better
yourself in a way that will help you in your next relationship, with other
people in general, or with your sense of self.

When Fear of Losing Clouds Your Judgment

*Marvin's wife, Estella, shared with her therapist how deeply remorseful she
was about the affair that led to the break-up of her marriage. She thought she
wanted out, but as the reality of the divorce became more tangible, she began to
second-guess her decision. Her marriage hadn't been as bad as she had thought it
to be only a few months ago. But now Marvin would not forgive her, and they
were locked in endless arguments that seemed destined for a long court battle over
parenting plans and finances. She was so frightened that she went out and hired
an attorney with a reputation for drawing blood. She didn't want to battle it out
in court, but she didn't dare trust Marvin not to exact suffering from her in retaliation for her behavior. She had no idea how far he would take this in anger,
and she felt she had to be ready for him at all costs.*

It is not uncommon for the initiator of separation or divorce to focus
initially on the excitement of a new life or love interest, to the exclusion of
all other considerations about the realities of divorce. The initiator suddenly becomes aware of how much she has to lose, often when relationship
ties are too severely fractured to resurrect the marriage. Estelle found herself facing many simultaneous changes and potential losses: place of residence, neighborhood, friends, time with family (children, in-laws),
economic security, routines, traditions, identity (being known as Marvin's
wife), and a future that is predictable in at least some respects. These postdivorce possibilities fill many people with a sense of dread, of fears that all
humans experience—of being lonely, not having enough money, making
decisions alone, dating, being single in a world too often oriented to couples and two-parent families.

Couples who go to trial are more likely to experience a greater number
of losses. They are more likely to lose parts of their family and friendship
network, some economic standing, altered relationships with their children,

and so on. It is often these very same fears, however, that underlie the interactions between disputing spouses. Mothers fight to have their children live only in one home during all school days, not only out of concern for the child, but also because the house is so quiet without the kids that it engenders panic. They experience the emptiness of missing the bedtime story, and the predictable fight to turn out the light when it is time for sleep. Fathers fight to have more weekend time with their children, even when the children try to tell them they need more time with friends, because the feeling that their parental authority or importance has slipped away prevents them from giving in on this point. For these fathers, the last thing they want is to be dads whose children don't want to be with them, but they can't find another solution without fear of losing their chance to affect their children's development in a significant way. Both parents' own feelings of insecurity, magnified by the divorce, heighten their fears about what their children are doing when they are not in daily contact with them.

These fears can result in failure to find solutions with which everyone can live comfortably. Instead, couples stick stubbornly to their positions, making up excuse after excuse not to reach an agreement.

Be honest with yourselves about your fears; write them down, and then examine them. Determine which ones are realistic, and which ones are unlikely to occur. Consider which ones could be diminished through settlement and cooperation. Walk through the legal walls you have been hiding behind. Your judgment will miraculously improve, and you'll recall what it feels like to see the first ray of sun after a summer storm.

PERSONAL ASSESSMENT

Is a trial really needed to resolve these issues? Is there nothing left to give in on? If so, then I have prepared myself thoroughly by orchestrating the best evidence, and the fullest documentation, in my power.

Have I selected the most appropriate witnesses for my case? Are they people who are interested in helping me or my children because they believe in me, rather than because they are friendly with me? I have found people whose opinions are based on experience with me and/or my spouse, and who do not have an ax of their own to grind.

Am I being as truthful and straightforward as possible? If my spouse is not, how am I dealing with it? I hope I am not becoming consumed with revenge or with proving the truth. I am keeping my eye on the big picture, and I am taking steps to end my spouse's ability to distort facts about me by separating our lives in as civilized a way as possible.

Am I being motivated by fear? How is it affecting my behavior, in and out of court? I am taking the time to understand my fears, and to put them into proper perspective. I am acting out of a position of strength, not fear.

7.

Taking Care of Myself and My Children: How *Not* to Get Lost

THE DECISION TO SEPARATE

The family that your children have known is about to undergo tremendous change. Divorce research has shown that children are rarely informed about their parents' pending separation and divorce prior to its occurrence. The younger the children, the less chance that they are told in advance about the divorce.

Parents' reasons for not informing their children are well intentioned. They are anxious and afraid themselves, and they have difficulty figuring out when and what to say. Some parents fear burdening their children if they say too much. Others are concerned that their children won't understand the reasons, and that the information will add to their hurt unnecessarily. Sometimes parents wait until the time seems right, and then events gather momentum, and the opportunity has slipped away. All of these reasons that parents wait to tell their children are understandable, but they are not helpful. Your children need to know. In fact, it will make the divorce more predictable to them, which will facilitate their healthy adaptation.

How Do We Tell the Children?

The first step in informing your children about the separation and divorce is for you and your spouse to sit down and talk about it by yourselves.

Decide if you are definite about separating; it is not helpful for your children to hear that you *might* do this. Once you have reached a decision, make an agreement about where the children will live and what kind of parenting plan your spouse and you will implement, at least on a temporary basis. You are then ready to speak to the children about your decisions.

A family meeting is a good forum to tell your children about your decisions. There are several advantages for your children if both of you can tell them together of your plans. Children will see that you intend to cooperate and work together as parents. It gives the message that although this is a painful turn of events, you will deal with it together. Also, it is an invitation to talk about an undesirable subject. By logical extension, your children will understand that feelings and actions of all kinds are acceptable fodder for discussion. Most of all, your actions show the children that you, as parents, are in charge and will continue to care for them together.

The first thing to tell the children is that you will be divorcing. You could say: "We have been unhappy for a long time because we fight so much. We have tried very hard to get along better and to work things out, but we have decided it is necessary to live apart. It is our best chance of preserving our friendship. We have decided to separate. We have decided that Mom/Dad will move out." Emphasize that you tried to work out your differences. Explain what you have done in simple terms: you have talked a lot, gone to counseling, or whatever else you have tried to do to save the marriage. The important message to convey is that this was a thoughtful decision, made with care and consideration for how painful it will be for the whole family.

Children need to be reminded concretely that they are not losing either of their parents. Tell them the obvious: that you both love them and will continue to love them. Parents divorce each other but they cannot and do not want to divorce their children. Reassure your children that they will have access to both of you, that they can spend time with the parent who is moving out during the week and/or on weekends. The time will start immediately, and they will be able to talk to the parent who is leaving the home on the telephone as often as they desire. Reassure your children that grandparents, aunts and uncles, and other supportive friends and caretakers will remain present in their lives.

Wallerstein and Kelly's study (see page 347) showed that children often feel responsible for their parents' breakup. This is especially likely among children who are preschoolers or just starting school, since this age group tends to be "egocentric"—they see the world as revolving around them. Not all children feel this way, and some who do won't admit to it. But tell your children plainly that the divorce is no fault of theirs, and they did nothing to make it happen. Nor can they do anything to fix it. This divorce business is between the adults. If you often fought, add that sometimes your fights were about them, and sometimes they were over other things. But the fights over them were usually about other things you were already mad about.

Your children will then need factual information. Explain to your children when their parent will be moving out; if possible, give your children information about where that parent will be living. If you have young children (six years or younger), they will be especially concerned about where they will eat and sleep, who will feed them and take care of them, and who will put them to bed and get them up in the morning. School-age children will want information about what will change in their environment: where they will go to school, when they will see their friends, and assurance that they can continue with the activities in which they are involved. Older children, preteens and teenagers, will want to know how financial arrangements will affect them. Will they have to give up their car? Can they still take karate lessons? If these things will not change for them, reassure them as such. If you are not sure, tell them you are not sure, that the details haven't been ironed out, but you will listen for their input about what's most important to them as you make decisions.

Finally, encourage questions. This demonstrates to your children that expressing feelings is not only allowed but valued; the capacity to express difficult feelings such as very deep sadness, anger, fear, and insecurity can replace the need to act out feelings that are submerged or in need of attention. It will serve your kids well throughout life to know how to talk about their feelings. This also teaches children that you can handle whatever feelings they lay on you, with the implicit message that you can also handle your own feelings and the divorce.

What if your children ask you personal questions . . . whose fault is it? Did someone have an affair? Do you hate Daddy now? You must use common sense and your understanding of your children to answer the questions in language and detail they can understand, given their age. Do not lie; it will come back to haunt you. Do not use blaming language. Some examples may provide guidance:

Question: Whose fault is the divorce?

PARENT TO SIX-YEAR-OLD CHILD:
Divorce happens because *two* people can't work things out. Mommy and Daddy are each angry about different things, and it is no one's fault.

PARENT TO EIGHT-YEAR-OLD CHILD:
When adults cannot get along and they decide to split up, everyone is angry and hurt because it is a very hard thing to do. Whose fault it is doesn't matter; more important is what we do in the future to try and stay friends.

PARENT TO ELEVEN-YEAR-OLD CHILD:
Getting a divorce isn't about fault. It is true, as you know, that Daddy has a new girlfriend and that I am hurt about that. But he is still a very loving daddy. If you are upset with him, you should talk to him about it.

Note that as your children get older, your answers can be more complex and more open. But do not give them information they didn't already have, and do not tell them more than they want to hear. Initially, your children may not appear to understand what is happening, or may fail to ask the questions that you would expect from them. This is because they don't want the separation to occur, and it may take time for them to accept even the smallest piece of information from you. Give your children a number of opportunities in the next few days and weeks to ask you questions about what is happening to the family. Encourage them to ask questions about what they fear most. You must not expect your children to understand the reasons and feelings why you separated, or to talk about their feelings in the same way as adults talk about their feelings. Children usually show their feelings through their behavior, which may change considerably at home, and at school, in the months after separation.

Using children as allies and pawns during separation and divorce is all too common. Parents who are feeling hurt, angry, or bitter may want to tell the children intimate details about why the marriage broke down, to persuade the children to think and feel as they do. It is very reassuring to have your child agree with you and become furious with the other parent. It also is a way to cope with your jealousy and desire for revenge. Parents may thus coax a child through questions to spy on the other parent, to tell them stories about the activities and behavior of the other parent. There have even been cases when a parent will feign illness, or exaggerate psychological problems, in order to obtain the children's loyalty against the other parent. There have also been cases where a parent will tell a child that the other parent does not really love him or want to be with him, but will want to see him a lot to hurt the caretaking parent. This hurts your child far more than it does the other parent.

Children often feel loyalty to both parents, and they quickly pick up on what each parent wants to hear. As a result, they tell both sides some version of what they want to hear, sometimes elaborating on events, exaggerating comments, or altering the tone of the parent's response, and thereby increasing the conflict between the parents. Using children as allies and pawns only confuses them. Researchers Johnston and Campbell (see Appendix, page 346) have shown that such behavior has long-lasting, damaging effects on the children's future development. Remember, it is you, the parents, who are divorcing. Don't expect your children to divorce your spouse, too. In most situations it is not healthy for them to reject the other parent, expelling that individual from their life, even if you are doing so.

HOW WILL MY CHILDREN FEEL AND REACT?

Your child's initial reaction is most likely to be denial mixed with tears and fears. Common responses include "How can you let this happen?" "How could you do this to me?" and "Isn't there something you can do to be happier together?" Younger children tend to deny, refusing to believe what they are being told. It is not uncommon for a young child to seemingly accept the divorce easily, without adverse reaction. The child may be young enough not to understand what it means, and this could work in his or her favor. Some young children will have questions and concerns that surface after a brief time. Others may not have concerns until they are older. Leave the door open for discussion, and monitor your child's behavior carefully. If there is no reaction at the present time, so be it. Wallerstein and Blakeslee report that some young children adapt to divorce over time better than older children, since their limited understanding and experience with life prior to the divorce buffers them from some of the intense negative responses (see page 347).

Older children cry and beg their parents not to split up. Many children are shocked, saying they had no idea the divorce was coming. Others say they are not surprised because Mom and Dad were fighting so much prior to the announcement. Whether or not they suspected does not seem to ease the way. It just allows kids to outwardly cope better, at least at first.

When the shock wears off, it is usually followed by fear, anger, and grief. Even when one parent was abusive, drinking too much, or not home enough, most children want the marriage to work out. As the feeling of loss sets in, children become anxious about what will become of them and, sometimes, they worry about the parent they perceive to be more vulnerable. Loneliness is pervasive among children in divorce situations because the parents they always turned to are not available. If parents do not actively encourage their kids to talk about their experience, the children may try to protect parents from feelings that they perceive to be an additional burden for the parent. They figure the parent has enough upset of their own. They then stop using their parent as confidante, which is not good for them.

Children of different ages have different reactions in the aftermath of the announcement. Preschoolers indicate increased fears of abandonment. They regress to earlier stages of development; for example, they may begin soiling their pants or wetting their bed again if they had mastered that behavior a short time before. Your child who loved day care now clings to your leg, wailing piteously about your leaving. She may be more cranky. Or she may seem not to have noticed, her denial working perfectly for her. This can scare parents, but it will not hurt your child to take more time before dealing with the event. Denial is wonderfully undervalued in our culture: it can give us the time we need to marshal our resources, allowing us to reach the next step. Young children take longer to cognitively and emotionally process complex relationships and events.

Young school-age children (six to eight years) are more likely to express their reactions in sadness. They are likely to mourn through yearning, like Madame Butterfly waiting at the window to see her love return to her. Their fears are ones of deprivation rather than abandonment; will there be enough time, attention, and money for them to live as they always did? Symptoms are manifested in academic difficulties and concentration problems. Sleep and eating disturbances are common, as are psychosomatic complaints—headaches, stomachaches, bumps, and bruises.

Your middle school child (nine to twelve years) is more likely to get angry than his younger siblings. This age is prone to loyalty conflicts, since friendships and teammates are just beginning to fully take over their imaginations and dominate their social world. This is the age most likely to become involved by their parents in the adults' conflict, signing up for one side or the other, but eager to be on a team and to have a common threat against whom to rally. Because of their sensitivity in this arena, and to their greater ability than their younger siblings to understand what is going on between the adults, they are used by parents to deliver messages, spy, or just report back.

Teenagers may try to understand all sides of the divorce, but they are focused on its effects on them. They are particularly vulnerable to parents' dating, since they may feel competitive about the new parental relationship and want the spotlight to be focused solely on them. They also may feel competitive with the parent, who is busy being concerned about her own attractiveness and sexuality instead of focusing on the teen's feelings in these domains. Teens need to count on their parents to counter their self-absorptive tendencies, not rival them. They also are anxious about their futures, and the divorce increases those feelings. They worry about having money for college and whether they will be able to choose a relationship that will last, or whether they are destined for the sadness they are observing in their own family. When the sense of loss becomes overwhelming, many become less focused and have lapses in concentration at school and in commitment to their extracurricular activities. They may appear fatigued, sleeping more than usual. Evidence of despair includes use of alcohol, drugs, or premature sexual involvement.

Some children of all ages, but especially teens, work at seeing both parents' perspectives. Their ability to do so can lead to increased social skills (especially in regard to problem solving), the development of empathy, and self- and other acceptance. These children often mature early, but one outgrowth of that maturity is the enhanced cognitive and social competencies and leadership abilities that accompany them. It is easiest for children to do this when they are presented with two parents of equal importance, and they are encouraged to develop lives with each parent and the families or homes that are created over time. When blaming and aggression are minimized and cooperation is maximized for the children's sake, they may feel the confidence and security that allows them to focus on their own tasks of growing up.

The question of how children fare over time has been studied by researchers who have followed small groups of families over time (for example, see Appendix, pages 346–47). The data consistently indicate that most parents and children cope reasonably well with divorce. The average adjustment period lasts from between eighteen months to three years. After five years postdivorce, about two-thirds of the children studied are coping well. Wallerstein and Kelly's small, Northern California sample provided the exception, as reported in a ten-year follow-up (see Wallerstein and Blakeslee, Appendix, page 349) in which about 40 percent of the children studied were still struggling with their feelings of sadness and grief. They had difficult young adult lives, especially the children whose parents divorced when they were middle school age or older. Their most distinct memory was the loneliness they suffered after divorce, as both parents were less available to them physically and emotionally. These findings remained consistent for some children twenty-five years after the divorce (Wallerstein et al.; see Appendix page 347).

Overall boys more than girls tend to become symptomatic after divorce. They feel rejected by their fathers, or just suffer from less closeness to their parent of the same gender. Most children live with their mothers after divorce, and mothers have an easier time parenting their daughters, especially being authority figures to them when the firm hand of discipline is needed.

Across the board, research has shown that the negative impacts of divorce on children are minimized and positive results maximized when:

1. The parents are in less conflict with each other and are more cooperative with each other.

2. The parents (especially the primary caretaker if there is one) maintain their ability to be nurturing and consistent caretakers.

3. Parent-child relationships are warm and close, with parents remaining parents and children remaining children; that is to say, that children do not take care of their parents or become primary supports for their parents and antidotes for their loneliness and sorrows. They are allowed to remain children, without the burdens of parental responsibilities and adult feelings.

Reducing family conflict is key! If you, as the parents, are able to establish a good and cooperative relationship before the separation, then your children will have the advantage and experience of a parental relationship that is based on respect, cooperation, and recognition of differences. For some families, the conflict and tension will continue during the separation period. If the fighting, arguing, and bitterness drag on for a considerable length of time, it is inevitable that the children will develop difficulties that will become evident either at home or at school.

If you are the sole parent involved with your children, it is important for you to remain as loving and emotionally available as you can muster, with a firm but appropriate hand when it comes to discipline. Involve other adults in your children's life who can be positive influences on them. If your children have been rejected or abandoned by a parent, help them understand that this did not happen because of some failure or lack in them, but that the other parent is not ready or capable of being a parent to the child at the present time. Tell them this over and over, *ad nauseum.*

It is difficult to determine when it is best to encourage another parent to be involved, and when this is detrimental to your child. Encouragement is often useful, but if you have to push too hard, it is not likely to work out for the child. You cannot mandate, by law or guilt, that someone act like a parent. If a parent keeps disappointing your child, not showing up or not calling when agreed, *and* if you are working too hard to keep this parent involved, let go. Find other men or women (as the case may be) to be close to your child. And leave the door open for a possible reentry when the parent is ready. As angry as this might make you, it could be best for your child to have more contact with the parent at another point in time.

How Can I Best Help My Children During This Early Stage of Divorce?

Your children have developmental tasks they must master relative to the divorce, just as they do relative to other challenges they will face in their lifetime. They need to be accepting of the divorce without becoming drawn into it, deal with feelings of loss and blame (self-blame and blaming their parents), and learn to look to the future again with optimism. There are many ways you can make this period easier for your children. Follow as many of the suggestions offered below as you can. Do not worry if you cannot meet all of them, but try your utmost to respond as suggested. Your children will benefit from any and all of your efforts.

Suggestion 1: Be Predictable

Continue your usual lifestyle and routine as much as possible, including activities, chores, and visiting family and friends. Continuity and predictability are ways you can reduce the disruption in your children's lives. Maintain rules and traditions. Have dinner at the same time on a regular basis, have the same expectations for homework as you did before the separation, and most important, maintain discipline! When scheduling changes are necessary, inform your children of plans that affect them. Get their input about what they want in the schedule. If either parent wishes to change a plan that involves contact with the children, tell the children well in advance and attempt to find an acceptable alternative if need be. Try not to be late for occasions that involve the children, for instance, picking them up after school, or after an outing. If you are paying child support, pay consistently and on time. Your children need to be able to rely on you.

Suggestion 2: Remain Involved.
If Not Involved, Get Involved

Some children feel that the parent who is no longer in the family home has rejected them. In order to reassure your children that you are still a part of their lives, remain involved. This means with homework and their friends, not just in time alone with them. If you were the parent who left the home, check in with the parent remaining at home regarding the children's sporting activities, school concerts, and weekend activities. Ask your children about these activities, show your interest. Telephone your children when you have not seen them for a day or two, just to say "hi." Do not take it personally if your children are not great conversationalists on the telephone. They will know that you are available and concerned. They will remember that you showed interest.

You may feel empty and distressed each time you see your children; assume that they will have the same feelings. It is not uncommon for parents in this situation to consider ceasing contact with their children because the transitions are so painful. If a parent disappears after separation, the child's worst fears are reinforced. You have abandoned them; now they believe they are not lovable. It is crucial that you maintain contact with them, no matter how painful it may be for you.

For most people, it does get easier over time.

Suggestion 3: Resist the Temptation to Be a Disneyland Parent

The parent who leaves the marital home, most often the father in our society, may fear that he will lose his children. You may believe you won't lose their love, but you fear that you will lose the chance to have ample say about their daily choices and what happens with them. This fear can add significantly to the stress and anxiety that is part and parcel of divorce. This impending sense of loss can lead to your feeling that you have to be a "Disneyland" parent.

It's all too easy for the nonresidential parent to treat time with their children as Disneyland days. Guilty or remorseful feelings about the divorce are allayed by making it up to the children through gifts and special trips. Trips to toy stores, movies, and events help push away the awkwardness at being together. They make the time special, and when time seems scarce, it feels like every moment must be perfect. However, your children need to continue to see you as a regular person, the usual Mom or Dad. They will need to spend quiet time with you, and they need you to be interested in their homework, their sports, friends, and all the things that concern them. If you spend your time with your children in "Disneyland," your children will come to look for this and the relationship between you and your children will become superficial. They will come to expect a fun time with you—gifts, activities, just the material goodies of life. And naturally, that is just one side of life and of being a parent.

Sometimes parents are unaware that they are competing with each other for the children's affections by lavishing the kids with favors. This does neither of you any good, and it can actually erode your relationship with your children. You risk becoming the fun parent, or the wealthy parent, but not the parent to turn to when it matters. Moreover, spoiling your child at this time does not do him any favors.

Another temptation when parents are unsure of themselves is to act like a friend rather than a parent. If your children are older, you may be tempted to take them into your confidence and tell them your troubles. If they are younger, you might substitute play for other parental functions. Your children need you to be a parent now. It is reassuring to them. Do not lower your expectations of them. Be gentle, give them slack as you judge that they need it, but do not change your style wholesale. If you were the "nice" parent, the lax disciplinarian prior to the divorce, you may have to work harder at balancing your normative style with the discipline that children need at both houses in which they spend time.

Suggestion 4: Listen to Your Children

Children often experience very different feelings than you do at different times during this transition. They may feel sad when you feel relieved. Try and listen to the feelings behind the words your children speak. Allow your children to express their anger with you and at their situation. Allow them to miss the other parent when they are in your presence.

Words are not the only way children express themselves. Younger children, and those who are feeling their emotions very intensely, do not use words to show their feelings. Learn to understand what they are feeling by watching their behavior. They may withdraw, indicating they are sad. They may act out in some way, which is telling you that they are angry.

Suggestion 5: Act Civilly to Your Spouse

There are several important components of being civil. First, try to co-operate together. You can disagree privately with each other, but try to present a uniform front as a parenting team. This will be especially helpful as your children mature, and when they need a safety net to keep them from wandering too far from "home" values. It is easier to keep them in tow if they know you are together on the rules and consequences of breaking the rules. Curfews, discipline, academic expectations, treatment of adults and other family members—these are basics you should try to agree upon.

Being civil means encouraging your children to respect the other parent. If you do not talk or act negatively about your ex-spouse, your children will not need to either. It is tempting to tell them stories about the other parent's lapses, but children who do not respect both of their parents have a harder time reconciling the half of themselves that is the genetic connection to the other parent. Your child is half of each of you. If she thinks that you hate the part of her that is like her mother, she may choose to hate that part of herself, too. Do not draw your child into rejecting half of himself or herself.

Suggestion 6: Be Cautious About Introducing New Partners

Before you introduce your children to a new love relationship, think about the experiences that your children are undergoing. Remember that your children are loyal to both parents, and they are wary, if not downright distressed, about how the future will unfold for their family. If you have a significant new relationship, many experts recommend that you wait to introduce the new partner to your children until your divorce is final. If you absolutely can't wait, or if you are carrying on in secret and it is driving you crazy, talk with the children about your friend prior to their first meeting. Leave plenty of time for them to get used to the idea and to come back to you with questions. Introduce this person on a gradual basis and in neutral territory rather than in their home. Allow the children time to develop a friendly relationship with this person on its own merits.

If possible, wait and see if your new relationship develops into a serious one. Children do not need a parade of new faces passing through their home or life right now. And you do not want them to become numb to each new partner, so that when you have found one you want to be serious about, they do not take you seriously.

Don't be surprised that your children will reject this new partner at first because of a sense of loyalty to the other parent. Children often feel that when Mom or Dad has a new friend that their other parent is being displaced. Or, more important, that *they* are being displaced. They have more difficulty if the new partner has children, as they fear they will be replaced by the new children. Go slow with this introduction phase. Let the relationship between the new partner and your children evolve with time. Under no circumstances should you introduce this new partner as your new love, or give them a cutesy name like Aunt or Uncle. If your new partner is rushing you, or won't give you adequate time, take a hard look at the relationship. It is not likely to be one which will enhance your life, or your family life, for the long haul.

Suggestion 7: Take Care of Yourself

Once you have started your divorce, the work of rebuilding your life has just begun. You will need to establish a consistent routine for yourself and your children that fits into your newly separated life. You will find this a demanding and disorganized time. The legal process in itself greatly adds to the stress. You have meetings to go to, paperwork to do, monetary matters to track, lawyers to meet with and to pay, and unless the divorce process is very amicable, all this happens against a backdrop of great uncertainty about the results of the process.

Allow yourself to have some time each day or week, even if it is brief, that is time simply for you. You need to be aware of your own stress level, and be able to pause when you are feeling overwhelmed or exhausted. You may find that the household routine will require that you ask the children to do extra chores and tasks. You may need to ask neighbors, friends, and family to help you at the commencement of your new lifestyle.

The single parent who is also employed or without previous social supports may find that the demands placed on him or her are overwhelming.

Single parenting, like becoming a parent for the first time, is exhausting because you have so much to do, all of which needs to be done immediately. There is no one to give you a break, to take over when you are tired, or to give you support in dealing with the discipline or management of the children.

Yet, with a sense of relief over having crossed the initial hurdles of separation and initiation of divorce proceedings, you may for the first time be able to organize and situate your life in a happier and healthier manner. The fact that you are solely in charge of running your home will enable you to establish what you want your home to be like and to feel like. Parents who are prepared to take risks and try new behavior will provide their children with a good example of positive coping with change and adversity. This will be a great advantage to your children as they develop.

Your children need to continue their own interests, friendships, and developmental growth spurts. They can do this more easily and with less worry if they see you doing the same things for your own life. It is very important that they see you taking time to rediscover yourself. Besides, your children will not always need you in the same ways. When you have a full and active life that supports their growth, you will have an easier time letting go of them when it is appropriate to do so.

How do you stay consistent and on top of their needs while working on your own day-to-day existence? You keep them at the center of your life but you build many concentric circles of support and interest beyond just them. In this way, divorced parenting is not different from parenting in two-parent families. You just have to work harder at it because there is not someone else reminding you to have a life. Allow yourself to be interesting and to have new hobbies. Be a person who tries new behaviors, reexamines her opinions, and makes mistakes. Your children will respect you and the fact that you are establishing a new, more flexible, and healthy family unit.

Suggestion 8: Be Positive About Your New Family Identity

Today some adults are discovering that the single-parent role is one of choice, and not of a transitional phase between partners or marriages. Single-parent families are different from nuclear two-parent families in that there is only one caretaking parent in each home who operates with fewer resources and often less income. The demands and challenges placed on single parents and their children can make this family unit more supportive of each other and close knit. If you as leader of a single-parent family maintain a positive attitude toward the future, viewing it as an unknown but welcome surprise, your children will find life exciting and full of promise. On the other hand, if you feel that separation and divorce confer a sense of shame and embarrassment, it is likely that the children will see themselves as less well-off than two-parent families.

During the process of exploring your own identity, your children can learn not only to support you but also to share in your new experiences with you. You may find that your children are proud to have a parent who is capable of maintaining a single household, who is also interesting and adventurous to be with as a person. Of course there will be times when the burdens and responsibilities get you down, and when you resent the demands that your children place upon you. If this happens, take some time out. Get emotional support from your friends and your family. Do something fun that does not involve the children.

Suggestion 9: Surround Your Children with Other Adults Who Are Supportive

Other adults can be resources for both you and your children. As soon as the separation occurs, it is important that you inform your children's teachers so that they may be prepared for any change in behavior that may occur. Have the teachers keep an eye on your children. Inform your children's friends' parents, as well, so they can keep in mind that your children will be undergoing many changes and stressors. They can be an extra pair of ears, eyes, and a sympathetic presence. You may also want to inquire about possible support groups at your children's school for children with divorcing parents. These groups tend not to carry a social stigma anymore, and are helpful in creating a place for children to share their experiences with other children who have recently undergone a similar change. Sharing stories, thoughts, and feelings can be invaluable to the process that you and your children will undergo. Self-help groups for children and parents have been proven effective for creating a sense of community during a lonely and stressful time for people who desire support, but don't need or want therapy.

WILL MY CHILDREN BE OKAY IN A DIVORCED FAMILY?

Parents often ask the question "Will my children be disadvantaged being raised in a divorced family?" One of the benefits of a divorced family is that your children are no longer exposed to the tension and conflict that marked their experience of living with both parents. Children's responses to their new status are often dependent upon how parents view their new status. If you as parent have a positive view of the future, this will significantly help your children adjust to and accept the new situation. Your children will have an early introduction to the emotional effects of loss and separation. This can cause long-lasting pain and insecurity. However, it also can be a valuable learning experience that will help them build resilience to life transitions and hardships. Children in divorced families have the opportunity to learn that relationships change, that their parents also change over time. Your experience may also show your children that they need not accept a circumstance in which they are unhappy, abused, or feel empty, that they can effect change in their lives for the better.

PERSONAL ASSESSMENT

Have I provided my children with timely, age-appropriate information about the impending separation and divorce? In particular, do the children now know what is going to happen, when, how, and what the living and access arrangements will be? Although informing the children in this manner is harder for me, it will help ease their fears of the unknown. Being as specific as possible about the parenting plans, as soon as possible, adds to their ongoing sense of security.

Have my spouse and I provided a unified front in our information? Have we either informed the children together or ascertained that we offered similar information, without inserting blame in the explanation?

Who is at fault is an adult issue; the children do not need to know what we each think about it. They will feel safer if we show them that we will still act together as parents on their behalf.

Have I taken careful notice of their responses to our announcement, and to the separation? Can I describe each child's reaction, and do I understand what his or her response means to the child? Have I noticed any reactions that are severe enough to invoke a higher level of concern? I have watched, listened, asked questions, answered questions, and feel confident that I am aware of each child's response to the separation.

Have I done what I can to ease the children's way in the aftermath? Have I been predictable, dependable, and as civil to their other parent as possible? Have I been thoughtful in my dealings with, and introductions of, a new partner in the presence of my children? During this time, I want to be vigilant about making this easier on all of us. I am continuing to be a loving and caring parent in ways my children have always known. I need to be cautious with any new relationship, not letting my own joy and excitement cloud my judgment concerning my children's need for me to move slowly and steadily into anything new. They are hurting and I must honor their perspective and timetable as different from my own.

8.

Legal and Residential Arrangements: Finding Familiar Paths for Your Family

Now that you understand what your children are likely to experience during the divorce, you are ready to begin thinking about creating a parenting plan that will work for both parents and is optimal to meet your children's needs.

WHAT ARE OUR LEGAL OPTIONS FOR RAISING OUR CHILDREN AFTER DIVORCE?

Increasingly, personnel associated with the courts agree that the terms used to connote parenting arrangements after divorce—custody, access, and visitation—are antiquated and pernicious. They harken back to a time when children were parents' property, and suggest that one parent is more of a visitor than a family member. These terms are being replaced with new ones such as "decision-making responsibility" and "parenting plans," which emphasize parental responsibilities over their rights. Nevertheless, legal and physical custody still are the primary designations after divorce, and must be understood as such. Technically, custody refers to caring for a child with regard to their safety and well-being. The courts have the power to confer both legal and physical custody.

Legal Custody

The parent or parents with legal custody have the legal right to make major decisions regarding the child. Major decisions typically refer to those pertaining to the child's health, education, and welfare. Commonly specified types of decisions include religious upbringing and education, choice of schools and/or special education decisions, medical decisions such as elective surgery, choice of doctors, and whether or not to have a child receive mental health counseling and/or medications. In sole legal custody, one parent has primary decision-making rights. In joint legal custody, such decision making is shared.

Joint legal custody

Joint legal custody is a label that was popularized in the late 1970s and early 1980s as a way to give both parents an equal opportunity to continue to be involved in decision making about their children's lives. One motivation behind the term was the belief that if the nonresidential parent remained involved in decision-making processes related to the child, that parent would be more likely to pay child support over time. Also, a growing fathers' movement spoke out about men's interests in continuing to have authority and a stake in their child's life through involvement in decisions about their upbringing.

Joint legal custody grants both parents equal power in making major decisions concerning the children's welfare. Typically, these are the health, education, and religious upbringing issues described above. The more day-to-day decisions about the children are usually made by the parent with whom the children live most of the time.

Joint legal custody works best when parents are able to cooperate with each other about decisions regarding their children. Parents who fight and use every opportunity to disagree about decisions that affect the children may be viewed as poor candidates for joint legal custody, although most states have statutes either allowing or encouraging joint legal custody unless the conflict is at such a high level that the parents are incapable of any joint decision making.

The types of situations in which joint legal custody might not be appropriate are the following: one parent is incarcerated; one parent lives very far away from the other; one parent abuses drugs and alcohol to the extent that it impairs his or her judgment; there is a history of violence between the parties and any unnecessary contact should be eliminated; or one parent suffers from a psychiatric illness that makes it impossible for that parent to use good judgment pertaining to the child's welfare.

For parents who are able to put their own differences behind them and work together for the benefit of their children, joint legal custody is a preferred outcome. Ideally, parents cooperate in making decisions, and they negotiate and compromise when they disagree. Not all parents can cooperate easily, and many parents write into their agreements that when they are stalemated in making a decision, they will use a mediator or therapist to help resolve the impasse.

Whether or not you are a joint legal custodian of your children, you need to make every effort to try and involve the other parent in decision making. Failure to do so often increases the other parent's sense of isolation, leading to hostility and retaliatory behavior. Obstructing your child's relationship with her other parent could thus turn into a legal problem for you or a psychological problem for your child.

Physical Custody

Physical custody describes where the child physically lives. Most children live primarily with one parent (called sole physical custody), spending a specified amount of time with the other parent (called either visitation or parenting access).When children spend fairly equal amounts of time with both parents, the court refers to this type of living arrangement as joint physical custody.

Joint physical custody

Joint physical custody takes various forms. Some children spend one week with one parent, and the next week with the other parent; others spend three nights one week with one parent, and four nights the next week. Various other permutations are also used (discussed later in this chapter), and as long as the children spend nearly equal time with each parent, the specific arrangement is not germane to the title. In this arrangement, children often think of themselves as having two homes.

Compared to joint legal custody, joint physical custody is a relatively rare event, with national estimates ranging from about 10 to 20 percent of divorced families. It is also a difficult arrangement to maintain; studies show that many families who begin in dual residence arrangements move to more traditional schedules over time. This is due to the difficulty of maintaining such arrangements, as they require cooperation, organization, and flexibility. This scenario typically works best when the parents live near each other and transportation to and from school and extracurricular activities is easily resolved, logistically speaking. It also works best when parents are able to communicate and cooperate with each other about scheduling matters, and the child's temperament is organized and relaxed when faced with multiple transitions. The pluses and minuses of such arrangements are discussed below.

Split custody arrangements: separating siblings

Generally courts will avoid separating siblings and placing them in different households. Under some circumstances, siblings are split up. This is a practice better off avoided if possible, but there are certainly circumstances in which it makes sense.

For example, if one child has special needs and the other child taunts or torments that child, or if the children have unique educational needs that are best met in different districts, split custody may be the preferred option. In some cases, a female child is very identified with the mother and a male child with the father to such a great extent that the children express strong preferences for living with their "identified" parent, even if it means living apart from a sibling. If your children are old enough to know what they want, and the situation makes sense given all other circumstances, consideration could be given to their preferences.

However, the children should not be divided for the sake of parental compromise. Childhood bonds between siblings are most likely to form and endure when the children grow up together sharing a home and family experiences. This aspect of the children's development should not be sacrificed for the parents' wishes.

SHARED PARENTING (CO-PARENTING) VERSUS CUSTODY

Custody refers to a legal arrangement, while shared parenting describes the actual activity between the adults. Often shared parenting, also called co-parenting, is interpreted to mean that parents are able to raise their children together, even if the parents are no longer marital partners. Cooperative and communicative parenting is optimal, but co-parenting can be effectively accomplished in less optimal circumstances, as long as parents can put aside their differences and stay focused on what their children need and deserve. This can take the form of parents discussing most aspects of child rearing. Or it can take the form of having each parent contribute primary decision making and authority in certain areas, with shared discussions when the parents are faced with complications or uncertainties.

For example, Juan and Maria agreed that through their co-parenting arrangement they both would spend significant amounts of time with their daughter, Valerie, each week. Juan would take primary responsibility for religious upbringing since that was of utmost importance to him; as an elementary school teacher, Maria would take primary responsibility (with input from Juan) for decisions about what kinds of preschool experiences Valerie should have before kindergarten. They would discuss any medical and mental health decisions, leaving fewer areas open to potential disagreement.

Researchers Ahrons and Rogers (see Appendix, page 347) discuss four types of postdivorce relationships between spouses:

- Perfect Pals
- Cooperative Colleagues
- Angry Associates
- Fiery Foes

Two of the four types can create an effective co-parenting alliance. Perfect Pals maintain close personal ties; Cooperative Colleagues are civil and cooperative, though their relationship requires frequent negotiation. Angry Associates and Fiery Foes, on the other hand, do not contain their conflict, and, therefore, children are incorporated into it in a way that makes co-parenting problematic, if not impossible.

Successful co-parents:

- Communicate and negotiate with each other about the children
- Respect each other as parents despite adult disappointments and personal differences
- Put past disagreements aside and concentrate on the children
- Share control with each other and adopt a hands-off attitude toward how the other person parents
- Tolerate differences in child rearing practices and values without labeling them as harmful to the child, and distinguishes between important and unimportant differences
- Value what the other has to offer as a parent

What Are the Benefits and Drawbacks of Shared Parenting?

Benefits of shared parenting accrue to both parents, as well as children. Some of the most salient advantages are:

1. The nonresidential parent is less likely to feel like a visitor or a money-making machine. The nonresidential parent is given ample opportunity to express his/her commitment to parenting, as well as love for the child. Feeling like an equally important parent leads to less hostility and resentment over time. It also leads to greater involvement in the child's life. Both parents maintain independent relationships with their children.

2. Both parents feel good about their ability to work together for their children. It helps them feel less grief or guilt about the ending of the marriage, as they are concentrating on positive ways of continuing the family rather than on the losses they all are experiencing.

3. The child has ongoing contact with both parents, and is less prone to feel like he/she must choose a favorite.

4. There is less chance that the family will have to return to court to re-litigate or enforce modifications. This results in less stress and money spent on the divorce process itself.

5. Both parents have more time to pursue personal interests and goals, such as school, work, time with friends, or hobbies.

6. Both parents get more support for parenting. When one needs help in a pinch, the other parent is more likely to step in and assist.

The disadvantages of shared parenting stem from the difficulty it can place on parents to disengage from the marriage and the past. Specifically:

1. More contact with the other parent can trigger jealousy, hostility, and resentment. This in turn can result in children being exposed to more conflict. Ongoing conflict and animosity between parents has been linked to long-term emotional problems for children.

2. Children often want two involved parents, but one primary home where their possessions and friends are located. This holds true especially for many teenagers, who don't want to miss a moment of their social life because they are making transitions between homes.

3. Shared parenting gives children more opportunities to play one parent against the other, as they do with married parents. This requires that the two of you realize what they're doing and that you don't allow them the power to manipulate you.

4. The more involved both parents are, the more difficult relocation issues can be down the road.

5. In situations where there is real or threatened physical abuse, contact between parents can be dangerous.

DO CHILDREN FARE BETTER IN SHARED PARENTING SCHEDULES THAN IN MORE TRADITIONAL CUSTODY SITUATIONS?

Like so many areas pertaining to the psychology of family law, our clinical wisdom far outstrips our knowledge based on research. Despite this limitation, we have some ideas about ways in which shared parenting benefits children and families.

Parents and children living in shared parenting arrangements, in which children spend significant amounts of time with both parents, report greater satisfaction with the arrangements than do their sole custody coun-terparts. The children see both parents more often than do children in sole custody arrangements, and the children like staying close to both parents. Children in families with joint legal custody, as well as those with joint physical custody, report greater father involvement than do children in sole custody families. The parents, both mothers and fathers, are happier with the arrangements, even when they were not initially in favor of them.

It is important to note, however, that these families may be self-selected, meaning that they were able to work out these arrangements be-tween themselves as part of their divorce. Most of these families were not involved in bitter custody disputes. Parents in shared parenting families generally have lower conflict from the beginning and describe their ex-spouse as an involved parent. Thus, in most studies people chose shared parenting voluntarily because of the values they share about parenting.

Although studies are sparse enough to be only suggestive rather than conclusive, there is some evidence that shared parenting arrangements ben-efit children in several ways. The children have fewer behavioral and emo-tional problems and report fewer negative experiences with the divorce. Boys derive special benefits from shared parenting, and the contact it af-fords them with their fathers. Adolescent boys, in particular, choose shared custody arrangements over more traditional ones. In addition, dual-residence teens of both genders report less depression and better grades than their sole custody counterparts. However, the research on this group also shows that children can do well in various types of arrangements as long as the parents provide support and firm guidance, combining warmth with parental control. This parenting style may be facilitated by shared par-enting arrangements.

Mental health researchers have been especially interested in the effects on very young children, as this is the fastest-growing segment of the di-vorcing population today. For young children, frequent father-child contact and the fathers' sustained involvement before and after divorce are associ-ated with a positive father-child relationship. Interestingly, fathers losing contact with children was less frequent among infants and toddlers who stayed overnight with their fathers. This would seem to recommend overnights as a vehicle for fostering paternal responsibility and closeness to their infants; yet many experts recommend forestalling overnights until

CONFLICT AND CONTACT

High contact with both parents coupled with high conflict between parents is not in children's best interests. There is no ambiguity about this! Children surrounded by continuous conflict demonstrate higher levels of aggression and regression. Alternatively, parents in frequent contact who are supportive of each other have well-adjusted young children, whether or not they spend overnights. It is not the overnights or the schedule in itself that is the critical link; rather, parents who work cooperatively and protect their children from negative involvements in the parental relationship can each spend more time with their children without harming them.

children are older. This paradox requires that parents take into careful consideration how well their children are able to tolerate separations from their mother, the child's temperament, and the strength of the father-child bond prior to divorce, and weigh all this against the likelihood of the father staying in the child's life over time if the paternal role is established as central early on. Children can bond with more than one person, but creating a secure environment with both parents necessitates that parents organize child care roles as soon as possible after separation, so that fathers establish themselves as another primary figure in the child's life.

Research points to the benefits of shared parenting defined as shared decision making, as well as shared time between two homes. A shared parenting label may denote and promote more contact with the less-seen parent. Parents who are sharing responsibility for child rearing enjoy having a legal status that advertises their joint authority and equitable involvement. And they stay involved with their children. However, involvement does not refer primarily to the amount of time fathers or mothers spend with their children. Research on fathers as the noncustodial, or less-seen, parent shows that the amount of time fathers spend with their children is not the most important factor for a child's healthy development. The amount of contact between father and child is important because it facilitates a closer parent-child relationship. But time does not automatically equal closeness.

⚖

STRATEGIES FOR SHARED PARENTING

Develop a joint plan for resolving conflicts—make compromises, and above all else, keep your kids out of the middle of your arguments.

Support each other's privacy—what goes on in the other house is none of your business unless it endangers your child.

Respect the other parent—talk civilly, use common courtesies, help your children appreciate and recognize the other parent's efforts to be close to them.

Communicate regularly with the other parent—use notes, e-mail, and faxes as well as phone calls.

Do your share of parenting and be clear about what you need and expect from the other parent in order to co-parent smoothly.

Problems or no problems, it is always a good idea to keep the other parent updated as to what is happening when the children are with you by sending a weekly, biweekly, or monthly letter along with school papers, sports schedules, report cards, drawings, and any and all other materials that may come your way by virtue of the time the children spend with you. A side benefit of sending written materials is that you can photocopy them and keep them in a journal so that you have them as indications of your attempts to keep the other parent informed in the event that co-parenting cooperativeness breaks down, and there are subsequent allegations that you were not cooperative.

The quality of time spent and the level of involvement in child rearing are consistently more important to child well-being after divorce.

DEVELOPING A SCHEDULE FOR LIVING ARRANGEMENTS

The decision about with whom children will reside primarily may be a stressful one and can add to the ongoing conflicts between spouses. Therefore, you may be tempted to defer to your children to avoid the conflict and decision making. It is true that for older children (usually ten years or older), the court will consider where your child wants to live. This does not mean that you should ask your child with whom he or she wants to live. It is not uncommon for children to tell both parents that they wish to live with them; sometimes they change their minds based on whomever they are speaking to at that moment. This may be a tactic to make each parent feel good, or the child may genuinely change his mind when with each parent. Children may choose the parent that they feel the most sorry for, scared of, or who has the least restrictive household rules. Your child is worried enough about the divorce situation without your adding to his concerns by asking him to choose between two parents.

If a child is given this decision, you run the risk of invoking guilt toward the parent who was not chosen. In addition, the parent not chosen could punish the child by showing displeasure. Down the road, your children may become angry with you for passing this responsibility on to them, when it is one decision they wish you had made.

However, children often do have a preference, based more on their own needs for familiarity within their home and neighborhood than on a choice of one parent over another. They want to be near their friends, with the parent who has the best computer, with the parent who has more time to spend, or with the parent whose home is most conducive to sleepovers with friends. Children can tell you where they'd like to live instead of with whom, which indicates that they want to be heard about *what* matters to them, not who. Having their opinions considered makes them feel included, valued, and recognized as persons with independent needs.

Along with your former spouse, talk to your children and encourage them to express their preferences for schedule rather than place, and be clear that the adults will make the final decisions.

WHAT ARE THE MOST COMMON LIVING ARRANGEMENTS AND SCHEDULES ADOPTED BY DIVORCING PARENTS?

The most common arrangement today is still for the children to live primarily with one parent and spend time with the other. How families spell out specific arrangements are as varied as families themselves. One familiar form is for the children to live with Mom, and spend time with Dad every other weekend and an evening per week for dinner. Sometimes the weekend ends on Sunday, and other times the children stay until Monday morning when they are dropped off at school. Variations on the theme include a cycle in which the child spends one overnight during one week, and a four-day weekend (or a three-day weekend) the following week.

Many divorce orders provide for "liberal and reasonable" access, without specification of a schedule. This works out fine when parents communicate effectively and are flexible with one another. This does not work when parents are unable to cooperate, but have entered into an agreement for "reasonable and liberal visitation" in order to expedite the divorce. To bring predictability and order into your lives, and your children's, you should specify a schedule in your divorce agreement. Having a schedule in place need not discourage both of you from being flexible about rescheduling when either parent requests modifications.

All kinds of details can be written into an agreement to forestall problems particular to your family. For example, if you feel that your time with the kids is often reduced when they are sick, which occurs particularly with young children, you can write into the agreement that if a child is sick and has to miss a visitation, then compensatory time will be scheduled if it is not too disruptive to the child's schedule. Similarly, if your spouse hires a baby-sitter to watch the children when you would normally be available, you can specify that you get first right of refusal for extra time with the children. This is especially important to do when the child sees a parent fairly infrequently. By the same token, using your spouse's desire to be involved with the children to call upon him/her every time you have some small need is taking advantage of the situation. You want your ex to be available for you without feeling imposed upon, and certainly the reverse would be true. The idea behind "right of first refusal for baby-sitting" is that the spouses support each other, and that the children maximize the amount of time with each parent, and minimize the amount of time with baby-sitters. In the event such a provision becomes manipulative rather than supportive, such as when it is used to influence how the other parent spends free time, it should be discontinued immediately.

Some Common Shared Parenting Schedules

For parents who want to share their children's time more equally, there are many possible schedules. Some that are used frequently are:

a. every other week
b. every two weeks
c. Monday morning through Thursday morning and Thursday afternoon through Monday morning
d. Wednesday morning through Saturday morning and Saturday morning through Wednesday morning
e. September through June and summers for parents who live in different states

Examples of how various arrangements could be worded in an agreement are offered in the Appendix (page 308) in a sample divorce agreement. Every schedule has different pluses and minuses associated with it. Which schedule works for your family will depend on how close you live to the other parent, your work schedules, ages of your children, their individual temperaments, school demands, hobbies, and activities. The schedule you choose should depend on how important it is for the children to be in the same house on weekdays (i.e., school nights) and how well your children adapt to the transition between homes. Can your children organize their schoolwork when they make transitions between homes during the school week? If they have religious, sports, music, or other training on a regular basis, then maintaining the consistency of such classes is important. Children shouldn't have to miss activities on a regular basis because they have to be at the other parent's house.

How children go to school and return home also will affect your schedule. Do they need to be driven, can they switch buses, are they in a carpool?

Do your children have a maximum amount of time they can tolerate being away from either of you? The length of time may differ for their primary caretaker and their secondary, and it is likely to differ for children of different ages. All such factors are considerations in determining the best parenting schedules.

ARE THERE ALTERNATIVES TO THE TYPICAL SHARED PARENTING PLANS?

Some less common, but important, variations on schedules also deserve mention. For reasons that will become obvious in the descriptions below, these arrangements are harder to maintain than more common ones, and they often require greater cooperation and sacrifice on both parents' parts. However, when values or circumstances dictate creative solutions, these are worth considering.

Parents who can successfully do it report great satisfaction with "nesting." In this arrangement, the children stay in one place, and the parents move out of the home and into an apartment or family member's home. Sometimes the parents share one other dwelling, other times they can afford to rent or own two different ones. Sometimes they each return to a parent's or friend's home as their secondary residence. Parents then move in and out of the family home according to the dictates of schedules that work best for them.

Sometimes parents live far away from one another. In these situations, children may spend school years with one parent, and longer holiday periods, vacations, and summers with the other parent. If the child is very young, the parent will have to do the traveling for a while and/or see his child less frequently than he or she would like. Until a child is ready to spend extended periods of overnights, these long-distance options don't work very well. Parents have options of briefer visits, sacrificing desired time with the children, or moving/staying closer to the other parent until the children are older.

When parents live near each other, they may choose to alternate the child's primary residence every other year. The children do not spend much time living between homes, but they do visit the other parent regularly. Each parent gets to be the primary parent some of the time, smoothing over the sense of one parent being the less central figure. This schedule, though often proposed, is counter to children's best interests in most situations. This arrangement erodes consistency in discipline across phases of life, as well as the child's sense of belonging in a home.

WHAT ARE RECOMMENDED SCHEDULES FOR CHILDREN OF DIFFERENT AGES?

Unfortunately, too little research has been conducted regarding children's responses to various schedules to offer sound empirical evidence about what types of schedules work for which types of children and families. This means that parents are still largely on their own in setting up a schedule—using common sense and compassion about what the schedule is like for your children are still the best guidelines. Experts in the field were consulted by a committee formed in the state of Washington to make recommendations about optimal schedules based on the "average" child's capacity to manage time away from the primary caretaker(s) and still feel secure, and to handle multiple transitions (see page 347). Their recommendations are summarized below.

The First Year of Life

In the first year of life, primary tasks for the infant include stabilizing physical routines of feeding and sleeping, and learning to trust the world through predictable contact that is nurturing and responsive to needs for feeding, diapering, and comforting on demand. Most children develop a primary attachment to the person who is responsible for their care, but they are capable of developing attachment to a second or third caretaker as well. Emphasis on predictability and familiarity facilitate healthy development for infants.

Most experts agree that for children under one year of age, the time spent with a "nonprimary" parent should be consistent, predictable, and regular. Anywhere from daily to as many times a week as possible for short time periods is useful. Overnights are not recommended, and separations from a primary caretaker should be kept to eight hours or less. The easier the child's temperament, and the more comfortable the parents are with the child in either parent's care, the more frequent the baby's time with the second parent can be without causing the child undue stress.

Having a primary home with two- to three-hour visits sprinkled throughout the week optimizes both parents' opportunities to learn about who their baby is and what the child needs.

Toddlerhood—The Second Year

The second year of a baby's life is dedicated to exploring and gaining confidence and familiarity with the world. To do this, the baby must feel secure enough in his or her environment that energies are available to commit to the tasks of seeking out a larger world. Care must be responsive and consistent, so that the baby begins to feel some sense of control over separations and reunions.

Children at this age can spend up to a day at a time away from the primary parent. Overnights are debatable. The committee from Spokane, Washington, advised no overnights. Solomon and George conducted some of the only research on this issue (see page 347), and they reported that for some toddlers, overnights were associated with signals of distress and less secure attachment to both figures in their life. In follow-up studies, they found that overnight visitation can disorganize children's attachment strategies, but such disorganization does not necessarily pervade the mother-child relationship. That is, the children may be more sensitive (e.g., anxious) around separations, but this does not necessarily carry over to longer-term problems. Moreover, in this author's own clinical experience with divorcing families, parents who have divorced early in their children's life report that their child spends overnights once or twice a week without exhibiting signs of distress. Since we do not know whether children will show stress symptoms later as a result of early separations, it is best to use caution in designing such arrangements. But they should not be discounted as options to consider.

Two to three full days, nonconsecutively placed, should work for many toddlers just starting visits. However, many children respond well to regular, full-time day care when such care is of high quality. Thus, children spending that time with another parent should be able to adapt as well.

Older Toddlers—The Third Year of Life

At this age, children are expressing their autonomy in more ways, actively initiating separations from parents to find out what else the world has to offer. They are discovering what is unique about them, how they are different and similar to other children around them. Children in this age group want to learn as much as they can about everything, and the world is their playground. In order to explore safely, they need consistent rules and limit setting, gentle but firm guidance, and assistance in managing their disappointments and frustrations when they hear the inevitable "No!" Verbal explanations of parental behavior is important, as the children are using language increasingly to manage their own behavior and to understand how to respond to new situations and feelings.

Older toddlers can spend as much as three days with the nonprimary parent. If the parent is familiar and an ongoing part of the child's care, overnights are more likely to be successful. Consecutive nights are still not recommended, and more than two nights per week may be too taxing psychologically. A conservative route indicates that when the child is in the latter half of the third year, you introduce one or two overnights and observe how the child manages. If this works, you could try another overnight later in the week, but be ready to back off if the child begins to send you distress signs, as discussed below.

Preschoolers—to Age Five

Children at this age learn to control their aggression and impulses, achieve a healthy sex role identification, and develop peer relationships. Clear roles and boundaries between parents are important, as children at this age are very rule-bound, and the world is more understandable to them when they abide by rules they can count on. Notice this age's emphasis on games that have rules, winners, and losers. It is all part of becoming competent and learning how to play new games, concretely and metaphorically. This age child also feels very powerful, and is learning to wield his masculine or her feminine wiles. Male and female children benefit from having relationships with fathers and mothers, as they discover how men and women are different, and what it means to belong to the gender into which they have been born.

For the preschooler, spending time in the nonprimary parent's home up to three nights per week is acceptable. Even two to three consecutive days are manageable for many youngsters. The every other weekend schedule may work well by this age, with additional time during one to two afternoons or evenings, and more frequent phone contact. No more than a full week should be spent away from either parent, if at all possible.

School Age—Six to Twelve Years

Children at this age are expanding their cognitive, social, and physical skills at lightning speed. Making distinctions among feelings, thoughts, and actions enables children to become socialized in ways that ensure their success in the world. They learn to understand the differences between what they wish and what they can make happen, what they do and do not have control over, and what is likely to happen and what is just a fantasy. Attachments to other people deepen, as children fall in love with friends, teachers, relatives, and other significant persons in their life. Skills related to grooming and adopting a physically attractive appearance, juggling multiple friendships and peer groups, dealing with anger and competition, and developing self-reliance are important hallmarks of this period. Developing clear values is also crucial to the child's ability to make sound decisions among competing choices.

A balance between structure and flexibility serves the children's developmental needs best at this stage. Children need less predictability and more freedom to make arrangements around their own activities, and no matter how much they love you, insisting that they stick to an arrangement that impedes their social life is likely to build resentment. Children can handle two to three weekends per month with mid-week stays toward the end of these years. Four to six weeks during summer and vacations are also possible, although some spacing of weeks away from one's primary home is recommended. Schedules in which parents share the week or month fairly evenly can be tested out during this period. Hodges's research (see page

347) indicated that children who are seven to eight years old prefer being with their nonprimary parent two to three times per week, while older school-age children (age ten and thereafter) prefer less frequent visits.

Almost any of the near equal arrangements or the weekend with evening contact schedules are consistent with the needs of school-age children. By this age, if conflict is minimal between parents, your children are capable of helping you design the best schedule for them by telling you their desires if they do not fear reprisal from, or feel the need to take care of, either parent.

The Teen Years

Teens are interested in sexuality, individuality, peer involvement, and achieving independence. Their primary tasks are to come to terms with their changing bodies and changing moods. Social responsibility and adopting a moral code of behavior are crucial challenges that usher in the beginnings of adulthood. Although children at this stage are notorious for pushing their parents away, they need you to hang tough with them in order to feel secure. Let them push, but you stay firm. They want to be heard and consulted about all aspects of parenting arrangements. They want the freedom to move between houses, sometimes to change their primary residence. Whether such moves are in their best interest depends upon the reasons and timing of their request: is this a chance to identify with the other parent and acquire some psychological space from the parent they feel most dependent on, or are they looking for lax rules and little supervision? Children at this age often believe they are more mature than they are, so be advised to gather input but to maintain final decision-making authority.

During this time, the schedules for younger children may still work well. But teens often request more spontaneity, drop-in times, and flexibility. Teens can benefit from every weekend away if parents live close to one another. If not, summers away are often welcomed by all involved. However, employment, girlfriends/boyfriends, and special projects generally provide the guidelines around which sensitive parents must conform.

⚖

AN ADDITIONAL NOTE ABOUT OVERNIGHTS:
WHAT'S ALL THIS ABOUT ATTACHMENT?

Despite the Spokane County, Washington, guidelines discussed above, clinical wisdom suggests that many children can tolerate overnights at younger ages than most professionals recommend. The guidelines emanate from concerns about what will happen to children's attachments to their "primary attachment figures," the parent to whom they first turn for emotional sustenance and comfort and to get their needs met. In American society, mothers are usually the primary caretaker when children are young.

However, the notion that overnights are deleterious to child attachment and sense of security has recently been called into question. Lamb and Kelly, two eminent researchers in this field, believe that current guidelines may not do sufficient justice to father-child relationships or children's abilities to cope with overnights (see Appendix, page 347). They point out that we have a lot of evidence now that babies form meaningful attachments to both parents at about six to seven months of age, even though fathers spend less time with the children than do mothers. While children often prefer one parent over the other, typically the parent who takes primary responsibility for their care, such preferences often diminish with age, often by eighteen months old. Moreover, relationships with both parents are strengthened by opportunities to engage around the rituals of eating, bathing, and bedtime. Children show sophisticated abilities to interact with multiple caretakers (not only parents, but grandparents and day care workers, etc.) by seeking out different people to meet their needs depending upon the person's qualities, or perhaps the mood of the child.

What all this points to is that it is important for both parents to have opportunities to care for their children, and it is important for children to have opportunities to have meaningful relationships with both parents. Overnights provide an important means of parent involvement: bedtimes are special moments in a child's day. Much discussion, cuddling, teaching, and sharing can take place around evenings or mornings. The younger the child, the more transitions must be built into schedules so that they have continuity in relationships with both parents. Transitions are not necessarily the evils once believed, although under conditions of high parental conflict, such transitions unduly stress the child and contribute to the development of problem behavior. Lamb and Kelly even suggest that by age two, many toddlers should be able to adapt well to two consecutive overnights with each parent. Of course, conditions under which such schedules are maintained are crucial. Routines around feeding and sleeping should be similar. Other factors to be considered include the children's age, temperament (how flexible or rigid), cognitive and language development (how well do they understand and make themselves understood), past experiences, and the presence of other familiar persons—notably siblings, but extended family members as well. The bottom line: If you are a father or mother who has been involved with your child from birth, know your child's needs and habits, have time to focus on your child when he or she is in your care, and share a mutual, loving bond recognizable to those who know your family, then overnights should not automatically be ruled out because your child is an infant or toddler.

COMMON MISCONCEPTIONS IN THINKING ABOUT SHARED PARENTING

EXAMPLE 1: "HE WAS NEVER INVOLVED BEFORE—WHY NOW?"

A common complaint from women is that their husbands were never interested in being an involved parent before the divorce, and now they want equal time after divorce. It does feel unfair if you were the primary parent, and now your husband and/or child prefer a schedule in which you have to give up valued parenting time. However, don't assume your husband is making choices just to anger you. Many men become better fathers after divorce, once they are emotionally freed from the restrictions they felt by the unhappy marriage. Predivorce father-child relationships are not always good predictors of postdivorce father-child relationships. It may seem unfair to you, but wouldn't you rather your child have more of his father than less? Even if you don't, this is the child's father, after all. And you did choose him to be the father. Divorce can open doors to positive changes for everyone.

Prior to divorce, Ellen had been the parent with primary responsibility for rearing the children. She took them to school, to the doctor, and to their activities. Although she and her husband worked for the same company, she left work if the children became ill during the school day. She views Bob as a good father, but emotionally distant, and too uninvolved in the children's daily life.

Suddenly, when she filed for divorce, he became Super Dad. He spent lots of time with the children, attended their soccer games, and contacted all of their teachers to introduce himself. Although Ellen was happy about this change in Bob, she was suspicious of his motives. She was sure he just wanted to pay her less child support, as he now wanted joint custody of the children. It was difficult for her to consider sharing the children for half of the week. Yet, at the same time, she was reluctant to discourage him because the children were so obviously delighted with his new behavior.

Many women fight their husbands' desire for joint custody in similar scenarios, seething with resentment. She can oppose his desires, or she can give him the benefit of the doubt that his motivation emanates from the heart, as opposed to financial incentive.

EXAMPLE 2: "SHE HAS ALWAYS CONTROLLED MY RELATIONSHIP WITH THE KIDS. SHE'S WORSE NOW."

In our society, couples with children generally develop complementary roles in which the fathers invest the bulk of their time in earning money for the family and the women take primary responsibility for child care. Because women generally spend more time with their children on a daily basis than do men, they have more knowledge about the children's daily routines, needs, and preferences. They are, in essence, gatekeepers to the children's world. In a divorce, the gate often swings closed in a defensive maneuver. The knowledge held by mothers gets clutched close to the breast, staving off further loss by hoarding it, sometimes lauding it over their spouse's head.

Men complain about this turn of events because they find gaining access to their children too difficult. Mom tells the kids not to answer the phone when Dad calls. Or she forgets to inform him of small but proud moments in the child's life, which he might have attended, if he'd known about them enough in advance. Fathers fear they will lose access to their children, as punishment for the time they spent providing the family income.

Billy railed at Stephanie for using every excuse she could think of to limit the time he spent with their ten-year-old son and eight- and six-year-old daughters.

She wouldn't tell him about their schedules and habits, and then filed motions in court stating that he was a derelict, uncaring father. He was so frustrated he was thinking about filing for sole custody to protect himself, although his lawyer told him he didn't stand a chance.

Stephanie does not think it is her job to tell Billy things he "should know by now." She always covered for him in the marriage, but she is now free of that responsibility. She doesn't mean to exclude him, but there is so much happening it is hard enough to keep track. She is sure that the children are not his priority because of what he does not know about them, and what he misses.

These two parents both think they are doing their part to protect their children and provide for their needs. Indeed they are doing what they know, and what they have always done best. But once there is a divorce, the old rules no longer pertain. It requires more work on both parts to equalize roles, information, and the chance to share child care. Sometimes mothers are controlling their children in order to wield power over their spouse, who has more power in the financial realm. Other times, it is just a perception based on differing roles within the family, and a real desire to structure the children's hectic lives in the face of divorce chaos, while protecting them from further hurt. If you or your spouse are gatekeeping, work with a competent mediator or couples' therapist to help you realign power and communication in the relationship without assigning blame.

WHAT ARE THE NECESSARY ELEMENTS OF A PARENTING PLAN?

Although your plan will be as unique as your own family, each plan has some basic elements upon which to build. In addition to legal and physical custody, you will set forth additional provisions to be followed by each parent, such as picking the child up from school if he or she is ill, and how day care will be selected. The less you plan to share parenting, the less detail you will need in your plan. The following components cover various possible arrangements, so some elements may not be pertinent to your situation.

COMPONENTS

1. Legal custody: Sole or Joint
2. Decision-making authority: Who has final say for . . .
    Schooling: private versus public, special needs
    Religion: where, when, and through what level
    *Medical: routine versus emergency treatments, medications, mental
      health treatment*
    *Routine Needs: medical/dental appointments, transportation to
      activities, homework checks, child care arrangements that cross
      transition times*
3. Physical custody: Joint or Sole; one primary residence or two
4. Residential arrangements: how often, how long, with each parent?
5. Holidays/summer/school vacations
6. Finances: who pays for what?
7. Methods for resolving impasses: decision-making processes between
    the two of you; when and how a neutral third party should be brought
    in
8. Plans for future and/or decision making: college expenses, schooling,
    travel, etc., depending upon what's important to your lifestyle

⚖️

LIST OF MAJOR HOLIDAYS

New Year's Eve, New Year's
Day, Presidents' Day, Martin
Luther King Day, Valentine's
Day, Good Friday, Easter,
Passover, Mother's Day, Me-
morial Day, Father's Day,
Fourth of July, Labor Day,
Rosh Hashana, Yom Kippur,
Veterans Day, Thanksgiving,
Chanukah, Christmas, Birth-
days

WHAT IF WE CAN'T AGREE?

Once you understand the emotional
issues and possible variations of parenting
schedules, it will begin to become clearer
to you whether or not you and your
spouse are headed toward a custody dispute. Because divorce is a time of great
emotional turmoil and feelings of loss,
sometimes parents are afraid that they
will lose their children. Both you and your
spouse will be spending less time with the
children (in the rare case when a spouse
disappears, of course, this would not be

true), but in all likelihood, you will continue to have sufficient quality time with your children, and you will also have some free time for yourself. While this may not sound attractive in the middle of your divorce, soon afterward you may be grateful for a little bit of adult time to pursue your own interests. Most parents, given time and the place to talk, are able to resolve disputes about their children. Sometimes, however, they need help.

⚖️

EXTENDED FAMILY

Consider visits with extended family as well. Many courts are enforcing grandparents' rights to see their grandchildren, even over the objections of the parents. If you are in such a situation, consult an attorney about the rights accorded grandparents in your state.

Using a Calendar

Your first planning step is to find a blank twelve-month calendar. First, chart out the activities for each of your children. List all fixed activities such as when they leave for and return home from school or day care, and when they need to be at each activity (e.g., baseball, music lesson, religious school, ballet, etc.). Use a full twelve-month calendar, because sports, school, and other activities the children participate in are seasonal. Use the child's school calendar and also mark in the school vacations.

Now, with a different colored pen, plot in your own time commitments. Include everything, whether it is work, school, church volunteerism, or any other activities that you pursue on a regular basis. Don't forget standing meetings and fixed appointments. It will begin to be clear how your schedule meshes with your children's and where the obvious holes lie.

Again using a different colored pen, chart out when your spouse has obligations, such as work or school. It should also be clear when your spouse is free to spend time with the children.

You can now start to draw up your parenting times. If you have to be at work, but your spouse is available, then the children could be with your spouse at that time. If you are available, but your spouse is not, then the children could be with you.

You can become more specific when you consider all of the children's commitments, which parent has historically filled those commitments, and which parent(s) is able to do them over the course of the year. The following questions will help you sort out different parenting schedules:

- Who does homework with them?
- What do the children do on the weekends?
- Do the children spend time visiting other relatives? Who would take them?
- How often do the children go to the doctor or the dentist, and who could take them?
- Have the children been absent from school often, and when they are sick at school, who picks them up?
- Who provides the children's physical care, such as bathing, changing diapers, arranging for sitters, haircuts?
- How do you each discipline the children and set structure for them? What are each parent's strengths in this realm?
- What kind of personal attention do you and your spouse each give to the children, such as teaching problem solving, reading and playing together, sharing activities?
- Who is responsible for the social activities: arranging birthdays, buying gifts, trick-or-treating, taking class trips, arranging to see friends and going to their parties, attending games?

On your calendar, each parent charts out desired time with the children given the information that you have assembled above. Don't forget to include holidays, Mother's Day, Father's Day, school vacations, (summer, winter, spring), special family occasions, birthdays, graduations, sporting events, try-outs, recitals, weddings, and birthdays of close relatives.

Give yourself some time when you are not working to be by yourself, or to make plans with adult friends. Although right now you might be very concerned about your children, you aren't going to be able to be as emotionally available to your children if you never have time for yourself.

Now compare your desired times to see where conflicts occur and focus your attention on those. Make some trades, compromise, agree to every other year for some issues (e.g., birthdays). If you still can't agree, you have at least assembled all of the information that will be necessary for pursuing mediated negotiations, or as last resort, a contested custody matter.

What Do I Do If My Child Doesn't Want to Visit?

You can try various resolutions when your child says he or she doesn't want to go to the other parent's house. Kids may say this because they have mixed loyalties, or just because they don't want to stop what they are doing at the moment, and this is natural. Also, children feel the same waves of anxiety, sadness, and the pain of missing that adults feel. They may experience such emotions when they arrive at the other home or return to their primary home.

It helps to have kids make transitions between homes with their favorite toys or objects. It also helps to put in words for them what they are feeling and to assure them their feelings are acceptable. How the transition is planned can make a big difference. For some children, they want to go right to their room and have some time to smell, touch, and know the place again. Being alone may be helpful. For others, leaping headlong into a jumble of activity may help them adjust by distracting them while they settle into the new location or parent.

From a legal standpoint, if there are court orders mandating that your child visit with the other parent, you are risking being held in contempt of court if that child does not visit the other parent. If the desire not to visit is unusual behavior for your child, try to ascertain what is behind it and modify your tactics accordingly. Begin to work on the problem by talking to your child to pinpoint reasons for not wanting to visit. Once you have discovered why your child doesn't want to visit, you can then begin working on your plan for dealing with the situation.

For example, if it is typical for your child to say he or she doesn't want to see the other parent because your child doesn't want to miss time with friends, insist that he or she go with the other parent, but talk to the other parent about trying to have the child's friends join in and spend time at the other parent's house.

If your child is a baby, some upset when leaving the home or primary parent is expected. If distress continues at least twenty minutes or more each time, consider changing the schedule to accommodate this stage of your child's life.

If you truly believe that it is not in your child's best interests to see the other parent according to the present schedule, then you must be prepared to prove that this is true. There are different situations under which this might happen, for example:

- you believe your children are being physically or sexually abused
- you believe your children are being emotionally abused
- you believe your children are being left in situations which could present danger (e.g., insufficient/inappropriate supervision)
- you believe your children are being exposed to things that are inappropriate, given their age or upbringing
- you see your children react poorly to visits, beyond typical difficulties with transitions

If you believe that your child is in imminent danger from the visits, you need to report this to the proper authorities immediately. Take your child to his or her pediatrician for a full checkup, and let the doctor know what you suspect. You also need to request that the court issue a restraining order for your children to protect them from the abuser. Stop allowing your child to visit under these circumstances, even though you may be facing court sanctions for doing so. Your primary goal is to protect your children, and if you are certain that the visitation is physically harming them, you need to stop the visits. Once the court is aware of the situation (which it will be, because of the restraining order) the judge can set the matter for a hearing so that you can present all of your evidence against visitation, and the court can modify the existing orders so that your children will be safe.

In other less exigent circumstances, your choices and plan of action are less clear. Sometimes problems happen during visitation, but it's impossible for you to tell if the situation warrants filing a *Motion for Modification of Visitation* in court. You can file such a motion at any time; the problem is deciding when it would be appropriate to do so. Don't file a motion you cannot back up with proof. If you want visitation changed and can't work it out between yourselves, you need to have solid reasons and evidence for asking for the change. Lots of children have a tough time adjusting to transitions, especially early in their parents' divorce and separation. But how will you know when it's appropriate to file for a modification of the court's orders?

If you think, but you don't know, that the visits are harming the children, then you need the assistance of a third party in order to determine how best to proceed. Have your children speak with a therapist or a school counselor if you think that something inappropriate may be going on, but are not in a position to prove it. Once they've spoken to a therapist or counselor, that person can let you know whether or not you need to intervene to change the parenting plan and the current way in which visits take place. You will need to determine whether your child is at risk for serious harm versus uncomfortable about things that can be corrected with minimal adjustments to schedule or types of visits. Examine your own behavior and make sure you are not giving your child messages that you need him or her to stay with you, for company, support, or to punish the other parent. This is an unfair burden to place on your child.

Other indications that children may need adjustments to the visitation schedule—or to something that's happening in your home—include:

- sudden behavioral changes that are aberrant from your child's normal personality (e.g., withdrawal in an outgoing child, sadness from a generally happy child)
- bursts of temper and moodiness
- aggression or violence toward others, pets, or themselves
- a sudden drop in grades at school

Find out why your child is behaving differently. If you cannot ascertain what is going on because your child is uncommunicative, or because you and your spouse view it so differently, consider having your child meet with a school counselor or a therapist. Choose someone who will not exacerbate problems, but will normalize what the child is experiencing and will help him deal with it. Someone who is experienced in treating people of your child's age, and who is familiar with divorce and family systems work, is optimal. When possible, include the other parent in your child's therapy. It is working together as parents that will provide the most assistance to your child.

If you're not able to address these issues as co-parents, then you will have to do it on your own. Once you've determined the reasons why the problems are happening, and have thought through possible solutions, pose them to your ex-spouse. See if together you can work with your children to modify the parenting plan to support them. If you reach an impasse, it's

⚖

CLASH OF PARENTING STYLES

Parents often report anger at how their spouse deals with their child, in ways that are not harmful but that undermine their parenting values. Common examples include letting him watch movies you don't think he is ready for, exposing him to rude humor or vocabulary, allowing him to be in the presence of people you think are unsavory characters, and so forth. As annoying as these things are, they are generally not matters with which the court will interfere. You should try and work things out with a mediator or therapist adult-to-adult, appealing to reason and concern for your child's well-being. Some of these differences you will have to learn to live with, and inculcates your own values when the children are with you.

time to approach a mental health professional and then the court about changing the visitation or custody orders.

CAN I RELOCATE?

Many parents ask "Can I relocate?" and the answer always depends on the individual circumstances at the time. Given our increasingly mobile society, it is not at all unusual for one spouse to need to move out of state, or even out of the country. Increasingly, the courts are trying to determine whether it is in the child's best interest to move, even if the child has lived with a primary physical custodial parent for quite some time.

The court will consider all of the factors that have gone into the original custody decree, as well as the reason for the move, the ability of the child to maintain contact with the other parent, what kind of visitation would be set up for the parent left behind (as well as extended family), and the living situation for the child in the new city or state.

If you think that maybe someday you might want to relocate, putting a notice provision with respect to relocation into your settlement agreement is important. Many such provisions call for 90 to 180 days notice before someone can move. A sample relocation clause is included in the Appendix (page 313). This notice gives time to negotiate or to ask the court to prevent the move while it is being worked out by the parents. Relocation is not a good bar-

⚖

RELOCATION: FACTORS TO CONSIDER

Be prepared to address:

- Any previous agreements between your spouse and you regarding relocation
- Number of prior moves
- Motives of the parent seeking to move and prospective advantages for the child and the moving parent
- Motives of the parent resisting the move
- Child's preference
- Child's connections to his or her current home, school, and community
- Child's ties to the community to which he or she may move
- Frequency and level of contact that can be maintained between the child and the parent who is not moving, along with a feasible, affordable plan
- History of moving parent in facilitating visitation

gaining chip, as it evokes a sense of threat, and often pushes the other person to become more intransigent and stubborn out of fear of losing contact with the children.

In most jurisdictions it will be up to you to prove that moving out of state is in the children's best interests. While you may have many reasons why it's in *your* best interests to move, is it really in the children's best interests? How will they maintain contact with the other parent? How involved are they in their school and school activities? Will close friends and extended family be left behind? How well does your child adjust to new situations?

The legal custody designation (e.g., joint legal custody) has little to do with whether or not you will be permitted to move. The actual circumstances of your case will be the determining factor. The more involved the other parent has been in the children's lives, the more difficult it will be for you to prove that it is in the children's best interests to move far away from your ex-spouse. Therefore, having sole legal custody doesn't automatically permit you to move with the children, and having joint legal custody doesn't automatically prevent you from doing so. Sometimes the court will say, "Sure you can leave, but your children will stay with their other parent." This has happened even when the children have always lived with the leaving parent.

WHERE CHILD SUPPORT FITS IN

WHAT ARE CHILD SUPPORT GUIDELINES?

Each state has child support guidelines, which mandate how much support each spouse must contribute toward supporting the children, based on factors which each state determines. The "guidelines" are actually very specific laws with specific calculations. Pick up a copy of your state's guidelines at your local courthouse, library, or a lawyer's office. Many are even posted on the Internet. The Appendix contains links for child support guidelines laws for each state (page 333). You can use the guidelines to estimate expected child support payments. Each state's calculations are different, but each takes into account what both parents earn and some of the children's basic expenses. Child support is also based on how much time the children spend with each of you.

Child Support and Income

In every state, both parents' incomes are the key pieces of information used to calculate child support. Income in this sense is income after deductions for taxes, and many states also deduct the children's health insurance premiums and day care costs. Other permitted deductions from income influencing child support vary from state to state. If there are factors that allow deviations from the guidelines, they will be listed in the guidelines. Typical deviations may include a child's extraordinary medical or educational expenses, extraordinary access expenses (like plane tickets to visit an out-of-state parent), and a child's own income or assets, which may be used for his or her support. Deviations are not permitted because of a parent's extraordinary credit card payments or car loan payment, or other expenses incurred by either of the parents. The law recognizes that your first responsibility is to your child, not to MasterCard or your landlord.

Most states consider any money that comes to you on a periodic basis to be income. This means that wages, commissions, bonuses, interest, dividends, worker's compensation, unemployment compensation, and even Social Security are considered "income" in most states. Income is income, even if you haven't received it yet. For example, suppose you typically receive a bonus each year based on your sales performance. The cutoff date for your performance record is June 30 of each year. You receive your bonus in December of that same year. If it's September, your bonus will be considered part of your income even though it hasn't been received by you yet.

Another example is stock dividends. The dividends are often automatically reinvested, so you don't actually have the cash to spend. Because stock dividends are earned, and you could choose to liquidate rather than reinvest them, they are deemed to be income.

Social Security comes with some complications, since it has special benefits for recipients with minor children. In most cases, the benefits that children receive directly from Social Security will be considered when child support is calculated. Typically, however, the government-provided benefit is only part of what the parent will be required to pay on the child's behalf. How Social Security is treated varies from state to state, and will be clarified in your state's child support guidelines.

There are special issues associated with earning capacity. One such issue is *salary history*. Most states include overtime, predictable bonuses, and commissions as income for purposes of calculating child support. If you have historically worked a certain amount of overtime, received a bonus each year, or earned a commission on sales, the court will most likely consider these "extras" as a part of your regular income for purposes of calculating the amount of child support due.

In order to be fair, and to protect yourself in the event of a dispute, be inclusive in your calculations. Review your overtime, bonuses, and commissions over the past five years. Have they been stable? Or were they linked to unusual circumstances that no longer exist? Are they regular, seasonal, or cyclical with the economy? Have market forces made bonuses erratic both in terms of amount and regularity? Has competition or new additions to the sales force eroded your commissions over time?

For instance, if you are a postal worker, and every Christmas you are required to work an enormous amount of overtime, average your income over the entire year. If your child support is based solely on your Christmas earnings, it will be much higher than is appropriate during the other eleven months of the year. If you work in construction, the summer months may be very busy, but you may be unemployed during the wintertime. If you are a day care provider, your summers are probably busier than the rest of the year. If you are a commissioned salesperson, make sure that your income history—and future—is presented realistically.

A striking example of this situation was Henry, a commissioned salesperson for an office supply company, which had been owned by his father. When his father retired, he passed his accounts on to Henry, who continued to work in the small, family-owned business. He earned a very comfortable living . . . until the office supply superstores invaded his territory. Suddenly, his little mom-and-pop enterprise was turned upside down as competition entered the marketplace, eventually forcing him to sell the business to a megastore. He was offered a job with the store, but had to start from scratch with no accounts to his name. His $350,000 per year income plummeted to less than $50,000. It was important that the judge take into account the new climate in which he was forced to work, and his new compensation structure. His salary history alone would have had devastating results, if the child support guidelines had been followed slavishly. The future became much more pertinent than the past.

Voluntary reduction of wages

If you have had a stable salary history, child support will probably be based on that history unless you can prove that the past is not applicable to the future, as in Henry's situation, above. When confronted with the child support guidelines and divorce, many people react by reducing overtime hours, delaying commissions or bonuses, or otherwise attempting to minimize their incomes, at least until child support is calculated and determined by the court.

This tactic is risky business. Typically, courts award child support (and alimony) based on earning capacity as opposed to actual earnings, and will not hesitate to do so when it appears that people have voluntarily reduced their earnings.

If your income has decreased, you will need to prove that your claimed income reduction is legitimate. For example, if your industry as a whole is shrinking (e.g., "defense contractors"), be prepared to offer industry information and statistics concerning this problem. If your work is seasonal, offer evidence of the past three to five years of these cycles. If competition has been stepped up with additional workers reducing available overtime, offer a statement from your employer outlining the changes that have been made in the workforce. If your commission structure has changed, and despite your best efforts you cannot earn what you used to earn, you will need to explain that as well.

Most important, you must prove that whatever reduction you've suffered in earnings is not your fault, and was not voluntary. If the court thinks that you've voluntarily reduced your income in an effort to minimize support payments, you risk being ordered to pay support based on previous available earnings, as opposed to your current actual earnings.

⚖️

EARNING CAPACITY AND STRESS

Many people find that their working capacity is lower during the divorce process, because they are stressed, spending so much time on their case, or in court. This constitutes a temporary situation, and will not alter your child support obligations. However, if depression or other psychological factors inhibit you from producing your normal amount of work, or maintaining your usual standard of living, explain this to the court and/or your attorney. You may be offered a temporary reprieve with a fixed time period, after which you'll be expected to resume your normal daily operations.

The most popular phrase divorce lawyers hear is "Well, if I have to pay *that much*, I'll quit my job!" That's no solution to the child support problem, however, because the court can consider your earning *capacity*, not just your actual earnings. So, if you reduce your overtime, quit your job, take a voluntary demotion, or do anything that voluntarily reduces your income, you take the chance that the court will base your child support on your prior earnings, not on your current earnings.

If you are contemplating divorce and realize that you will not be able to maintain your current salary after the divorce, i.e., you cannot work twenty-five hours of overtime a week and still see your children, reducing your salary now without later reprisal from the court will take planning. You will need to prove that your salary reduction was not voluntary or spiteful. A legitimate way of reducing your salary might be to change careers with the blessing of your spouse. Another way is to reduce your overtime gradually, so that there's not a sudden drop in income. You may want to ask for a transfer to a different department where overtime is not available or required, or where the salary is less (and perhaps the workload is less too). Asking your employer to delay or defer a raise, commission, or bonus may reduce your salary but be careful about this, as you're required to be honest about your assets and income. If you're entitled to a bonus, and you don't list it on the financial statement you provide to the court, you may be found to have fraudulently misrepresented your income or assets—and the ramifications of such a finding by a judge will be much worse than the child support you would have paid!

Oftentimes forgoing a raise, promotion, or bonus punishes you as well as the recipient of the support monies. For example, in Connecticut in 2000, support for one child is around 21 percent of your net income. So for each $1.00 in your pocket, you keep 79 cents. And that money doesn't just disappear, it is part of your parenting responsibilities to provide for your child's welfare. That commitment was made when you decided to have children. Divorce can certainly put a different spin on the feelings associated with support; try and separate those feelings from your sense of obligation and powerful desire to care for your child.

CHILD SUPPORT VERSUS CUSTODY AS A FINANCIAL DECISION

For the parent paying child support, the amount may seem astronomical. "Given the dollars involved, the children should be living like kings." For the recipient, the money is never enough. The recipient is "shopping with coupons, wearing hand-me-downs, and eating leftovers—and still the ends never meet."

Most people drastically underestimate what children cost. They also underestimate what maintaining two households costs. While you're living together as a family, you're paying for one family home, one set of toys, and one set of clothes. When you separate, you're suddenly paying for two homes, two sets of toys, and almost two sets of clothes. Not all of the additional expenses have to do with the children directly: there are two mortgages or rents, two sets of home insurance, and two sets of household items. And your children's needs are increasing with age: dancing lessons, soccer dues, hockey equipment, and field trip entrance fees.

Statistically, men who pay child support fare better economically than women who receive child support just two to three years after the divorce is finalized. The child support guidelines adopted by each state were designed to even out the incomes of the custodial versus noncustodial parent. For those who pay support as ordered, and those who receive it, the finances are evening out somewhat. However, other societal factors work against equality, such as the differences in wages between men and women doing the same jobs. Also, parents who see children only on weekends and days off are free to work overtime during the week, and to pursue career-enhancing activities when the children are not with them.

When spouses become embittered about their side of the "lopsided" financial picture, each spouse blames the other and both grouse about their finances. If you are feeling angry about how little you get, or how much you pay, try to sit down together and assess where the money is going. Use general categories rather than details about how you each spend your money; the divorce obviates that obligation to each other. But look at broad categories and ascertain whether in fact someone is "getting screwed" or whether there is just less money to spread around. Becoming more realistic about your finances may improve relations with your spouse enormously.

Although the advent of child support guidelines has decreased the tendency to use child support as a bargaining chip in custody negotiations, it still happens. Many parents ask about reductions in child support for shared custody situations. Other parents ask for reductions in support based on split custodial arrangements. The laws of most states recognize that these situations are special, and may warrant an adjustment to the amount of money that one parent pays to the other. Exactly how much the support amounts vary depends on the laws of each state. Some have complicated calculations based on the percentage of time spent with each parent, and other states treat each case separately, based on the facts.

In either case, using time with your children as a substitute for child support doesn't pay off, in money or metaphoric terms! The money you hoped to save by having the children with you winds up being paid, because the children actually have more needs than provided for by child support guidelines. So you spend the money anyhow—you're just writing the check to the grocery store rather than to your ex-spouse. That may feel better, but it doesn't change the amount of money spent. Some parents consistently refuse to buy their children something they request, or spend any money on them, because "it costs too much," regardless of how large or small the request. In many of those families, the children are raised in middle-class neighborhoods, where the now-divorced parents refuse to treat them like other local children are typically treated. Sometimes parents cannot afford much of what their children need/want. In other cases, the parents simply continue their conflict through the children. This indirectly punishes your child for the divorce, and unfortunately, the message is not missed by most children.

Perhaps you really don't have the money. But if you deny money that you do have to your children, and then spend it on yourself or a new family, you will be paid back with the children's resentment. You will pay child support for up to twenty-one years. Your children are your children for the rest of your life. Many parents wonder why their children are so angry at them, after one parent uses money as a bargaining chip with the other. The parent may have secured some money each month, but earned a lousy relationship with the children that is far more painful than budget cuts. The moral of the story: check your motivations and do not count your pennies at the expense of the big picture over time.

WHERE CHILD SUPPORT IS SPENT

If you pay child support, you don't have any say in how it is spent by the recipient. That sounds harsh, but it's true. If you are legitimately concerned that you're paying support and that the recipient is buying drugs, taking expensive vacations leaving your child at home, or making other inappropriate expenditures, you should look at changing residential custody arrangements, not controlling the child support. Each state's guideline calculations take into account the fact that the person with whom the child lives will have to have a larger home or apartment because of the child—perhaps a newer, larger car and any number of "hidden" expenses (insurance, fenced-in yard) over and above the obvious ones like school lunch and diapers.

If you are concerned that the support you pay will not be used for the children's benefit, you may wish to negotiate specific payments that you can make directly on behalf of your children in exchange for a reduction in the amount of support you are required to pay to the other parent. For example, you could put the money into a trust fund for the child's college education. Or, you can pay the day care provider or school tuition directly, and receive a dollar-for-dollar reduction in your support amounts. You can work to fashion an agreement that assures that the basic needs of the children are met no matter how financially irresponsible the other parent. Use an attorney or mediator to assist you in creating a plan.

At all costs, however, keep the interests of your children in mind. You want them to have the best that you and your spouse can afford, and all of the opportunities that they would have had if you had remained married. Don't let resentment about your loss of control of money interfere with what your children need, and what they deserve.

PERSONAL ASSESSMENT

Am I doing everything I can to create a positive co-parenting environment that allows our children to have maximum access to and support from each parent? Creating a viable shared parenting arrangement requires a lot of patience and turning the other cheek. My children will benefit, and over the long run, it will help keep our divorce a productive experience.

Do the living arrangements, decision-making plan, and actual schedule fit with who my children are at the present time? Gearing the schedule to the age and developmental needs of each child helps ensure its effectiveness.

Is the parenting plan specific enough to cover most likely situations at present and in the near future? Do we have a backup plan for resolving differences that will inevitably arise? Specificity helps maintain predictability and keeps boundaries straight. Our plan supports our separateness without seeming burdensome. It leaves space to offer and ask for flexibility as needs arise.

Am I doing my part to maintain the plan and ensure its effectiveness for my children and all involved? Am I letting negative emotional responses left over from the marriage interfere with implementation? If we each do our best to make this work, it will work out well.

Are our child support payments determined accurately and with fairness? Child support can be financially burdensome, but it benefits my children. I still wish to provide for them in the best way I can. That is one way I can protect them from negative impacts of divorce.

9.

Contested Custody Cases: Hazardous Territory and Loose Footing

WHEN TO CONSIDER A CUSTODY BATTLE

Engaging in a contested custody dispute is a last-resort proposition because it usually produces two losers, and no winners. It may be warranted if you believe that your children's current situation places them in serious physical or psychological danger—not discomfort, but danger. Your sense of danger is discriminated from one of discomfort when the custody and access arrangements create serious problems for your child (not you!) by seeing or living with the other parent. If you feel the child will be exposed to physical or sexual harm, or to persons and behaviors that compromise the other parent's ability to care for the child properly or make sound judgments about her needs, *and* if the situation cannot be mediated or ameliorated with outside help, then you may need to contest custody or visitation. Examples include a parent who is using and/or dealing illegal drugs, having multiple sexual encounters that the child witnesses, or who is experiencing an abrupt shift in mental functioning, such as psychotic episodes that involve the child. In these cases, it could be necessary to fight with a parent who is not thinking or acting rationally in order to protect your child.

When you are determining whether or not to contest custody, you must carefully weigh the costs. There are your legal fees, your children's legal fees (children are appointed lawyers or guardians—or both—in contested custody cases), and fees for the court-ordered evaluator. Sometimes these costs can be greater than what you'd expect to pay for your child's college education. However, the costs of a contested custody matter reach far beyond the literal dollar cost of your case. You and your children will feel stressed beyond human endurance during the process. Contested custody trials, and matters that are headed toward contested custody trials but which ultimately settle, can be extremely time consuming, emotionally exhausting, and damaging to a family unit. Do not underestimate the trauma that this will cause your family if you and your spouse are unable to reach an agreement concerning your children's upbringing. If you are holding out on the schedule in order to win some other concession, financial or otherwise, think again. Ask yourself, "What makes it worth it? Are the costs to my ongoing relationship with my spouse and to my children worth holding out for? Will the schedule my spouse wants me to agree to inconvenience me, sadden me, or actually harm the children or me?"

Courts are set up to assist you in reaching your own agreement about your children. However, when parents are unable to resolve their differences, the court will step in to assist. The "assistance" requires that your lives and past decisions get examined in minute detail, by you, your spouse, the evaluator, and the judge. You may have to testify about your spouse's faults and shortcomings in the same detail. You will also have to listen while your spouse testifies about every perceived misdeed and defeated expectation, and every criticism your mate has of you, your parenting, and your relationship with your children. After that, you also have to listen while the court-appointed evaluator testifies about your strengths and weaknesses as a parent, and about how your behavior has affected the children during the divorce process.

After the trial, after listening to all of that testimony, win or lose, you have to continue to operate as a family. You will have to attend your children's bar mitzvahs, First Communions, school plays, soccer games, and even their weddings . . . a whole lifetime of activities in which your children need both you and your spouse to participate. Maintaining a civil relationship will be very difficult after a contested custody trial. If considering one for yourself, visit a trial in session. Most cases are open to the public, and you can sit in and watch the proceedings.

Assuming you've considered the costs to your children and yourself, examined your own motivations, and still decided it's best to proceed with a contested custody case, you have a great deal of planning and work to do to assist your chances of success. That planning requires understanding exactly what a contested custody case entails.

TELLING YOUR CHILDREN ABOUT WHY YOU ARE INVOLVED IN A COURT BATTLE

You should explain to your child that Mom (or Dad) and you have become very angry at each other, and that you are no longer able to make decisions together right now. The one thing you agree on is that you both want very much to have the child in your life as much as possible from day to day. You know the child can't be in two places at once, so you are asking the judge to help you make a plan. The court will make the decisions, and Mom and Dad have agreed to abide by them. If the situation includes a mental illness, you might wish to add, if your child is capable of understanding, that Mom/Dad is not well (describe the type of illness) and is not able to make good decisions right now. You have asked the court to help you because the court is neutral and will help find the best situation for your child. Reassure your child that the decision is not in his or her hands.

THE SPECIAL FEATURES OF A CONTESTED CUSTODY CASE

The court will often order mediation if you have not already tried to mediate your disputes with the help of a neutral third party. When trial seems imminent, the court may order an attorney for the children, or a guardian *ad litem* (Latin for "for the case"); these professionals act as advocates on the child's behalf, charged with separating the child's needs from the demands of either parent. The court may also order a psychological evaluation. An evaluation of the family provides the court with information needed to ascertain the family's special strengths, problems, and issues. These components are then used in a series of court proceedings, such as a pretrial and trial, which follow the same legal format described in Chapter 6.

Court-Ordered Mediation

In the course of a custody trial, the court will often ask you first to try and mediate the dispute with an officer of the court, which we will generically refer to as the Family Relations Office. You also have the option of obtaining a private mediator. Typically, you will sit together with a mediator (sometimes two), and you will be expected to discuss what your concerns are about the other spouse and his or her abilities to care for the children and address their needs, and to explain what you would consider an ideal situation.

The more reasonable and willing to negotiate you are, the more likely it is the mediator will be able to help you resolve the matter. Mediation is not about "strategy" or about "winning." It is about being reasonable, organized, and succinct. By the time you get to the mediation, you should be prepared with your idea of a viable custody and visitation plan. You then want to organize yourself to present it in the best way possible. Focus on the future, not the past. Always listen very carefully to what is being said by your spouse. Try not to let your excitement about making your presentation result in a failure to listen to what your spouse or the mediator says.

Attorneys and Guardians for Children

If you have a contested custody matter that cannot be solved by the initial mediation sessions, the court will generally appoint either an attorney or a guardian *ad litem* to represent your children. The children's attorney represents their legal interests just as your attorney represents yours, voicing their wishes and advocating for that position. The guardian *ad litem*'s job is to give neutral information to the court about what is in the children's best interests, irrespective of their wishes. Typically, older children will get an attorney appointed, and younger children will get a guardian, especially if they are too young to talk. Some children are appointed both an attorney and a guardian, but this varies across states. It is the attorney's responsibility to determine what the children want to do, and the guardian's responsibility to determine what is in the children's best interests. Typically, the attorney or guardian will conduct his or her own investigation into the situation, consulting with the children, their teachers, counselors, babysitters, pediatrician, and other professionals. If the children are too young to talk, these ancillary investigations become even more important. Because of their investigative roles, and the special backgrounds experienced attorneys for children and guardians *ad litem* have, they can be a useful resource for parents in custody disputes, offering a child-focused view of the case.

EVALUATIONS OF THE CHILD AND FAMILY

When parents are disputing child issues, then in addition to the court-appointed advocates, the court typically orders an evaluation of the family to assist the judge in making decisions for the parents. The purpose of the evaluation is to provide the court with a full picture about the individual family members and their relationships to each other. This information will assist the judge in making decisions about parenting arrangements, depending upon the factors to which that judge decides to give most weight.

Courts with a Family Relations Office may conduct this study for little or no cost. You may also wish to ask for an independent custody evaluation, which is typically performed by a social worker, psychologist, or other mental health professional that the court deems competent to evaluate your case for custody and visitation issues. Either you or the court could request and/or appoint an independent evaluator.

Court-sponsored evaluations conducted by Family Relations officers typically include the following elements: the evaluator will speak with the parties together, separately, with the children alone, with the children and each party, with the teachers, day care providers, doctors, extended family, and anyone else who has contact with the family and who would be able to comment on the parties' parenting abilities. The Family Relations Office study is a nuts and bolts analysis of the family situation, and the parental roles within that family situation over the last several years. Court-sponsored evaluations have the benefit of being less expensive, and utilizing court-related personnel who have a great deal of experience with the judges and attorneys of the local judicial district. They are often expert investigators, within the standards of their practice.

However, there are several drawbacks to Family Relations officers. You aren't likely to have a choice about the evaluator assigned to your family. Quality varies from officer to officer. Most officers are well qualified and approach each situation with common sense, proficiency, and caring. Their years of hearing the same types of stories over and over again, and speaking with the same teachers, as well as their experience with the family court judges has sharpened their skills in recognizing patterns of family interaction and predicting the likely outcomes of cases.

Another drawback is that the backlog of cases in many districts leads to a four- to six-month process for many evaluations. That is a long time in the course of a young child's life. Over six months, many routines are established that may be harder to change for your child or yourself. Before deciding whether to take advantage of services offered by the court Family Relations Office, ask your attorney, friends, and courthouse personnel about the reputation of Family Relations in your jurisdiction.

If you elect to hire an independent evaluator, the evaluation could take three to four months' time from initiation to report dissemination, but rarely is a case resolved that quickly. Costs vary depending upon the breadth of evaluation required. One study recently indicated that evaluations conducted by a psychologist cost an average of $3,000 to $4,000, although the cost is often even higher.

So why hire an independent evaluator to do an evaluation when (if) the court has one available free? Having a licensed psychologist or psychiatrist review the situation will give a broader perspective to the court than will a Family Relations study. While the court Family Relations Office's and the psychologist's roles may appear, on the surface, to be the same, they are actually complementary. The outside evaluator may offer training and background that the Family Relations officers do not possess. For example, a psychologist may include psychological assessment using standardized tests (personality, to assist in diagnosis, or to uncover underlying emotional issues), open-ended or projective tests aimed at uncovering deeper psychological concerns or problems, and interviews with the parties and the children that focus more on the inner world and health of each family member. A psychiatrist offers special expertise when family members are taking psychiatric medications. Since these professionals have more experience and training in accurately diagnosing issues such as depression, alcoholism, personality disorders, and other more serious mental disorders that clients may have, their work can supplement, rather than duplicate, the work done by the court Family Relations Office. These professionals should also have specialized training in talking with children, and in understanding their conflicts from what they say, what they do not say, how they behave, and what their play indicates.

For lawyers, litigants with a psychological history often present more complex cases in terms of client communication and bringing the client to an understanding of the risks, benefits, and possible negative outcomes in the event of custody litigation. The assistance of an evaluating psychologist or other professional can be invaluable.

Sometimes when a client feels that the court Family Relations officer has not given him or her an adequate opportunity to explain the situation, it is helpful to have an independent evaluator appointed to give the client an additional opportunity to bring to the attention of a professional the problems that the client perceives. Sometimes the process itself assists an individual in coming to terms with the issues of the custody and visitation matter, by giving the client additional opportunity to be heard. The extra input and respect that the evaluator's role commands can be helpful in settling the case, even if it doesn't differ from the recommendation of the court Family Relations Office.

Typically, the evaluator will be permitted by the parties to communicate with the court Family Relations officer and the attorney for the minor children or guardian *ad litem*. In this way, each professional can assist the others in understanding the total picture of the family and its dynamics. It should be underscored, however, that neither Family Relations nor independent evaluations are confidential; the court is entitled to full information contained in the evaluation.

HOW IS AN EVALUATOR CHOSEN?

Evaluators are most effective when one neutral professional is agreed upon by both parties. When choosing an evaluator, find someone with the appropriate background and experience. The parents in the family being evaluated are in a state of extreme emotional turmoil, yet they will be trying to make the best impression possible. The children may feel torn between two parents who cannot separate adult issues from children's issues in the dispute. The evaluator you choose must be prepared for these conditions. He or she must, therefore, have a thorough understanding of the boundary issues that must be kept clear in a custody evaluation. Experience, training, and absolute integrity on the evaluator's part will keep the evaluation a fair and effective tool in helping the court reach a custody decision.

It is helpful if the evaluator has experience testifying in court. Of course, even the most talented professional once had no experience, so this is not a prohibition for the selection process, but a witness who knows how to handle himself or herself can be crucial if a trial is involved. Equally important as other aspects, choose an evaluator with whom your attorney can work. The evaluator should not be a "hired gun" who will automatically testify for a client based on a personal relationship with the attorney, or who is known for personal biases (e.g., for mothers or for fathers). Rather, the lawyer should trust that the evaluator's opinion is sound and will hold up under scrutiny. Respect among the professionals involved in the case can also help settle it, as they guide you based on what they learn from one another.

WHAT HAPPENS IN AN EVALUATION?

Find out in advance what the evaluator's procedures will be so that you can prepare yourself—emotionally as well as with any collateral information you wish to introduce into the evaluation. An example of such information is a list of people with whom you'd like the evaluator to speak. Once you know what to expect, you will be more comfortable with the process. Generally, evaluations will consist of some combination of the following:

• Meeting with each parent and each child alone several times to learn family history, individual developmental histories, concerns, and desires for the outcome of the dispute, strengths and areas of deficit, and how each parent thinks about the child as an individual

• Observing parent and child interactions to ascertain their relationship. Often the evaluator will make observations in each parent's home so that the child is comfortable and the situation is at least as realistic as can be under the anxiety-filled circumstances.

• Speaking with collateral sources: others who know the parties, especially the children

• Psychological assessment using standardized and open-ended questionnaires and instruments

• Assessing extended family and community networks of family members through discussion with family members, community sources, and/or observation

WHAT ARE THE CRITERIA CONSIDERED IN AN EVALUATION?

The methods used in an evaluation are designed to provide the court with information it needs to determine a child's best interests when the parents cannot make such decisions for themselves. The concept of child custody evolved over the years from a presumption in favor of fathers to one in favor of mothers throughout the nineteenth century, with the term "Best Interests of the Child" introduced in 1881. In response to changing social conditions that have brought more parity in social roles between men and women, gender is no longer viewed as the basis for deciding child custody. More recently, the term has been interpreted to connote a variety of factors as determined by the Uniform Marriage and Divorce Act (1974), expounded upon by individual states. Each judge can give different weight to the factors that have been delineated as important.

Which factors any given judge will ascribe as most important will be determined on a case by case basis. This is one reason why it is so scary to let a judge decide for your family how your child's living situation will be arranged. It is impossible for anyone, including the attorneys and mental health professionals involved, to predict the outcome of any particular situation.

The court will consider any and all of the following factors:

• The quality of the emotional ties between each parent and child
• The capacity of each parent to love, educate, guide, and raise the child

• The capacity of each parent to provide food, clothes, and medical care

• Each parent's special abilities and particular disabilities (e.g., health, mental health)

• The psychological functioning (at school, home, and in the community) and developmental needs of the child

• The child's need for stability and continuity with regard to past living arrangements

• The parent's values concerning parenting

• The potential for inappropriate behavior or misconduct that might negatively influence a child (e.g., alcohol or drug use, sexual conduct, criminal activity)

• A parent's capacity to encourage the other parent's relationship with the child

• The wishes of the child when the child is of sufficient age to articulate a well-reasoned preference (this age differs in different states but generally begins between the ages of eight and twelve)

Some of the more salient and ambiguous factors require descriptive explanations:

Emotional Ties Between Parents and Children

The most important part of the evaluation for most evaluators is observing how each parent relates to the children. The court will consider relationships between each parent and child, past and present, with an emphasis on the present. The evaluator will assess how close, or "bonded" the child is to each parent to determine who is the primary caretaker in the child's life. All children need at least one primary person, although they can easily be attached to two or more people. The primary person is typically the one who has spent more time with the child, but this is not always the case. It is generally judged to be the person to whom the child turns when ill, upset, or tired. It is the person who takes off from work to do not only the routine care of the child, but the emergency care, as well. In your family, who disciplines the child on a regular basis is a crucial element, especially for children old enough to get into trouble when parents exert insufficient, inappropriate, or ineffective discipline. If you feel that your closeness to the child has diminished over time, take this opportunity to renew your connections. Bear in mind that all parents and children experience ebbs and flows of emotional connection over the course of the child's development. This is an essential part of growing up and becoming an autonomous being.

Capacity of Each Parent to Best Serve the Psychological Needs, Development, and Growth of the Child

The evaluator will be interested in the structure that a parent provides for a child, the ability to provide clear boundaries and firm but fair discipline, in addition to the nurturing and caretaking abilities. Ideally, the evaluator will hope to see a blend of structure, warmth, and affection shown to the child. This combination optimizes parenting. During every stage of your divorce it's important for you to assess the quality and degree of your parenting devotion and involvement, for you to use this time as an opportunity to increase the time you spend, and enhance your relationship with your children. However, in the event of a custody dispute, you will continually and consistently want to demonstrate your best capacities and attitudes.

A controversial issue in children's care is whether or not a parent's work hours are a detriment to his/her case. Nowadays, many young children spend time in day care, and this is not a negative factor in itself. On the other hand, if one parent is much more available than the other parent to spend time with the children, you need to take a hard look at why there is a custody battle between you.

Current circumstances are most important to the court, but if you or your spouse have engaged in past behaviors that were severe enough to impair your judgment and ability to parent, these matters can also be considered by the court. Such behaviors may include losing your temper with the other parent or your child and acting rashly and harshly, especially if it was done in sight of witnesses whom the other parent will now enlist in his/her behalf. More extreme examples include ongoing verbal or physical abuse of the other parent, the children, or even pets.

If this describes you, you will want to be able to state clearly how your past behavior does not relate to the present situation, and how you have changed. If this pertains to your spouse, and is ongoing, document in as much detail as you can what the past problem was, including any supporting materials such as police reports, doctors' reports, child abuse reports, and so forth. You will also need to be able to explain why this past behavior impacts your spouse's current ability to be a good parent.

Parental Health or Mental Health Disabilities

The fact that your spouse has some physical or mental health problems doesn't automatically prove that person is unable to be a competent and caring custodian for your children. However, when someone's health or psychological disturbances interfere with the individual's ability to be a consistent parent or to use good judgment, that will be a factor in a custody case. If your mate's condition prevents him or her from caring for the children (e.g., your spouse can't get out of bed in the morning) or from making rational decisions in the children's best interests, be sure to bring these problems to the lawyer's or evaluator's attention. These are real concerns that will also concern the professionals involved.

Inappropriate Conduct or Behavior

The courts frown on certain kinds of behaviors known to be destructive for children. Examples include alcoholism or leaving young children at home unattended. Other examples include pumping the children for information about the other parent or household, having children deliver messages, using transitions between parental homes as opportunities to create a disturbance. These behaviors require careful documentation and support, as they signal poor judgment and control on the part of the parent.

Often parents try to apply this factor loosely, drumming up examples

⚖️

EXTENDED FAMILY

If extended family members have been a part of the child's life on an ongoing basis, this fact will be considered by the court. These extended family members' roles and the support that they have given you, your spouse, and your children over time are important for your children's well-being. Even if the extended family members with whom the children have had a relationship are related to you only by marriage, and the divorce will dissolve the legal relationship, your willingness to continue to facilitate these relationships will be seen in a positive light by the court. Similarly, the impact of a nonrelative, especially a new significant relationship, is fair game for consideration by the court. Evaluate whether you are spending time with someone of solid character, who will make a good impression on the judge, Family Relations officer, and independent evaluator.

for the court of the other parent's instability and misbehavior. It can be very difficult to untangle "he said, she said" examples, and often such attempts wind up reflecting poorly on both parents, canceling out the intended effect on the evaluator or judge. Skip the drama, and use only those examples that show a serious incapacity to provide the kind of parenting a child of your child's age needs. If you are the parent accused of such behavior, take care to obey all court orders, especially protective orders requiring you to stay away from your spouse or former home, even if you believe the charges are unfounded.

Capacity to Encourage the Other Parent's Relationship with the Child

Nothing will ruin a custody case faster than the perception that you have withheld visitation or created obstacles to the other parent seeing your children. Keep a diary and/or calendar of your efforts to keep the other parent involved. Also include any efforts that the other parent has made to exclude you, or to minimize your time with your child.

⚖️

AFFAIRS AND CUSTODY

In many courts, the fact that one spouse is having or has had an affair will not be a major consideration in a typical custody case. If that parent's sexual activity affects the child, however, that is a different story. If the parent is leaving the child unattended while he or she pursues romantic interests, or if the child has witnessed such activity, this will impact your case. Obviously, if you are the one engaging in such behavior, stop immediately. If it is your spouse, be sure to keep a record, and apprise your attorney. It hurts your bargaining power, if not your case, when you bring a new partner into the child's life before you are divorced.

HOW CAN I MAXIMIZE MY CHANCES OF ATTAINING A SUCCESSFUL OUTCOME?

Present Yourself in a Positive Light

How you present yourself throughout the process is extremely important. Try to be pleasant and cooperative in your demeanor. Be as succinct and organized as possible in setting forth your version of a workable parenting plan. Use the calendars you wrote up in Chapter 8. Be brief, but complete. Anticipate what your spouse's plan will be, and be prepared to explain why your spouse's plan is not in the children's best interests, or why it won't work. Be ready to explain why your spouse is not the parent better able to handle areas of concern. Use specific examples. When you are describing your spouse's behavior, be descriptive without being judgmental. Labels like "crazy" do not illustrate well, but examples of "crazy" behavior can paint a colorful picture for the evaluator of what life is like with your spouse. Highlight your concerns and explain why you are concerned about these behaviors or actions. Directly answer all questions asked without going into a "he said, she said" rendition of the marital fights of the last six months. Negotiate in good faith. It may be difficult to do this when you are upset and stressed. Solid preparation on your part will ensure that you are at your best.

Do your utmost to present your positions without appearing obstinate, demanding, or controlling. Never say, "I *let* my spouse _____." Rephrase that sentence to say, "I've been willing for my spouse to _____." Understanding that you need to present yourself as a rational, caring human being to the psychologist

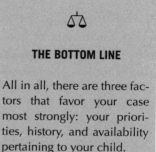

THE BOTTOM LINE

All in all, there are three factors that favor your case most strongly: your priorities, history, and availability pertaining to your child.

rather than as a vengeful, bitter litigant is crucial. That doesn't mean that you should compromise on what you think is in your children's best interests just for the sake of being reasonable or reaching an agreement.

What to Avoid Doing

Do not link issues about your children with financial issues during the evaluation. You are presumably concerned about the stability of the children, not using them as a vehicle to obtain an advantage with regard to the family finances. Never mention money or the house in a custody study unless specifically asked by the evaluator. If your concern is for the children to remain in the family home, and you are worried about how you can afford to do so, then state that as a concern rather than as a separate financial issue.

Avoid insults and counterattacks on your spouse. Such responses can detract from the positive impact of a well-reasoned response to criticism leveled against you. Instead, put a positive spin on your behaviors, concerns, and actions. For example, if your spouse thinks you are too much of a disciplinarian, explain this by outlining your concerns about giving the children structure, and describe how you are firm but fair (assuming that this is true). Use these disagreements to highlight the differences in parenting styles between yourself and your spouse, and for you to articulate why your approach is better than your spouse's approach, and better for the children. Do not rely on nitpicking details as your examples. It is not helpful to an evaluator to hear the arguments about every time your spouse was twenty minutes late for his or her time with the children. Now is the time to be the best parent you can be, and to rise above continuous battles in order to focus on the best possible evaluation outcomes for your children.

How Does the Court Use Evaluation Recommendations?

The court-sponsored evaluator is expected to make recommendations to the court. This is almost always the case when Family Relations officers are involved. Independent evaluators vary as to whether they make final recommendations or choose only to provide the court with information to make its own decisions. Either way, while courts are not bound by these reports, they rely very heavily on them. Once recommendations have been issued, you must consider them carefully. Your chances of refuting them, or petitioning the court to have them stricken from the court record, are slim to none.

The evaluator usually recommends legal and physical custody (sole or joint) and a parenting schedule for each party. The recommendations may be written, oral, presented separately to the parties, or to the parties together in the same room, with or without attorneys. Recommendations may also include other elements. For example, the evaluator may recommend that either the parents or the child continue or begin therapy, that the child receive special education services, or that medication for parents or children is continued and monitored. Assessment of children's special needs or parenting vulnerabilities may translate into a recommendation concerning parenting in the future.

IN THE EVENT OF A TRIAL

As in any trial circumstance, collect material evidence whenever possible so you can offer viewpoints other than your own, which is obviously biased. Day care providers often have sign-in and sign-out sheets that reflect which parent dropped off and picked up a child. Doctors' records, school attendance records, report cards, teacher reports, and receipts are sources of evidence. Journals and diaries can be useful, as well. For example, if you are separated and your wife always gets the children to school late on the days she's responsible for their transportation, the school attendance records coupled with your visitation schedule can be evidence of her irresponsibility. If the teacher's notes say that your child never has his homework with him on the days after he's spent time at his father's house, then this is evidence that his father isn't taking his parental responsibilities seriously with respect to schoolwork.

Think of people who could be witnesses to your activities with your child. If

LIFE UNDER THE COURT'S MICROSCOPE

During your divorce, you are, in effect, under a microscope. Both the court and your spouse are examining every aspect of your behavior. Sometimes, spouses even hire private investigators to follow estranged spouses around. While not all of the information is pertinent, it is unsettling to have people watching. Your behavior will be scrutinized closely during this process.

you are your child's soccer coach, perhaps an assistant coach would be willing to write a letter or testify, if need be. Neighbors, day care providers, friends, relatives, and everyone else who has seen you be a parent to your child are all possible witnesses. People who have seen you often, and know you as a parent, are the best witnesses. Any one example is not sufficient in itself, but when you have multiple examples that indicate *regularity, consistency,* and *familiarity,* witnesses matter. Nonrelatives are better than relatives, for obvious reasons, but relatives can serve as witnesses, too.

You will need to be careful in how you approach potential witnesses, as many of them may know both you and your spouse and will be reluctant to get involved. Perhaps those who are reluctant would be willing to vouch for your abilities as a parent, without criticizing your spouse. Those who are familiar with your circumstances, have known you well for a period of years, and who are willing to speak out about inappropriate behavior on your spouse's part are the best witnesses, but explore the possibility of asking others to come forward to help you as well. A handful of well-selected witnesses is more powerful than a laundry list of mediocre ones. Have your witnesses work with your lawyer about how to describe things accurately and adequately, so that your story is clear and convincing.

Some witnesses may provide a letter to the court supporting your position. An example of a helpful letter is:

I have known Jennifer for fifteen years. We are neighbors, and our children play together and go to the same school. I am also acquainted with her husband, Ralph. Last year Jennifer and I served as room mothers for her daughter Betsy's class. This entailed chaperoning on three field trips, assisting with two craft projects, and providing refreshments for three in-school parties. Jennifer is always willing to help . . . etc., etc., etc. I also know Jennifer's husband, Ralph. Last summer I saw him scream at Ralph Junior when Ralph Junior fell off his bicycle. Ralph Junior began to cry, but Ralph Senior continued to yell. I was concerned, so I went over . . . I saw similar events on four other occasions, which began to make me worry about Ralph Junior.
  Judith Neighbor
  Address + Telephone Number

Use of Therapists as Witnesses

Asking your therapist to testify in court on your behalf, or to speak to a court-appointed evaluator, can greatly assist you in your case. Your therapist knows you well, and will be able to comment on your concerns about your children's well-being, your efforts as a parent, and your problem-solving abilities. Judges typically find that therapists who testify on their own client's behalf, and who do not testify about the other spouse if they have not interviewed that person firsthand, are helpful to the court.

While there are other limitations and drawbacks to your therapist's testimony, it may be helpful to the court by providing information and insight about you. Remember that your therapist probably has not met your spouse, and may not have met your children. He or she, therefore, can only comment on you, and not on people that he or she has not met or treated.

By calling your therapist to testify, you are waiving your therapist-patient privilege, i.e., the confidentiality of your discussions with your therapist. Prior to such testimony, everything that your therapist and you discussed was covered by a special therapist-patient privilege, and was confidential. When you ask your therapist to testify for you, you give your permission for your spouse or his or her attorney to question your therapist about your diagnosis, relationship, and treatment. Before you embark in this direction, decide whether or not you feel comfortable forfeiting your confidentiality. Sometimes people are surprised by what they learn when their therapist testifies. If your therapist is not experienced in giving testimony, it is easy for him or her to be caught off guard by the opposing lawyer, and to have difficulty explaining to your advantage. Also, many therapists strongly encourage you to leave them out of the dispute, so that they can be most helpful to you in the ways for which they are best trained, and which are most respectful of the confidentiality of your relationship.

If the court-appointed evaluator wishes to speak to your therapist, you will also lose your confidentiality privilege. Under these circumstances, however, it is usually best to permit your therapist to speak to the evaluator unless there is a compelling reason to preserve the confidentiality of your relationship.

There may be circumstances under which you will need to waive your therapist-patient privilege in order to help your case. For example, if you are claiming that you need alimony because you are unable to work because of a psychiatric disability, your privilege will be waived for that issue. In addition, some courts have determined that by pursuing a custody matter you have voluntarily put your mental health into question, and in order to decide that question, the court needs therapy records that would otherwise be confidential. Therefore, when you make a custody claim, you must assume your mental health records will no longer remain confidential.

Of course, if you are unable to get out of bed in the morning to fix your children breakfast, or if you have been diagnosed with a severe mental illness that affects your ability to parent your children, these situations can adversely affect your custody claim. It is likely that your spouse will attempt to make an issue of your disabilities in your case. If your therapist can testify about the progress you've made, the efforts you've put in to getting better, and your adherence to a therapist's plan, the testimony will probably make the best of a less-than-optimal situation.

⚖️

WITNESSES FOR HIRE

In no case or circumstance does it make sense to hire competing independent evaluators to produce a battle of the experts. All you do is double your
headaches, economic costs, and often the experts present opposing testimony that leaves the court will little help in the end. Choose one neutral
evaluator carefully. Check into the person's background and make sure the
individual has no biases that could adversely affect you. Then agree to
abide by the evaluation, and stick to it, even if it is unfavorable to you. Any
reputable expert will work with you to improve the recommendations for
all parties, as the parties show their ability to work together or compromise.

How Do I Help My Children at This Stage?

You can help your children most by doing everything in your power to
keep them separate from the court contest. Be careful what you say on the
phone or to visitors; children usually have much more information than
parents think they do, albeit filtered through their own eyes and ears. Do
not talk to your children about the dispute, except to inform them of its initiation, to answer their questions, to assure them of both parents' continued
love for them, and your desire to be their parent in all respects, whatever
the dispute's outcome. Do not grill your children about the other home or
use them as informants, detectives, or messengers. Your information must
come from elsewhere. If you cannot find it, and your children are not complaining to you directly, then perhaps you are blowing issues out of proportion.

Pay attention to the stress level your children are expressing. They may
be manipulative or angry. They may be echoing your complaints about the
other household; you'll especially want to note if your spouse reports the
opposite. Then your children may be "telling" you they are caught up in
loyalty conflicts. They may be demonstrating increased anxiety around
transitions between parental homes, or between their primary home and
day care, school, or after-school activities. They may be regressing in their

behavior, going backward to a previous developmental step. Or they may be discipline problems at home or at school. If you pay close attention, you may be able to trace the change in behavior to specific events, such as the house being sold or a parent's move to another town. Or you may observe a slow deterioration as the custody dispute wears on.

In any case, when you note negative changes in your child's demeanor or behavior, you should first talk directly to your child (assuming he or she is verbal) to ascertain what the child understands about the behavior, and to learn more details about what the child is feeling. Talk to the child's attorney or guardian to discuss changes you might make to facilitate improvement. Certainly, notify a teacher or therapist already in the picture.

If, upon discussion with other professionals involved in your child's life and in the case, you decide that either you need more information than the child is giving you, or that he or she needs professional support, don't wait until the dispute is over. Seek help immediately. You might benefit from individual therapy or, if your spouse is willing, counseling specifically geared toward helping the two of you help your child. Or you could have your child seen by an outside mental health professional. Parents often feel at this stage that so many people are involved in the dispute that they are loathe to invite one more person in, especially with time and money already scarce. Your child did not ask for this dispute, and shouldn't bear the brunt of it. So if at all possible, you should get short-term help, or just provide someone not connected to the dispute for your child to talk to confidentially. It may help the child manage his or her stress level, and cope with the ongoing dispute, whatever its length turns out to be.

WHAT DO I DO IF I THINK MY SPOUSE HAS TURNED THE CHILDREN AGAINST ME?

All too often parents will say that a child does not want to go with the other parent during their scheduled time. This may be manipulative on a parent's part. In many instances, however, the behavior is emanating from the child. This behavior, or verbalization of a wish to reduce time with the other parent, may be an attempt by the child to appear loyal to the primary custodial parent, because the child senses that this parent has some leftover upset feelings toward the other parent. In cases like this, the child needs to be encouraged to go on the visits until the child feels that he or she is not dividing loyalties between parents simply by visiting with the noncustodial, less-seen parent. If need be, consult a therapist for help with these issues.

The field of law and psychology has created a term for when a child does not want to visit the nonresidential parent, and expresses that refusal with venom and vehemence. The child shows disregard for the parent, maybe even hatred. The term is Parental Alienation Syndrome (PAS). PAS occurs when children become allied with one parent to a degree that they refuse to have any contact with the other parent. The hatred they express often reflects the feelings of their primary parent. They become echoes of one parent's disdain for the other. This may be communicated directly to the children, until that parent cultivates negative feelings in the children that become deep-rooted and unmalleable. When parents deny that they have conveyed such feelings to their children, it is often true that they have not discussed how they feel directly, yet they have conveyed their attitudes through unconscious communications that the children pick up.

If you think you are the victim of PAS, you have several options open to you.

1. Your option of least intrusive means is to talk to your child yourself, and/or to have someone whom the child and you both trust (e.g., a grandparent) talk to the child. Tell your child how much he/she means to you, how much this rejection hurts, and how much you want to work on your relationship. Ask your child what is getting in the way of your trying together. Sometimes this minimal intervention is sufficient to begin changing the situation, but not usually.

2. You can file a motion with the court for contempt of a visitation agreement, in order to have the court enforce your parenting plan. If the court finds the other parent guilty of contempt, it can levy financial, detainment, or other sanctions through changes in parenting orders.

3. If you have not done so already, you can request an evaluation in order to clearly demonstrate that the alienation has occurred and is being reinforced through the other parent.

4. You can request therapeutic intervention. The therapist will work with the alienated parent and child, separately and together, to reunite them gradually.

One of the sad aspects about alienation is that forcing your children to see you when they don't want to often just reinforces their view of you as an ogre or a bully. Your efforts are invariably "misunderstood" through negative misinterpretation or attribution of intent. Even if the court forces your children to see you, it may not improve your relationship. A therapeutic route is always a better bet than a legal one. However, often you cannot change your children's opinions, no matter what you try. You may then have to wait it out. Keep in contact from a distance, dropping notes or calling occasionally to remind your children that you care, that you are abiding by their wishes, but that you want things to be different. It may take years, but if you have been wronged, children generally figure this out on their own. It is sad for all of you when you realize you have wasted precious time, but your children will appreciate how you hung in, and will feel loved and appreciated. This seems like a meager reward compared to what you endured, but in the end, you are likely to find one another again.

The rejected parent isn't always so pure and wronged, however. Parents whose children have been turned against them have generally contributed to the situation by acting in demanding, controlling, arrogant, or selfish ways that lend support to the other parent's accusations. Examine your reflection carefully in the mirror. Are you ready to understand your role in what has happened? Children rarely turn on a parent so completely without some provocation, unless the alienating parent is so vulnerable that the child must support that parent to help her cope with the divorce. In this latter situation, it is difficult to fight such strong influences. The passage of time, patience, and the alienated parent's consistently nurturing behavior (given *any* opportunity) can combine to gradually soften the child's position against that parent.

PERSONAL ASSESSMENT

Have I tried every avenue in my power to avoid a custody dispute, and am I so sure my child is in danger that it is worth the heavy toll it will take on all of us? If my convictions are sure and clear-minded, then I can proceed with authority rather than self-righteousness.

Have I gone about the process in the best manner available to me? Have I hired competent professionals (attorney and mental health) who will represent my interests vigorously without fighting for its own sake? Do I have confidence in the evaluator we are using? I will need someone the court and I trust, and I have selected with care.

Have I prepared every step of the way? If I can answer "yes," then I have done my legwork, I have documented my concerns, enlisted support for my case, and followed the guidelines provided for my demeanor and behavior in and out of court. These will lead me to the highest ground.

Have I observed my children throughout the process to gauge their reactions and to detect when they need help coping with the legal dispute and its accompanying stresses? I am on the right track if I have not lost sight of the reason I am doing this, and my children are still in the forefront of my thinking, feeling, and actions.

Have I made my problems my children's? Have I done anything to undermine their relationship with their other parent; alternatively, have I given them reason not to trust or respect me? Am I willing to be party to the pain I am creating for them when I encourage their negative feelings toward their parent, or could I make the situation any easier for them? If I cut out the other parent from their life, I do get more of their time, but there is less of them because a part of them has been cut away, too.

10.

Domestic Violence and Other Forms of Abuse: When the Route Is Really Dangerous

When verbal or physical violence has been a part of your marriage, or is likely to be a troubling part of the picture during divorce, our recommendations change radically. This book is about collaborating and cooperating first and foremost, putting your children's needs before your own, sometimes at what seems to be an initial cost to yourself. We believe that a cooperative, constructive strategy is a long-term one that will serve you and your family better over the years, although it will mean making some sacrifices initially. This advice changes when violence enters the family equation. You will need a strong advocate who can stand firm with and for you as you waver throughout your divorce journey. If you cannot afford an attorney, check with your local legal aid office, bar association referral service, and domestic violence shelter for a free or low-cost attorney referral.

DEFINITIONS OF VIOLENCE

There is no one definition of what constitutes physical or verbal abuse. We refer to physical abuse as hitting, slapping, grabbing, pushing, biting, kicking, or any more severe form of physical touch or restraint that is likely to invoke fear and/or cause injury. Verbal abuse consists of verbal assaults about one's character (name calling), threats to harm the spouse or children, and threats made with the intent to coerce or scare—including threats of homicide. Abuse may also take the form of imposing control such as enforcing isolation, forbidding someone to leave the house, locking someone in a room, or other degrading behaviors in public or private. It may also encompass stalking and harassment. Persons who make such verbal or physical assaults on their partners are referred to by the legal system as batterers, and their behavior is frequently referred to as domestic violence.

Although both men and women can be batterers in relationships, women are at greater risk for serious injury, due in part to their smaller size and less muscular physique. Women are the victims in 95 percent of known cases, while men are abused by their spouses in 5 percent of reported cases. However, new research suggests that men may be victims far more often than previously known. Therefore, we will address this section to women victims, but the facts and advice stated herein will be useful to men who are concerned about their own safety at the hands of their wives.

Divorce represents a crisis point for abused women. Through divorce, they have an opportunity to leave the abuse, and to make a new life. They are also at serious risk for the act of leaving in and of itself. National statistics indicate that 40 percent of all women murdered are killed by a spouse or boyfriend. Many of these women are killed in their own homes. Women are most seriously at risk soon after they leave their husbands, or announce that they are leaving. The potential for violence is also high during custody disputes. Disputed custody contests exacerbate violence among persons prone to angry, abusive responses. When the control that is part of an abusive relationship is threatened, would-be batterers up the ante to regain it.

PATTERNS OF ABUSIVE RELATIONSHIPS

Abusive relationships tend to follow a cyclical pattern that recurs throughout the relationship. Many times some of the warning signs were present early in the relationship, but they seemed muted. Other times behavior prior to marriage is controlling and demanding, but never reaches a violent stage until after the marriage or a child is born.

The cycle has three fairly predictable steps:

1. A period of building tensions in which small incidents become more frequent, and the batterer expresses irritation and frustration with his

partner's appearance, behavior, or imagined relationships with other persons.

2. Next, an acute incident causes an explosion. The batterer "blows" like a pressure-filled chimney, shooting anger and venom at the spouse. The incident usually results in actual violence or threats that are serious and barely related to the incident, and the intensity of the reaction is far out of proportion to the incident itself.

3. Next follows a period of loving contrition, where the batterer apologizes and tries to woo back the affections of his victim. This is where most women are vulnerable, as they willingly believe promises that such behavior will not be repeated. Then the cycle starts all over again.

There is another pattern to the violence. It is an intergenerational transmission of the battering behavior and the attitudes that underlie it. Women who were abused as children, physically or sexually, are more likely to become battered wives as adults. Similarly, a risk factor for becoming a batterer is witnessing your parents' violence as a child. Studies compiled by the National Organization for Men Against Sexism show that boys who witnessed their father beat their mother were three times more likely to beat their own wives. However, it is important to note that many abusers do not have a history of witnessing domestic violence, and many who did witness such violence do not themselves become batterers.

The causes of domestic violence are not yet completely understood. However, many factors contribute to its inception. Domestic violence, and other types of violent behavior, have been linked to neurological impairments, such as head injuries. Violence between spouses is also associated with binge drinking and with the onset of early alcoholism. The most clear correlate with battering, as noted above, is being abused as a child or witnessing violence.

SETTING CLEAR BOUNDARIES FOR YOURSELF AND YOUR CHILDREN

Oftentimes, your situation does not meet the level of serious violence where you have to flee, but you are subject to ongoing intimidation. This is

⚖

INDICATIONS THAT YOUR PARTNER HAS GONE TOO FAR INCLUDE:

getting angry at you when you disagree; punching holes in walls; throwing objects (aimed at nothing or at you); destroying belongings; threatening to hurt you or leave you for the purpose of creating fear in you; physically restraining you from leaving home; putting pressure on you not to work when you want to; insulting or ridiculing you; becoming jealous of your friends, activities, or hobbies; making you account for your whereabouts at all times; using promises and lies to manipulate you or to get you to forgive an angry behavior; isolating you from friends or family; making you ask permission to go out or make a career move; threatening your possessions, pets, or children's safety.

also a form of violence or battering. Understand that when you are being victimized, your children are at risk for being hurt, too. Furthermore, you are teaching them about your expectations for relationships, a kind of learning that they may carry with them throughout their life and repeat when it is their turn to become involved in intimate relations. Set standards for how you will allow yourself and your children to be treated.

Do not allow behaviors that feel uncomfortable, frightening, or intimidating to become acceptable to you or your children. These behaviors are forms of abuse even if you do not fear for your safety. Make it clear to your spouse that he can no longer seek to control your life or your actions. If you do fear for your safety, you will need to take additional steps to stay safe.

WHEN YOUR CHILDREN ARE INVOLVED AND AFFECTED

Children can be affected by parental violence in several ways. They can be injured during an incident between their parents; they can be traumatized by fear for their mother and their own sense of helplessness in protecting her; they can blame themselves for not preventing the violence or for causing it; they can be directly abused themselves; and they can be neglected by parents who cannot care for them properly due to the violence in their relationship. Studies show that parents underestimate how often and to what extent children are witnesses to parental violence. Both mothers and fathers report that children are witnesses less than the children report when given the opportunity to respond for themselves.

WHAT IF MY CHILD HAS WITNESSED THE VIOLENCE?

Over 3 million children are at risk of exposure to parental violence each year. Most research suggests that as many as 75 percent of children from violent homes observe their fathers battering their mothers, with reports ranging from 68 percent to 87 percent. It has been noted that in some instances the violence is most likely to occur when the children are present, as the father seeks to further humiliate his wife. The amount of hostility and verbal abuse turned on you can and does affect your children. Research shows that children who witness such behavior show long-lasting effects.

Children are prone to suffer from parental violence in four ways:

1. Immediate trauma
2. Longer-term adverse effects on their normal development
3. Living under high levels of stress on a consistent basis, with the trauma that fear of harm to oneself and one's mother inflicts
4. Exposure to violent role models

Children who have witnessed violence report fear, worry, confusion, and stress. They experience problems regardless of their age at the time of the violence. Children as young as one year were observed to regress in their behavior so dramatically that they were incorrectly diagnosed as mentally retarded. Preschoolers demonstrate more yelling, hiding, shaking, stuttering, and aches and pains in their heads, stomachs, and bowels. Children older than about six years of age may identify with the aggressive parent, growing up to be aggressive or abusive themselves. This is especially true for boys who have watched their fathers berate and abuse their mothers. Girls are more likely to display passive, withdrawn, and dependent behavior. They also are more likely to become targets of abusive fathers; they are 6.5 times more likely to be sexually abused by their fathers than are girls in nonviolent homes. In the long term, girls are likely to repeat their mothers' behavior, falling into abusive relationships.

Other problems experienced by children who witness their mothers being abused include pervasive anxiety, fear, sleep disruption (e.g., nightmares, bed-wetting), and school problems. Depression, low self-esteem, low self-confidence, and insecurity are internal symptoms recorded by researchers. Difficulties with academic achievement and concentration, absenteeism, and conflict with other children are more externalized symptoms also commonly found among children who witnessed violence at home. The children are often less socially competent than their peers, as they are more isolated and feel shame about their families. By adolescence, children who witnessed violence have more behavior problems, are more likely to get into trouble with the law, and are more likely to commit violent acts outside the family. One study suggests that these children are arrested by police four times more often than nonabused children. Some adolescents express their distress by running away, abuse of alcohol, or suicide attempts. In divorcing families where violence was frequent and ongoing, research has also traced the development of personality disorders that are difficult to change and require long and intensive therapy.

ASSESSING AND ACTING WHEN YOU ARE AT RISK

How Do I Recognize Whether I Am at Risk for My Partner's Abuse or Escalating Violence?

If your spouse is controlling, jealous, possessive, and threatening in several of the ways described above, you are at risk for being hurt during your divorce. The risk increases for women if their partners own or have access to a gun, have a history of abusing alcohol or drugs, have stalked them in the past, or threatened violence or suicide. When you are the one leaving or your husband and you are involved in a custody dispute, you should be especially careful. If any or several of these descriptors fits your relationship, you should assess the likelihood of conflict escalating into violence with the help of an attorney or mental health professional, and you should take necessary precautions.

In the meantime, you can informally assess what the risk is for you of continued contact with your spouse by asking yourself these questions:

- Is the frequency of the violence increasing?
- Is the severity of the violence increasing?
- What is the frequency of alcohol or drug use? How often is the point of intoxification (drunkenness) reached?
- Has your spouse threatened to harm the children?
- Has your spouse threatened to kill you or your significant other?
- Has your spouse threatened to coerce or hurt you sexually?
- Have there been any suicide attempts or threats made?
- Are any weapons available to him, and have they ever been used in fights before?
- Does he have any known psychological problems?
- How close do you live or work to each other?
- How often does control get exerted around contact with the children by him? By you?
- What kinds of life stresses is he currently experiencing? How have these changed recently?
- Does he have a criminal history?
- Is there a new relationship in your life? Does he know? How has he acted about it?

If the answers indicate that you have reason to fear, and that trouble seems more likely at the current time, then you should proceed with immediacy and care.

What Do I Do First?

Make a safety plan. Have ready to take with you:

- an address book with important names and numbers: doctors, school personnel, teachers, police, a domestic violence hot line, shelters, and trustworthy friends and relatives

- documents: driver's license, insurance information, car registration, copy of house deed, passport/green card/work permits, Social Security card, birth certificate
- household information: mortgage book, unpaid bills, debt information, insurance papers
- copy of any restraining orders already in effect
- money and credit cards
- medications
- children's favorite personal possessions, such as blankets, stuffed animals, bottles
- change of clothing for each family member who might flee with you

If you are planning an escape, call a lawyer who is experienced with the special risks and needs in domestic violence situations before you do anything else. If there is no time, call after you have left your home. Do not allow a confrontation, just leave without notice and get to a safe place.

WHAT CONSTITUTES AN ABUSIVE RELATIONSHIP AS FAR AS THE COURT IS CONCERNED?

For legal purposes, various types of abuse are categorized as either:

- **Verbal abuse that does not present a threat of actual danger:** e.g., "You're stupid, lazy, and irresponsible and I hate you."
- **Verbal abuse that may constitute a present threat of physical danger:** e.g., "I'm going to get a gun and shoot you" or "I'm going to burn down the house."
- **Verbal abuse that may constitute a threat to commit a crime:** e.g., "I'm going to take the children and move to another country and you'll never find me."
- **Verbal abuse coupled with a history of physical abuse:** e.g., "I'm going to give it to you just like last time" or other innuendos that refer to previous physical instances.
- **Restraining you from leaving without actually physically touching you:** e.g., blockading you in a room or in the house.

• **Violent behavior that takes place in your presence but doesn't hurt you:** e.g., throwing a heavy object in your direction that isn't intended to hit you and doesn't hit you, or putting a fist through a wall. Intent to intimidate is present.

• **Sexual assault:** e.g., any unwanted physical sexual touching or fondling.

• **Physical abuse:** e.g., slapping, punching, tripping, shoving, or any other unwanted or menacing physical touching that happens at least once. It need not cause a bruise or injury.

Once you are able to categorize the type of abuse you are receiving, you can then decide when and if to bring it up to the court.

If the abuse is physical or violent in any way, or is verbal but threatens physical violence ("I'll burn the house down with you in it"), you may qualify for a restraining order or an order of protection. In addition, this type of violence can be a factor in property distribution and alimony if your state considers the reasons that the marriage broke down in property division and alimony orders. Therefore, even if you elect not to obtain a restraining order or order of protection, you may still wish to raise violence as an issue pertinent to your case.

If you have been subjected to abuse that is predominantly verbal—badgering, insulting, screaming, and the like, but doesn't include threats to physically hurt you—then you are probably not entitled to a restraining order or order of protection in most jurisdictions. This type of abusive behavior, however, also may be considered by the judge in dividing assets. You may also use this information in a custody dispute, as evidence of your spouse's deficiency as a parent. You will need to discuss this with your attorney to decide if it would be worthwhile to pursue a claim for sole custody on this basis.

Other types of abuse include threats toward your children. If the abuse is either physical or of a violent nature toward your children, or involves threats to kidnap them, then you may be able to apply for and receive a restraining order or order of protection on behalf of your children. This is described in more detail in a later section of this chapter.

TYPES OF PROTECTION AFFORDED BY LAW:
RESTRAINING ORDERS AND ORDERS OF PROTECTION

Most jurisdictions permit the filing of court pleadings known as a temporary restraining order or order for protection under circumstances in which domestic partners or family members find themselves under a present threat of physical abuse at the hands of domestic partners or other family members.

Temporary Restraining Order

If your spouse has been physically abusive or threatening to you in the immediate past, you may qualify for a temporary restraining order. The general standard for such a restraining order is that the person against whom it is granted must be a relative of yours by blood or by marriage, or someone with whom you have lived. That person must have put you in a position where you are under a *present threat of physical abuse.* That means that if your spouse abused you two years ago, and in some cases two months ago, you will not qualify. You do not need to have bruises, black eyes, or broken bones in order to qualify. Threats such as "I will burn down the house before I give it to you," menacing actions with handguns, pushing, shoving, and physical restraint may all qualify as abuse sufficient for a restraining order. You need not have the police involved in most cases in order to qualify.

You can hire an attorney to help you obtain such an order, but it isn't required. Most courts have set up the process so that you can apply for and obtain a temporary restraining order without a lawyer. The procedure includes filling out appropriate forms, available at the court clerk's office. You then tell a judge a brief explanation of the history of abuse and why you are afraid at the present time. The order goes into effect immediately. The order forbids your spouse from coming near you, into your home, or into your place of work, calling to harass you by telephone, placing any physical restraint on you, or assaulting you. Even coming near you is a violation of the restraining order, and your spouse could be arrested for doing so. Thus, you may wish to obtain a TRO before the divorce papers are served, in order to protect yourself. For many, seeking a restraining order will be the last step toward a divorce after many episodes of abuse or threats, or both.

A follow-up hearing is then scheduled within a few days or weeks to give the person against whom you have the order a chance to tell his or her side of the story. If the restraining order is continued after the hearing, it usually stays in effect for several months, depending upon your state's laws. This order provides special relief for special circumstances, and should not be used inappropriately in an effort to simply have your (nonabusive) spouse removed from the family home.

Order for Protection: Criminal Court Relief

A temporary restraining order is a civil remedy, as opposed to a criminal remedy. If the police become involved in your case, you may also be entitled to a criminal restraining order, sometimes called an order of protection or a protective order, through the criminal court and the police department. A civil restraining order is separate and in addition to "or instead of" a criminal order. You can obtain such an order by contacting the local police department, but typically they are automatically issued by the criminal court after your spouse (or other abuser) has been arrested.

Below we refer to a restraining order for both civil and criminal types of orders.

HOW SHOULD I PREPARE TO SUCCESSFULLY OBTAIN A TEMPORARY RESTRAINING ORDER?

Document your legal grounds for applying for an order. When physical violence occurs, file a police report, or go to the doctor and tell the doctor the details about what happened. This will create an account of the severity and frequency of your injuries.

Take photographs of your injuries as documentation.

You should document both physical abuse and emotional abuse.

It is also important to tell close friends, family, psychologist, or family therapist when incidents occur. These people will then be in a position to corroborate your claims of abuse and be a witness for you, should that become necessary.

Even if you do not pursue a restraining order at that time, save these materials in a safe place. At the very least, take notes. Two, three, or eight months from now, you may not remember the time, place, and date as well as the details of the incident. Unfortunately, you never know when you might need this documentation.

If you have none of this kind of documentation, but feel that you need a restraining order, apply for one anyway. You do not have to have documentation in order to qualify for a restraining order. It helps, but it isn't necessary in most cases.

How Do I Enforce the Orders with My Spouse?

Once you have your restraining order it is very important that you adhere to the guidelines of that order. Regardless of whether your partner is abiding by the restraining order, you must. For instance, if you see your husband or wife in a parking lot, supermarket, or department store, simply turn around and walk away. You can always go back another time to do your shopping. Seeing your partner during the times when the restraining order is active can be a highly emotional experience. You may experience a rush of feeling when you see or hear from your spouse. Such feelings can evoke deep-seated anger and resentment for what the person is putting you through, and it is not unusual to initiate a verbal altercation or argument with your partner. Or, the sense of loss may well up again, and you may feel as if you want to hold on to your partner even if just for a moment. Despite these feelings, once you have obtained your restraining order, you must abide by it. Going to counseling with the person who has abused you or threatened to abuse you is permissible, but permitting that person to come to your house or meet you even in a public place may compromise your safety. If the order says that the person is to have no contact with you, you should have no contact with that person either. If, in a moment of weakness, you invite your spouse to meet with you at your home, and he becomes violent, the police may not show up fast enough to remove him before you are harmed. That could be true especially if the police have heard from you before after you have invited him in, and you are not taken seriously.

Juliet obtained a restraining order after her husband hit her, yet despite the order he was following her in the car, and calling her on the telephone at all hours of the day and night. A sense of sadness and loss regarding the marriage compelled her to meet with him for coffee. On the telephone her husband was sweet and considerate. During one of these coffee dates an argument started. Juliet asked the manager to call the police. When they arrived they determined that they would send Juliet and her husband on their way without making an arrest; after all, Juliet had agreed to meet her husband voluntarily. Juliet's husband continued to call her and harass her and she tried to have her husband arrested in violation of the restraining order. Because of her previous agreement to meet him, however, her husband had sufficient evidence that she was a willing and complying partner in their meetings, and the restraining order was not extended by the court. This left Juliet in an extremely vulnerable position.

BOTH MEN AND WOMEN CAN QUALIFY FOR A RESTRAINING ORDER

Men need to think about a restraining order as well. In these days of readily available handguns and other weapons, any physical threat must be taken seriously. Is your wife calling you repeatedly at your workplace or at night?

Michael's wife could not bear being separated from her husband. Her sense of loss and fear for the future caused her to become extremely anxious and hysterical. Since she was convinced he was seeing another woman, she would call him at two, three, and four o'clock in the morning just to see if another woman would answer the telephone. "I'll kill her and you!" she'd scream into the phone. During the course of the day she would call him at his office, screaming abusive remarks to his secretary and also to him. Michael's boss, finding him distracted from his work, spoke to Michael about the need to control his wife. Michael spoke to his lawyer about this, a restraining order was issued, and the harassment stopped.

WHAT THE ORDER CAN AND CANNOT DO FOR YOU

A court order is useful for self-protection in cases in which the person against whom the order is issued will abide by it, or is someone who will violate the order in such a way that the police will arrest him or her. The order provides legal protection, which means that a police officer can arrest the violator and the court can impose criminal and civil penalties (like jail time and fines) on anyone who violates it. But restraining orders are pieces of paper. They are not shields.

The vast majority of people against whom restraining orders are issued abide by them. For these individuals, the threat of legal action and even criminal penalties are enough to keep them away from you. Take the physical precautions you feel are necessary to protect yourself. Get an unlisted telephone number and do not tell your batterer your address. Install outside security lighting; install an alarm system; change the alarm code. File a copy of the restraining order with your children's school. A few people feel the need to test the order by violating it in some small way, such as parking in front of your house or calling on the phone, and a quick call to the police allows law enforcement officers to enforce the order.

An extremely small number of people, however, completely disregard the court order. Intent on causing harm, they are undeterred by the possible punishments of violating the order. These people are extremely dangerous. They are also rare, but you must be prepared for the possibility that the person from whom you need protection will not be stopped by a court order to stay away from you and take reasonable precautions to protect yourself. If you believe that the person might violate the restraining order and place you in physical danger, utilize self-defense techniques and common sense to protect yourself. Contact your local domestic violence agency or coalition for information on how to obtain an advocate to walk you through the steps needed to ensure your safety and negotiate the legal system.

⚖

SOME IMPORTANT WAYS YOU CAN PROTECT YOURSELF:

- get an unlisted telephone number
- do not tell the batterer your address
- keep a certified copy of your order with you at all times
- install an alarm system in your home; if you already have one, change your burglar alarm code
- change the locks on your home
- install outside security lighting
- carry pepper spray or Mace (if legal in your state)
- never walk to your car alone
- never walk anywhere in the dark alone
- check the interior of your car with a flashlight or natural light before getting in
- alert your neighbors and local police of the situation
- find safe shelter, such as an abused women's shelter, if you still feel in danger
- file a copy of the order with your children's school and alert them of its existence
- call the police every time the order is violated, no matter how small the violation

CHILDREN'S INVOLVEMENT IN THE LEGAL PROCESS

Although children may be integrally involved in the violence cycle at home, from a legal standpoint, it is extremely unusual for a child to actually be called as a witness in family court. Typically, a family court judge will let you testify about what your child said or did in an abuse situation, even though technically such testimony is considered "hearsay" and is therefore inadmissible. Most family court judges feel that protecting children is a more important goal than excluding hearsay evidence, and will let you testify.

In the event that a judge decides that your child ought to testify, the court will appoint an attorney, or a guardian *ad litem*, to represent him/her. The role of these children's representatives is discussed in Chapter 9. The court may also make special arrangements to protect your children, such as closing the courtroom, or having the child testify in the judge's chambers rather than in court. Again, such practices are quite rare. Children's attorneys, guardians *ad litem*, family relations studies, and psychological studies have made the necessity of children's testimony almost obsolete. Even when the "children" are actually adults, the damage that such testimony can do to a family is oftentimes deemed not worth the benefit derived, since it requires the children to testify against their own parent and is potentially damaging for them emotionally.

What If My Child Is the One Being Abused?

Violence toward a spouse is often a precursor to direct child abuse. Nearly half the men who abuse their partners also abuse their children. Children who both witness violence and are abused themselves suffer the most negative long-term consequences. These children are at highest risk when the marriage is dissolving, the couple has separated, and the father is committed to continuing to assert control over the lives of his wife and children. Some men, after their initial rage, let go. Others become more enraged following marital separations, as they fear losing control over their wives and families. These men are the most dangerous to their children. Older children face the special problem of being assaulted when they try to intervene to protect their mothers and to stop the abuse. Daughters are more likely than sons to become their fathers' next victims. They may experience physical or sexual abuse.

Compounding this problem, women who are abused are less able to care for their children. Researcher Walker (see page 348) reports that eight times as many women report using physical discipline on their children while living with their batterer than when living alone or in a nonbattering relationship. Symptoms experienced by abused children are similar to those described for children who witness their parents' violence (pages 263–64), but their problems at all levels are more severe.

Special Legal Steps to Take When Violence Involves Children

The same types of legal protection are available to children as to adults, such as restraining orders or orders of protection. As the parent, it is your responsibility to bring these actions on behalf of your children when necessary. The same procedures described above apply to children's restraining orders.

In addition, suspected child abuse should be reported to the child's pediatrician and the police. As a parent, you must protect your child, but the reasons for reporting abuse to your child's doctor and the police also include protecting yourself legally. All states have laws that require parents to protect their children, and by failing to make the proper reports to authorities and to seek proper medical treatment for your child, you put yourself at risk of being charged with child abuse or neglect. Your child's teachers, day care providers, and doctors are also all required to report suspected abuse. Failing to protect your children against abuse or failure to seek proper treatment for them when they've been abused may be interpreted as neglect on your part. In the worst-case scenario, you could lose custody and your children could be placed in the protective care of the state.

SHOULD ANY CHILD INVOLVED IN A VIOLENT FAMILY BE FORBIDDEN TO SEE THE OFFENDING PARENT?

Many courts have the power to order visitation even for a parent who has abused or threatened to abuse a child. Before a court does so, however, it typically orders a family study to be performed by either the Family Relations Office or a psychological evaluator. This procedure is described in depth in Chapter 9. Once the family has been evaluated, the court may still order visitation, depending upon the outcome of the evaluation. You can be confident that the court will do its utmost to assure that the children are not placed in a dangerous situation as a result of court orders.

There are several opportunities for the court to put safeguards in place in the event it decides that it's in the children's best interests to visit with a parent who has been abusive in the past. If visitation is to take place, insist on supervised visitation and transfer of the child. There are several types of supervision. One-on-one supervision requires that a third person be present and that the visitation occurs in a designated place. Visits can be informally supervised through a family member or more formally through a professional supervisor. The court can even order that supervised visits take place in a clinical setting, such as in a psychologist's office, or at a visitation clinic specifically set up to handle such visits. Exchange supervision specifies when, where, and how the children are transferred between parents. Off-site supervision designates a neutral location, such as a playground or local fast-food restaurant and a neutral drop-off site, such as a relative's home or a public place. This form of supervision is least restrictive, and often precedes the slackening or dropping of the supervision once the danger period has passed, and if you believe that you and your children are no longer threatened. The danger may be reduced if the batterer receives some therapeutic assistance or intervention. The court can order the abusive parent to receive counseling or to take parenting classes as a condition of being permitted to see the children. Anger management classes are common to most areas, often serving as an alternative to prison time after an arrest for domestic violence. However, the efficacy of such programs is unknown.

Some state laws hold that violence toward the mother does not constitute ample reason to deny fathers their rights of access to their children. However, recent articles published in the Albany and Boston University Law Review journals report that approximately 85 percent of states (forty-six states and the District of Columbia) have passed laws requiring that a batterer's violence be considered a factor in custody and visitation disputes. All states adhere to the "best interests" standards, however, and so while violence may not be a specific statutory criterion in many states, it will be considered in every case in which it is present.

Even if the batterer is not considered a viable candidate for joint custody, many courts will protect that parent's right to access through visitation. Many batterers terrify their spouses by using visitations as an opportunity to continue the abuse. The court must decide when batterers should be completely deprived of their parental rights, and when allegations of threats made are part of the ongoing battles waged by two angry parents. At times, parents wield unfounded accusations as swords against one another in an attempt to gain an advantage in custody cases. The court's job then becomes one of not only assessing the truth of the accusations made but also to assess the psychological impact on the children, as well as balancing the constitutional rights of parents to raise their own children.

Given this complicated landscape, it's essential to document all allegations with photos, witnesses, or any other evidence that shows when and how threats are made that are later denied. Take note of when the children are present for the abuse, and how they experience direct or indirect consequences of the abuse. See Chapter 9 for advice on how to substantiate allegations.

Ultimately visitation depends upon what the court finds to be in the best interests of the children. If the children know and are attached to the abusive parent, and the court believes that the children are safe when with that parent, visitation may be ordered. On the other hand, if the court cannot assure the children's emotional or physical safety, visitation may be suspended indefinitely, until the situation is remedied.

WHAT IF MY CHILDREN DON'T SEE IT MY WAY?

A subtle form of emotional blackmail occurs when the batterer tries to seduce your children with promises, luring them to believe that he is the perfect father and gentleman. Young children, in particular, are vulnerable to becoming confused by the difference between their mother's attitude toward their father and what they see and experience themselves. In such a case, you have two options. If you feel your safety is compromised in any way, you must insist that your children accept your judgment on the matter and take precautions to prevent the batterer from having any contact with you, or more contact with your children than the court requires. Talk to your children about your fears and the reasons for them. You do not need a lot of detail, especially with children who have not yet reached adolescence. Explain to them that you are keeping them and you safe. If they are obviously emotionally attached to their father, tell them that you know they love their father and wish it could be different; you hope it can be in the future. As soon as you believe that you are all safe, you will support their having a relationship with him. If they get angry at you, stand your ground. Someday they will understand. For now, it is one of those times that being a parent means doing the hard thing "to" your children in order to do something "for" their optimal development. Be sympathetic, but remember that you have nothing for which to apologize. Maintain your parental authority, even if you don't feel it. If you feel that your husband is being manipulative, but you believe the children are safe and that access is desirable for them, you might wish to set up visitation so that they can benefit from seeing him without your safety being compromised. To facilitate this, a skilled attorney with experience in domestic violence issues is essential. If you do not have money for a private attorney, contact your local domestic violence resources and they can help you find an attorney.

Explain to your children that although their father and you cannot see each other right now because Daddy is so angry at you that it is too dangerous, you believe that he loves his children and will not hurt them. You know they love him, and you will do what you can to help them have a relationship with him.

EMOTIONAL BLACKMAIL OF CHILDREN

Battering men use custodial access to their children as a method of terrorizing their spouses or retaliating for the marital separation. This is not surprising, since it is one of the few tactics available to an abuser after separation. Custody battles are one kind of threat that abusive husbands use to bring their wives to heel.

At times, an abusive father will threaten his children, saying that unless they side with him, he will disappear from the children's life. Afraid of losing that parent, children may acquiesce. Using the visitation time as a brainwashing opportunity, these batterers work on their children's fears to induce compliance with their views and wishes.

ABDUCTION

A corollary to such threats are child abductions. It is estimated that forty children are abducted each hour in this country. More than half of those abductions are found to be short-term manipulations around custody orders, but many involve concealing the child's whereabouts for a longer period of time. Most of the abductions are committed by fathers and 41 percent of them occur between the time of separation and divorce. A majority of the abductions occur concurrently with domestic violence between parents.

Take all precautions and prepare as if the worst *could* happen. Make sure your children's passports are in a safe place, along with their birth certificates. It's possible for your spouse to obtain copies, but it's unlikely that your spouse will follow through on a kidnapping threat before you have a chance to obtain a court order against him or her if the children's passports cannot be found. If you believe that abduction is a realistic possibility, you need to obtain a court order forbidding your spouse from removing the children from the country, or perhaps even from your town or state, until the court can investigate the situation and make appropriate long-term orders. Seek a restraining order or injunction if you believe that their other parent may take the children within the next few hours or days. As described above, these types of orders can be obtained immediately after such a threat is made, without your spouse being present. Your spouse is then given an opportunity to be heard, but typically ten days to two weeks later. Alert the police to the situation; although they cannot make an arrest unless and until something illegal actually happens, put a statement on file. If the police are familiar with your situation, you have a better chance of faster action if something does happen in the future. Also alert your child's school or day care provider, and restrict access to your child at pickup time to yourself or another trusted family member. Instruct the school or day care provider to call the police if anyone else shows up to pick up the child from school, and to notify you immediately.

When domestic violence is involved, divorce is especially emotionally difficult and fraught with challenges. Move carefully and be informed. Although this journey will be especially challenging, it is well worth the effort to sever yourself from the cycle of terror and violence. Once you've moved beyond this part of your past, you and your children can begin to look forward to a calmer and more peaceful future.

PERSONAL ASSESSMENT

Am I in danger of becoming, or am I already a victim of, domestic violence? If so, I need to acknowledge this, take precautions for my own and my children's safety, and begin making changes in my life. I will have more self-respect, and my children will have a stronger, perhaps better, parent.

Have I . . . taken the precautions I need to? . . . documented the abuse? . . . obtained a restraining and/or protective order from the court? . . . and enforced it as needed? This is one of the most painful moments in my life, but it is an essential step toward freeing myself and my children and leaving a bad situation behind for the potential of a better life.

Have I taken additional precautions if my spouse has an especially violent temper? The law can be a partner with me, but it cannot protect me in and of itself. I must protect my family myself, with any help from friends or family I can muster.

If my children are safe but are being manipulated by my spouse, have I made it my problem rather than theirs? Have I protected them when necessary, and allowed them to see their father when they are not the ones in danger? We brought them into this world together, and if physical safety is not an issue for me or them, I must control my desire to punish his controlling behaviors by controlling his access to his children. They will someday be mature enough to decide for themselves who we each are to them.

11.

Life After Divorce: When the Horizon Beckons Anew

P art of the healing process of the divorce is dealing with the details that establish you as an independent person, fully separated from your spouse. Even small things such as making sure that your (and your spouse's) mailing address has been updated to prevent unnecessary reminders of your married days will assist you along the trail to healing and moving on with your postdivorce life.

FOLLOW-UP TASKS

After your divorce has been finalized, there are a number of details that you can take care of on your own, without the help of a lawyer. However, before we discuss those, there are a few pieces of paperwork that you should have a lawyer finish for you:

• Preparing the judgment documents for the court to sign (you may prepare this yourself with the help of the clerk's office if you did not hire a lawyer to represent you).

• Preparing any Qualified Domestic Relations Orders for pension, 401k, and some IRA divisions, and following through to see that the pension administrator's office distributes the funds properly. A judgment awarding you a share of a pension or other retirement fund is difficult or impossible to enforce without a Qualified Domestic Relations Order.

- Drafting and recording house deeds and/or mortgages.
- Preparation of new wills and trust documents. Your divorce invalidates your old estate plan, so update it as soon as is practical to do so.

Most other follow-up tasks are easily done yourself. Taking care of these things personally will enhance your sense of independence and competence in handling your new life. It also saves you money.

TO-DO LIST

- Double-check that you have closed your joint credit card accounts.
- Change utility bills into or out of your name.
- Sign over your automobiles as provided in the court judgment and obtain personal car insurance.
- Explore tax ramifications of any alimony you receive. Alimony is taxable to the recipient and a deduction for the person who pays.
- Consider other tax ramifications: transfers of property between spouses as part of a divorce is not a taxable event, but selling assets once they've been transferred may trigger tax consequences, so check before you sell.
- Update your estate plan, as the dissolution of your marriage will invalidate your will and may affect your other estate-planning documents. If you haven't asked your divorce lawyer to prepare a new will and estate plan, find a probate attorney who will assist you.
- Change the beneficiaries on your life insurance, 401k, pension, and IRA accounts. Contact your bank or insurance company for proper forms. Notify each insurance company of proper beneficiary designations.
- Update your mailing address with credit card companies, banks, motor vehicle department, and insurance companies.
- If you have changed your name as a result of the divorce, get a new Social Security card, driver's license, and credit cards. Notify your bank, stockbroker, and children's school.
- Close any joint safety deposit or post office boxes; open new ones if desired.

• Update your address with your lawyer's office. Sometimes changes in the law may affect your case, and your lawyer will need to contact you.

A few additional tasks and accompanying paperwork will need to be completed:

OBTAIN A CERTIFIED COPY OF YOUR FINAL JUDGMENT

Keep a certified copy of your judgment on hand to show official proof of your divorce. Order one (or several) from the court clerk's office as soon as your divorce is finalized because it may take the clerk's office a few weeks to process your request. You will need to give the full name of the case and the year in which you were divorced, and pay a nominal fee. A certified copy is needed when applying for loans (when your credit is still intermingled with your spouse's credit), to change titles on a home or car, to obtain mortgages, and in some states to remarry. Get a certified copy while you are still reorganizing your life, and keep it among your important papers.

CREDIT ISSUES

Obtain a new copy of your credit report. Make sure the joint credit card accounts you closed have actually been closed and the credit agency files have been updated. If your spouse has damaged your credit, pursue your right to clarify—or correct—your credit record.

HEALTH INSURANCE

Apply for COBRA health insurance benefits from your former spouse's employer, if appropriate. If insurance is available through your employer, sign up to participate if you have not done so already.

SOCIAL SECURITY

If you were married for at least ten years, you are entitled to make a claim against your spouse's Social Security. This is not as exciting as it sounds, because you must choose between receiving 100 percent of your benefit and 50 percent of your spouse's benefit at the time you become eligible for Social Security. For those who have worked, typically their own benefit is larger than half of their former spouse's benefit, but it's worth reviewing.

You can get an estimate of your Social Security benefits by filling out an Estimation of Benefits form at your local Social Security office or online at: http://www.ssa.gov.

RECORD KEEPING

1. Keep records of payment or receipt of alimony, child support, and any other support payments made to, or received from, your former spouse. Keep all of your canceled checks in order of payments made, and keep a calendar for all payments received. The easiest way to do this is to keep these records in a separate envelope. If there is ever a question about whether or not you paid or received money for support, alimony, or medical bills, all of the records are in one place and you don't have to sift through years of canceled checks.

2. Keep records of all of your children's medical visits, insurance claims, insurance payments, and insurance denials, and your payments to providers or your spouse for the children's care. If you take a child to the doctor, send or request a copy of the bill or receipt from your spouse and submit the claim form in a timely fashion. Again, keep these records all in one place so that if you're ever questioned about what you paid, you don't have to sort through years of bank records.

3. If co-parenting with your spouse is still a sticky issue that has potential to resurface as a conflict in the future, keep a record of how the visits with the other parent went, and if there were any specific problems. This can be done on a calendar or in a journal. Keep the records in one place in case questions arise in a dispute later on.

4. All child support and custody matters are modifiable when circumstances change if (a) you return to court and (b) demonstrate that the change was substantial enough to warrant a change in previous orders, typically about a 15 percent difference in the amount of the required payment. If a change of circumstances occurs, you may be entitled to a modification of child support or alimony payments (either higher or lower). A change in circumstances may also warrant a change in legal or physical custody arrangements for your child.

5. For your income taxes, assemble all Social Security numbers for children you are permitted to claim as a deduction, and for a spouse to whom you paid alimony. You may also need a copy of your judgment or IRS Form 8225 to prove who gets to claim the children as exemptions on their taxes, if applicable. From the IRS, request a copy of Publication 504, which deals with divorce tax issues. If you have questions about your taxes, including capital gains taxes, contact an accountant, tax professional, or your lawyer for professional assistance.

6. Contact your child's school and let the school know the divorce is final. Update the school about your address and your spouse's, and where school notices should be sent, emergency contacts, school pickups and drop-offs, and so forth. Unless there are specific reasons not to, such as in case of ongoing hostility and conflict that has potentially dangerous ramifications, encourage a free flow of information toward both parents.

WHAT KINDS OF CHANGES MAY NEED TO BE MADE IN THE FUTURE?

Although your court case has been finalized, and you are divorced, there are certain circumstances under which you may need to return to court in order to have orders modified or enforced. These typically include orders related to custody, visitation, alimony, or other financial arrangements.

IF YOU DO NOT HAVE CHILDREN

If you do not have children, the divorce may be the end of your case. For most childless couples, once the property division and issues of spousal support have been decided, they no longer have any dealings with the court, and the judgment is considered final in all respects.

The circumstances under which your judgment may not be final include the following:

- If either you or your spouse was untruthful about your assets and/or liabilities, the court's judgment may be reopened due to fraud.
- If both you and your spouse made an honest mistake as to the existence or value of an asset, the court's judgment may be reopened to deal with that asset.
- If you received alimony, or if you pay alimony, and the order is not designated as "not modifiable as to duration or amount" you may seek a modification of the alimony order by petitioning the court. Typically, alimony orders are modifiable unless they *specifically* state that they are not. The procedure for a modification is outlined on page 287.
- Both you and your spouse have a short time in which you can appeal the court's ruling. This assumes that your case went to trial, and was decided by a judge after hearing evidence and testimony. Appeals are possible, but rare, in cases where spouses reached an agreement for an uncontested divorce. If, after the trial and upon request by either party, the appeals court finds that there was an important error made in the ruling on your case, the appeals court will send it back to the trial court for a new ruling. Often this creates need for a new trial. The appeals court cannot typically "fix" an erroneous ruling; a new trial must be held.
- If either of you does not follow through on the court's orders, enforcement proceedings may be necessary. These proceedings do not reopen or change the court's judgment. They are simply a mechanism to have the original orders enforced. Enforcement proceedings are discussed on page 288.

IF YOU HAVE CHILDREN

If you have children, all of the above scenarios apply to you. In addition, orders concerning children are always modifiable in the event that there is a significant change in circumstances. Such changes may affect:

- Child support
- The children's health insurance
- Provisions for life insurance benefiting the children
- Access plans
- Legal custody designations
- Joint custody problems: disputes over schooling, religious training, health issues, and other parenting issues that impact the children but don't rise to the level of a custody dispute
- Enforcement of court orders: nonpayment of child support, failure to transfer property pursuant to the court judgment, failure to abide by visitation orders, failure to pay court-ordered debts, and the like

The way that a court changes its orders is through a Motion for Modification. Either of the parties, or the children's attorney (if one has been appointed), can bring such a motion. Basically, the motion sets forth what the original orders are, an outline of the changes that have taken place, and a request for a modification of the orders.

For example, if your children live primarily with the other parent, and you pay child support, but then your children come to live with you, you might file a Motion for Modification indicating what the old custody and support arrangement was, the fact that the children now live with you, and a request that the custody and child support orders be modified.

Modifications can be by agreement, or they can be contested. If they are agreed upon, it's a simple matter to file the motion and present the agreement in court to be approved by the judge on the court date. Even when the modification is amicable, it's a good idea to formalize the modification with the court so that the orders are enforceable.

If the modification is not agreed upon, a motion is filed as in the above example, but on the date that the motion is scheduled to be heard, a hearing is held. The process is very similar to a hearing that is held as part of a divorce, with the only difference being that the court will hear only evidence about the issue in dispute. All other aspects of the court's judgment remain the same. Although your Motion for Modification pertains to post-divorce issues, the procedures used are the same. For custody modifications, you may also want to reread Chapter 9, Contested Custody Cases.

When the disputed issue is the amount of child support, alimony, or spousal support that is being paid, you will first want to determine if you qualify to have the orders changed. For child support, each state's child support guidelines determine how much each party's income needs to change in order to qualify for a modification of the orders. The guidelines also outline what kinds of custodial arrangements or circumstances may warrant deviation from the guidelines, another indication that the order may be eligible for modification. If you're not sure about whether you qualify for a modification, check the guidelines.

As for alimony or spousal support, you must first determine that the order is modifiable. If your judgment states that the orders are not modifiable for any reason, your chances of modifying the orders are extremely slim. If they are modifiable, make sure that you meet the criteria for modifying the orders both as set forth in your court judgment and in your state's alimony laws.

Be certain that you qualify before filing a Motion for Modification of any type. Since returning to court is such an expensive process, both emotionally and financially, return to court only if you expect a worthwhile outcome. You may wish to consider consulting an attorney for advice on your chances of success before you make your motion.

ENFORCEMENT OF ORDERS

If either party does not follow through on the court's orders, the other party can begin enforcement proceedings, typically called a Motion for Contempt of Court. A Motion for Contempt of Court sets forth what the original orders required, a description of how they were not followed, and a request for a remedy of the situation.

For example, if you are to receive child support but your former spouse fails to pay you for several weeks, you can file a Motion for Contempt stating the original orders, the date of the last payment, that payments have not been made, and that an arrearage has accrued. Your requested relief might include asking that all outstanding arrearages be paid, for a wage withholding for child support (if one is not already in place), for your court costs to be paid by your former spouse, and even additional court sanctions or incarceration if this is not the first time that your ex-spouse has fallen behind in payments.

The court then sets a hearing date. If you are able to resolve the matter, you can present the court with a written agreement outlining your solution on the hearing date. If you do not have an agreement, the court will hear the matter according to its regular hearing procedures. Courts typically follow the same basic procedures for hearings both before and after cases go to judgment.

EMBARKING ON YOUR NEW FAMILY LIFE

HOW CAN I RE-CREATE THE HEALTHIEST LIFE FOR MYSELF AND MY CHILDREN?

Despite the fact that divorce puts children at risk for long-term problems, most children of divorce adapt well, and within a few years of the divorce, feel happy and content in their lives. The key is to move through the divorce with as little disruption as possible to the important people, places, and activities in your children's lives. Throughout this book, we have recommended routes to take to keep your children's development on course as projected. During the postdivorce phase, you can breathe a little easier, now that the worst is over. However, don't let down your guard too far. Your children still need you to finalize the transition to a new life that feels satisfying and full for all family members. Here are a few areas to keep working on:

HOW DO I HANDLE DISCIPLINING MY CHILDREN?

When you and your children are hurting and in transition, the natural temptation is to ease off on your expectations of them, to coddle them just a bit more than usual. Coddling can be healing, but your children also need you to maintain house rules and regulations. This makes them feel safe by sending them the message that hurting does not equate with giving up on what is important. You don't want to give the divorce that much power in your lives. It is important that each parent establish himself or herself as an effective disciplinarian, regardless of who administered discipline before the divorce. Continue to maintain the same expectations as you always have: for household chores, completion of homework before TV, bedtime, and so forth. Explain rules clearly as well as the consequences for breaking rules. When a rule is broken, you must follow through on your stated consequences.

Special circumstances may warrant an occasional exception. If your child is having an especially hard day or week, you may soften your requirements a bit. Perhaps ballet has started up again for Sara, and Dad used to be around to pick her up. Sara is sad as she comes into contact with another small change of a routine that had a big place in her heart. So maybe she can stay up later tonight to cuddle with you. But do not let responsibilities slide on a daily basis.

Many parents find it much harder to enforce discipline after the divorce. They were used to sharing the responsibility, and it helped to have someone else back them up. Also, you are juggling more roles now, and you may be drained by the end of the day. And if your children aren't feeling too worried about you, then, like all children, they are likely to test your resolve to see how these new arrangements are going to affect them.

Research shows that maintaining nurturing but structured parenting provides children with a sense of security that helps them adjust to the divorce. It keeps their relationship to you stronger. And it firmly establishes you as a single parent who can be counted on to know and do what is best for the children, even when it is hard for you. This is especially important for moms and sons, who tend to have a tougher time with each other on the discipline front as the boys get into middle school and older.

Discipline is not the most pleasant part of parenting, but it is one of the keystones. It rises to the forefront in importance during any life transition or milestone, and at this critical juncture your attention must be sharp and your intentions steady. You will reap the rewards for years to come.

Routines

You have put so much energy into unraveling your married life that it may be hard to realize when it's time to put the pieces of your new life together. Establishing new routines is one way of helping your family to move on from the divorce, by creating daily and special patterns that come to feel familiar. On a daily basis, work to save time for doing some small things together with your children. Maybe it is taking a run, or having a hamburger after a sports or music practice, or getting pizza on Friday nights to start off the weekend. Have some special routines as well; the group ice cream party after the dance recital, for example; or the theater performance each child gets to pick for the family to attend when he has an excellent report card.

These routines give children a sense of security and memories of happy family life. They establish predictability after a period of havoc and great change. Such stability is relieving to everyone. Even if you have to cancel or change commitments on occasion, convey to the children that some routines are priorities and will not drop by the wayside.

WHAT ABOUT MY OWN DATING AND SEX LIFE?

Meeting Someone New

Now that you are in the final phases of the divorce, you must turn a greater amount of attention back to yourself. When you are ready to begin meeting new people or dating again, there are a number of ways to go about it. The common complaint: "I can't meet people because I am not the singles' bar type" is no longer a valid excuse. If you want to meet other unattached people, here are some opportunities that could fit into your lifestyle.

If you are active, get involved in a local sport. Many single people join town-sponsored volleyball, golf, tennis, or softball teams. Recreation centers such as the YMCA/YWCA or Jewish Community Centers also sponsor intramural sports. Joining a gym is an excellent way to get into shape and meet single people in a safe environment. Many gyms host events to familiarize members with each other. If sports is not your thing, consider a dancing group. Square dancing, folk dancing, and ballroom dancing have all gained popularity in recent years. Open events are usually listed in the weekend section of local papers.

If you are less actively inclined, consider special events at museums, lectures at a nearby university, openings at art galleries, readings at bookstores, and exhibits at the library to spotlight local talent. Tell friends and colleagues you are interested in meeting new people, and convey your interest in being invited on outings. Meeting a new date through a friend in common is a popular and effective way to socialize.

You may also try the singles groups (e.g., Parents Without Partners, church groups) listed in your local paper each week. Or join a reputable dating service. The biggest drawback to these services is that they can be expensive, so do some research before you join.

The Internet and personal ads also provide numerous opportunities for meeting people from afar. Web sites such as www.cupid.com are devoted to introducing singles to each other, and they have huge followings. If you choose to meet a potential date in person, be careful to meet in a public place away from home, to protect your privacy and safety.

Make your dates fun and minimize the stress that accompanies returning to the world of singles. If the date is low-cost, you will feel less pressure at the end of the night to see each other again. But do something you really want to do.

Margie always went to the orchestra at a nearby college campus on her new dates. The concerts were good, and the price was reasonable. That way if the date was unsuccessful, she always felt that the night was not wasted.

From New Date to New Romantic Interest

When you meet someone who interests you, try to be clear with yourself and the new person what you want, when you want it, and how you would like it. Communicate clearly and verbally about your interest and the degree of intimacy you are ready for at the present time. Be as clear as you can with yourself about whether you want to be hugged or sexually involved, and what such actions connote to you about expectations for intimacy and commitment. One of the painful mistakes people make when dating after divorce is becoming sexually involved because they need reaffirmation about their own attractiveness, and because it may have been a long time since they were sexual. But what one person hopes is the beginning of a long-term relationship may be just an interlude for the other person, who is not ready to be tied down again. One is left feeling rejected and unlovable, and the other feeling like a heel.

Telling and Introducing Your Children

It is always easiest on your children to refrain from introducing new people into their lives until either you have been separated for a substantial amount of time, or better still, when the divorce is concluded and the family has settled into new routines and clear parenting arrangements. When someone is a new friend, introduce him or her as such, and keep their contact with your children casual and friendly. When the relationship is taking a more serious course, tell your children about it in advance. Tell young children that having best friends is important, and just as you have female friends, you also want to have a special male friend (or vice versa). Tell them that you want them to have friends their own age, and you need someone to love who is an adult like you, but that doesn't change or compete with what is unique about your love for them.

For older children, give some more details. You might say that you have found someone you want to be close to, as you were close to Daddy (or Mommy). When the relationship progresses farther, you might tell them that it is someone you think could be very important in all of your lives in the future. Be careful to tell them that it may not work out, that you are still exploring. This will allow them to maintain some defensiveness toward the new relationship, to minimize the pain if it is a relationship that the child cares about and it does not work out in the long run.

Give your children time to ask questions, and to express their concerns. Perhaps a few days or even weeks should go by before you introduce them to your partner. Let their curiosity peak, and let them get some information from you that will help them form their opinions favorably. Most likely, they will worry about whether they will still be Number 1 in your life, and whether they will have to share you with new stepsiblings. They will worry about whether this new person will want them to be a part of everything as you always have, and they want to know that you will be happy and not led astray. It is also likely that they will not like the new person at first, especially if they are feeling protective about your ex-spouse. Allow them time; usually when the relationship is a good one, children come around. If your children do not, ask yourself the hard questions about whether you are viewing this relationship clearly, and whether the timing is optimal, or whether it is just too soon.

Share with your children that you have concerns, too. Talk through which family rituals you will maintain "just you guys" and which will be expanded to include the new partner. If some routines have to be left behind, discuss what those are and the reasons for it. When your children are too young to discuss such matters, show them all this through demonstration. Reassure them about your love and devotion, and be careful not to let important routines or rituals slip by.

How Do I Establish New Family Traditions?

When children recall their fondest memories of growing up, they remember family traditions that were associated with important people and fun times. Whether you are a single parent, or joining two families into one new one, create new family traditions in place of old ones from the divorced family. For example, one New England family began replacing turkey with lobsters on Thanksgiving Day. The family used paper tablecloths instead of china, and they created a big, festive mess in the dining room, all of which the children loved. Another family began spending Christmas Eve in a soup kitchen, since they had little family left with whom to spend time. The experience made all the family members feel good, and they discussed the meaning of Christmas in a way that replaced the previous focus on gifts.

The elements to include in new traditions are threefold: people, values, and an event or day on which the same activities take place each year. How many people is less important than including people important to your new family. The values expressed indicate what your family wants to perpetuate, such as giving to those less fortunate, spending time with extended family, making music with beloved friends, traveling to experience a new place or culture, or learning something new. Sometimes, given parenting schedules, the day upon which these events are celebrated can be shuffled as well. Use this opportunity to forge new, important, and meaningful traditions in your family, irrespective of the calendar date.

Bring new families together to increase your child's sense of family, but be careful to accommodate to your children's needs for the first few years while they are adjusting. Do not wipe away traditions specific to them and you unnecessarily; preserve some of them or incorporate them into your new plans. Do not expect your children to feel comfortable right away in a new home with new family no matter how welcoming. They will need some time to work through old loyalty conflicts, or plain old resistance to change.

Often when divorcing parents create a parenting plan, they decide to alternate holidays each year—e.g., "In year one you take July 4 and I'll take Memorial Day, and next year we'll switch." This gives each parent some time with their children at each holiday, but it is not always the best schedule for children, or for the development of new family traditions. Another suggestion is to keep schedules the same from year to year. Let one parent have every July 4, and the other every Memorial Day. That way your children become familiar with the routines, and they and you can plan to have a particular kind of May and a different kind of July holiday. You, on the other hand, can make other plans for the day you are not with your children, and you can create new traditions that include family, friends, coworkers, or time alone. This continuity gives meaning to each holiday, and takes away the stress of trying to decide how to spend the holiday each year. As children get older and want to include friends or even boyfriends/girlfriends in their plans, it helps to have clear expectations for all important events.

Making Co-parenting Easier

The rules of making co-parenting easier over time echo the rules of thumb that make all co-parenting succeed.

Communicate directly with your ex-spouse. Do not make assumptions or inferences, and do not leave the communication to your children or other third parties. Unless you have found someone (such as a new partner or an in-law) who has the skill to provide a buffer without inflaming either of you, the best way to hear information is directly.

Unless you are friendly with each other, plan your discussions by having an agreed-upon agenda and stick to the subject. Above all, do not digress into blaming about the past.

Keep your expectations realistic. One reason you divorced is to free yourself of the constant disappointments you experienced in the marriage due to different values, lifestyles, or personalities. Do not succumb to fantasies of magical transformations now. Try to know the minimum you need to about your ex's home, life, and daily existence. As your children mature, you will need to negotiate less about the children's routines. Parents often become curious about the other's life, but what they learn makes it difficult to control hurt and resentment. Ask little and know nothing. Your ex-spouse will become a less central figure in your inner life, and your disappointments will be fewer.

Dealing with the Pain of
Sharing Your Children with Your Ex

The relief of not having to deal with your ex-spouse on a regular basis is often replaced by the pain parents feel as they realize what it means to share their children for a lifetime. Like having children in the first place, no amount of information about the realities fully prepares you for the actuality on a day-to-day basis.

Divorce can turn every holiday into a reminder of the division of family ties. Also, there are many events such as parent-teacher conferences, graduation ceremonies, religious celebrations, and children's weddings that over the years force ex-spouses and their families into contact with each other. If your divorce was amicable, these events may not be so emotionally charged, and some parents even choose to spend important family occasions together. But for others, each event is laden with psychological complication. Perhaps you are the wife who must face your ex-husband and his new wife and baby at a family event. Or maybe you are the husband who finds himself sitting next to the brother-in-law who turned against you during the legal process. The best time to deal with these potentially uncomfortable situations is early in the divorce. Conduct your divorce with enough dignity and grace that you are able to be pleasant to each other, and can appear in public together without fearing that your hostilities will override the happy occasion at the center of your meeting. If possible, remain amicable with your ex's family; if they reject you, continue to treat them with distant respect and cordiality.

If you have not succeeded at this, concentrate on your child's desires to have his/her family members be civil to each other, and remind yourself and your ex-spouse that this event is not about either of you. It is about your child, and your feelings are not the important ones. All eyes are not really on you, they are riveted on your child, as they should be. Unless you choose to make the event about both of you, your roles can be relatively minor. To accomplish this, pack up your hurt egos and your anger, and store them at least until the event is over. You and your former mate should stay low-key at the event, and surround yourselves with people by whom you each feel supported. Be cordial and move away from your ex and his/her family, acting polite but as indifferent as you need to feel. Observe your child and focus on how it feels to see her/him smile and laugh, relaxed about the family and concentrating on making this day a positive memory.

Time is a natural healer, and this all will get easier. This is especially true if you work on letting go of your anger and remorse, and stay above trying to make a point for the public to see what you have to bear. Do not be a martyr or an instigator. If you do not rub salt into the wounds on a regular basis, you will find it easier to deal with your ex and to share your children over time. In the end, it is not what you think of your ex as a partner or parent that matters, it is what your children know. Let them have their own experience, though it may differ from yours. And let them make up their own minds, and act accordingly. Trust the children whom you have raised to make the most of both parents and to strive to be different, and a little bit better, than either of you.

WILL I EVER BE FREE OF THE COURT'S REACH?

One of the greatest shocks parents express is their dawning realization that the divorce is finalized, but the court process may not end there. Parents can take each other back to court throughout a child's life to modify child support or parenting plans. If conflict continues, complaints of straying from agreements and motions to enforce previous orders could tie a family up in court for years. The legal system is thus used as a police power—to enforce and protect—but it is not well suited to this role in the area of family law.

One of the most lethal fallouts from a legal dispute over divorce is that it sets the stage to continue such disputes for years to come. Avoid such possibilities at all costs. Better to compromise on some issues now than to negotiate over them for years to come. The financial toll alone is devastating. The emotional toll is equally weighty. Most people who resort to litigious solutions find themselves bitterly disappointed at the end. Their lives become subject to the court's almost continual observation, like fish in a fishbowl. Over time, this results in an erosion of family privacy, sense of decency, and confidence to raise children. The message you give your children is that you are not capable of raising them, and that you must turn to the court to make important decisions. Your children deserve better! Be mindful of the court's long reach, and take steps to finalize your involvement in the legal system as soon as possible.

In addition to conducting the entire divorce with the end point in mind, write into your agreement steps you will take to avoid further legal actions down the road. Agree to discuss any actions before bringing lawyers or the court into the dispute. Furthermore, agree to mediation by a legal or mental health professional in the event of a change in circumstances or more serious disagreement. However you decide to manage future conflicts, the key is to maintain full parental authority and keep control of your own lives. As the parents who love these children best, you are the best equipped to plan their route and steer their course. Even if you do not know the terrain, you do know your destination.

PERSONAL ASSESSMENT

Have I followed through on the paperwork that is necessary to complete my divorce case? Have I established new record keeping procedures that will help me keep track of issues like support payments and asset management? The more organized I am, the less time it will take me to deal with the day-to-day details of our divorce judgment. This gives me more time to pursue the things I'd like to do rather than focusing on the unpleasant past.

Have I set appropriate house rules and boundaries? If I establish a new structure for our household and establish myself as a disciplinarian, I will provide my children with a sense of security that will help them adjust to the divorce.

Have I set up new routines for our household? Have I established new holiday plans? If I create new traditions for our family, both day-to-day and special, I will create lasting memories for my children of the good times we shared together. If I do not have children, setting up my own new routines and holiday traditions is still an integral part of building my new life.

Have I thought out my motivations in dating and meeting new people? Am I really ready to take this step? If I am honest about what I need and want, as well as what I'm capable of giving, I can create new, healthy relationships based on honesty and communication.

Have I considered my children's feelings before I introduce them to a new friend or love interest in my life? Am I considering their needs, or only my own? If I am sensitive to the divided loyalties and confusion my children may feel over the breakup of our marriage, I can better foster a good relationship between them and a new partner in my life.

Have I thought through ways I can make sharing my children with my ex-spouse easier? If we are having problems, am I acting out of my own anger or frustration, or am I putting the needs of my children first? If I am able to put my children's needs above my own and bite my tongue when my ex starts to pick a fight, I can look forward to a time when making decisions with my ex about our children will be easier and less stressful. By refusing to succumb to the temptation to ask my children about my ex-spouse's home life, I can distance myself from my ex and focus on my own new life.

Have I exhausted all possibilities of settlement before I resort to asking the court for help in resolving differences that arise after divorce? If I can work on creating new ways to solve problems, I will free my family of the court's interference in our ability to live our lives the way we choose.

12.

Conclusions: At the Summit

Your divorce is complete and you have begun the final acts of transition from your old identity into your new life. You have reached the top of the summit. It is our hope that as a result of the plans you made with the help from this book, you *are* confident that you 1) made the best decisions you could at the time for yourself and your children; 2) that your decisions were well reasoned and not knee-jerk responses to emotional reactions; 3) that your choices minimized the pain your family felt during the divorce; and 4) that you are headed toward a healthy future. These were the goals of your trip.

The view is clearer now, forward and back, and you probably have a list in your head of ways you behaved that you are proud of, as well as some things you could have done differently, or better. Learning from our mistakes is one of the benefits of travel, or transition, in this case. As you reflect upon the journey and its value, return again to the ten emotional guideposts we listed in Chapter 1. Do you feel most of them accurately describe how you conducted yourself throughout the legal process? Did you use your emotions to gain understanding and inform your choices, rather than be led astray by them? If you are disappointed with some of your responses, and the outcomes that emerged from the divorce process, it is not too late to start engaging your former spouse at a higher level. It is not too late to support your children's right to have two parents from whom they learn about life, for better or worse. It is not too late to reach out to someone from your ex-spouse's family who has been important to you, but with whom you lost touch when the divorce led your two families down different paths.

Most important, take what you learned about yourself during this journey, and utilize it to shore up your strengths and enhance your future. Most people report that a divorce instructs about what's important in life, what you can't live without. If you have children, they are usually at the top of the list. Also, extended family, friends, jobs, and neighborhoods take on a greater value. As you turn to head back down the mountain, glance behind one more time at the summit, and appreciate the view. It may be a long time before you have such clarity again. Remember whence you came and where you are headed. Then journey forth.

APPENDIX

INFORMATION TO PROVIDE TO THE SHERIFF OR REGISTERED PROCESS SERVER FOR SERVICE OF DIVORCE PAPERS

Name of person to be served: _____

Residence of person to be served: _____

Most likely time to find person at home: _____

Home telephone number: _____

Business name & address of person to be served: _____

_____

Business telephone of person to be served: _____

Most likely time to find person at business address: _____

Automobile make: _____ model: _____ year: _____

color: _____ license plate: _____

Physical description of person to be served: _____

_____

Facial hair? _____ glasses? _____ race? _____

Any special service instructions or problems: _____

_____

Your name: _____

Your home telephone: _____

Your work or alternate telephone: _____

Your address: _____

_____

May sheriff leave papers at the abode if the law doesn't require in-hand service?   yes   no

Additional information (owns a gun, dangerous or violent in any way, please call first, etc.):

Photo?

SAMPLE FINAL DIVORCE OR LEGAL SEPARATION AGREEMENT AND EXPLANATION OF PROVISIONS

This agreement is a model for a final divorce or legal separation agreement. Although similar to an interim agreement, as described in Chapter 4, the final agreement typically contains much more detail than is necessary in an interim agreement—i.e., division of tax exemptions, college education expenses, duration of alimony or spousal support, and other issues that are important but may not apply immediately to the parties' circumstances. Interim agreements ordinarily deal only with the immediate needs of the parties, leaving the details to be worked out later.

AGREEMENT

THIS AGREEMENT, made in triplicate original, by and between *(name)*, now of *(address)* (hereinafter called "WIFE"), and *(name)* now of *(address)* (hereinafter called "HUSBAND").

Witnesseth:

WHEREAS, HUSBAND and WIFE, whose maiden name was *(maiden name)*, were intermarried in *(place and date of marriage);*

WHEREAS, HUSBAND and WIFE have *(number of children)* children who are issue of their marriage, to wit:

(name), born on *(date of birth),* and
(next child, etc.)

WHEREAS, in consequence of disputes and irreconcilable differences, the marriage of the parties has broken down irretrievably; and

WHEREAS, the parties desire to enter into an Agreement concerning the alimony, the disposition of property, and other rights and obligations growing out of the marriage relationship.

NOW, THEREFORE, in consideration of the promises, Agreements, and mutual undertakings herein contained and for other good and valuable consideration, the parties covenant and agree with each other as follows:

This alimony section is in two parts: one provides for alimony and the other does not. When alimony is part of your agreement, be sure to specify whether it is modifiable as to the duration of the alimony or the amount. If you wish to place limitations on duration of alimony, for example, that alimony is only modifiable in the event that the receiving party suffers from a physical disability making it impossible to work, then this needs to be written into the agreement specifically.

1. Alimony

Neither party shall claim nor be entitled to alimony from the other, and each hereby specifically waives the same, and each shall forever be barred from claiming alimony from the other.

Or

The WIFE/HUSBAND shall pay to the HUSBAND/WIFE alimony in the amount of $_____ per week. Said amount is/is not modifiable as to term, and is/is not modifiable as to amount.

The following sample is written as the husband paying the wife alimony but it could just as easily be for the wife paying the husband alimony. The point is that in order to limit alimony payments in any way, there must be an agreement and it must be spelled out specifically. The limitations placed on the amount and the length of alimony are two separate negotiation points. You can choose which provisions to make modifiable or nonmodifiable. For example, the amount may be modifiable, but may end after a specified number of years. Or, the amount could be consistent and the length of time it's paid may be left open to modification. In the alternative, you can keep both the amount and length of time alimony is paid subject to the court's modification.

Provisions for Nonmodifiable Alimony

The HUSBAND shall pay to the WIFE as periodic alimony the sum of $_____ by cash or check until the first to occur of the following events: the death of either party, the remarriage or cohabitation of the WIFE, a modification, suspension, reduction, or termination under the provisions of the State Statutes, or _____ years from the date of the entering of a decree of a dissolution of the marriage of the parties.

As to the amount and duration of said alimony payments, the term of the HUSBAND's obligation to pay alimony to the WIFE shall not be modified as to amount or to extend beyond said _____ year period under any circumstance whatsoever, and the court shall not modify the amount or term of payment of alimony except to suspend or terminate it absolutely before the expiration of said _____ year term, and in no event shall the court extend the term beyond said _____ year limitation, even in the event of the disability of the WIFE, medical condition of the WIFE, or any and all other intervening circumstances, foreseen or unforeseen, that may impact the WIFE's ability to provide for herself financially.

2. Child Support and Custody.

This is the section in which you specify whether you will share joint legal custody, or whether one of you will have sole legal custody. Physical custody should also be specified. Usually this is phrased in terms such as: the parties shall share joint legal custody of the minor children, who shall make their primary physical residence with the father/mother.

(a) **Custody.** The parties agree that they shall share joint legal custody of their children. They agree to discuss the children's upbringing, health, education, religious training, and general welfare on a regular basis. Both parents shall have input into the decision-making process on these issues.

Both parents also agree to keep each other informed of the child's activities when the child is with each parent. They agree that they shall share copies of the children's school schedules, special events and activities, back-to-school night, teacher conferences, extracurricular activities, report cards, and the like. Both parents agree to participate in the children's homework and schooling and they agree to work together to facilitate the children's development.

Both parents agree to encourage the children to continue to maintain their relationships with each party's extended family.

In the event that the parties are unable to agree on major issues affecting the children's upbringing, health, education, religious training, and general welfare, they agree to participate in at least three mediation sessions in order to attempt to resolve their differences prior to filing any actions in court to resolve these matters. The mediator shall be selected jointly by the parties. In the event of a dispute over the selection of a mediator, the parties agree to consult the Academy of Family Mediators for a referral. In addition, the parties also agree that in the event that any or all of their children are involved in counseling or therapy, that the children's counselor shall be consulted about the children's best interests with respect to the matter in dispute and that this input shall be shared with the mediator.

The parties agree that they shall share parenting time with the children according to the schedule outlined below, and that the children shall make their primary residence with the mother/father [or: the parties shall share joint physical custody of their children].

Whether it's called parenting access time or visitation, terms of time with the noncustodial parent should be specified. To the extent possible, also include holidays, school vacations, time with grandparents, and how to resolve any disputes that arise.

(b) Visitation.

Local parents, primary physical custody to mother:

The parties agree that the children shall make their primary residence with the mother during the school week. The father shall have uninterrupted time with the children on the second and fourth weekend of each month from Friday after school until Sunday evening at 7:00 P.M. and every Wednesday evening from after school until 8:30 P.M.

In the event the child is too ill to spend time with the father or otherwise unable to visit on a regularly scheduled day (e.g., school field trip, special event with mother's family), makeup time will be scheduled so that the child does not miss time spent with the father.

The parties agree that they will alternate holidays as follows:

Mother in even-numbered years, Father odd-numbered years:
New Year's Eve and New Year's Day until noon
President's Day
Spring Break
Mother's Day (each year with mother)
Independence Day
Columbus Day (if school holiday)
Veteran's Day (if school holiday)
Christmas Eve to Christmas Day at noon
Child's birthday

Father in even-numbered years, Mother in odd-numbered years:
New Year's Day until January 2
Martin Luther King's Birthday
Easter
Father's Day (each year with father)
Memorial Day
Labor Day
Halloween (overnight)
Christmas Day at noon until December 26
Saturday after child's birthday

Holiday visitation shall supersede the usual school-year parenting schedule.

Summer Vacation

Each party shall have three weeks of summer vacation time with the child. These weeks may be scheduled with 30 days' advance notice to the other party, and may be scheduled as 7 to 21 uninterrupted days so that vacations can be planned.

Both parties agree that the child shall have regular telephone contact with the other parent while with the vacationing parent. The vacationing parent shall provide (in writing) the name, address, and phone number for each date on the itinerary for the scheduled vacation time to the other parent at least ten days prior to the scheduled vacation time.

Both parties agree that summer camp is a priority, and both agree to participate in the selection of a camp each year for the child. Camp shall be selected no later than May 31 of each year so that the parties may schedule their respective time with the child around the camp schedule.

Camp and vacation scheduling shall supersede the ordinarily scheduled parenting time that each parent enjoys during the year. The school-year parenting plan shall stay in effect all year except during camp and vacation visits.

Telephone Contact

The parties agree that the child shall have regular telephone contact with the other parent when in either parent's care. Phone calls shall be placed and terminated so as not to interrupt the child's homework and bedtime schedules.

Local parents, shared parenting schedule:

The parties agree that they shall share their time with the children as follows:

Week 1

Children shall be with the mother from Friday after school until Tuesday morning dropoff at school, and with father Tuesday pickup from school until Saturday evening at 4:30 P.M.

Week 2

Children shall be with the mother from Saturday evening at 4:30 P.M. until Thursday morning dropoff at school, and with father Thursday pickup from school until Monday drop off at school.

Week 3

Children shall be with mother from Monday after school until Friday dropoff at school, and with father from Friday after school until Wednesday dropoff at school.

Week 4

Children shall be with mother from Wednesday pickup after school until Monday dropoff at school, and with father from Monday after school until Friday dropoff at school.

Summer Vacation

The parties shall continue the shared parenting schedule, with pickup and dropoff times to be designated by the custodial parent's work schedule on the day he or she has the child. Example: If father has child and parenting time is ending, dropoff time at mother's home is one half hour before father's workday begins. Pickup time for mother is one half hour after her workday is finished. If either or both parents are not working, dropoff time shall be 10:00 A.M.

If the child is in daycare, camp, or other summer activities, the parent who has the child is responsible for transportation to/from daycare, camp, or the activity.

Out-of-town father, primary custody to mother:

1. The father shall have weekend visitation on the first, second, and third weekends of every month. The father shall pick up the children at 7 P.M. on Friday and drop the children off by 7 P.M. on Sunday.

2. The parties shall alternate holidays. In the event that the weekend schedule interferes with the holiday schedule, the parties shall rearrange the weekend schedule so that the party who is to enjoy the holiday with the children shall be able to do so.

3. During the summertime, the father may have visitation on his weekends beginning Thursday evenings at 7:00 P.M. provided he notifies the mother by Monday of that week that he wishes to have the children

that weekend and the mother has not already made plans for the children. The mother agrees that her consent to occasional Thursday additions to the schedule will not be unreasonably withheld.

4. School vacations shall be divided equally between the parties (except summer vacation), but the holiday schedule shall supersede the division of school vacation time—i.e., school vacation visitation shall be arranged around the holiday schedule with each party having the children during half of the school vacation time whenever possible.

5. The father shall have two weeks of vacation time with the children arranged at least thirty days in advance. The weeks may either be continuous (i.e., fourteen days at a stretch) or the father may vacation with the children twice for seven days each.

Child support needs to be specified, typically in terms like: The husband/wife shall pay to the wife/husband child support in the amount of $_____ per week, which amount is in conformance with the guidelines for child support.

(c) **Support.** The father shall pay to the mother child support in the amount of $_____ per week. This amount is in accordance with the State Child Support Guidelines for child support. Support shall be paid via an immediate withholding order for support, and the mother's attorney shall be responsible for preparing the withholding order paperwork.

The parents agree that when the first minor child reaches age eighteen (or the age of majority in your state), that child support shall be reevaluated for the younger children in accordance with the State Child Support Guidelines.

Whoever has the best health insurance through his or her employment should probably be designated as the person who is primarily responsible for keeping the children insured. If there are two policies available, one can act as a backup, or you can keep the children insured on both policies, if that is cost-effective. If you believe that exchange of medical insurance information could become a problem, the court can use a specific court order to direct the insurance company to allow each parent equal access to insurance information and reimbursements.

(d) **Health Insurance.** The HUSBAND shall provide and maintain health insurance for the minor child(ren) as provided through his employment. In the event that the HUSBAND no longer has insurance available to him through employment, and the WIFE has insurance available to her through her employment, then the WIFE shall be responsible for providing and maintaining health insurance for the children as available through her employment.

In the event that neither party has health insurance available through employment, then the parties shall either provide and pay for a private-pay policy, dividing the premiums equally, or they shall divide the child(ren)'s medical bills equally.

The parties shall divide equally the children's uninsured and unreimbursed medical, dental, therapy, orthodontia, and health-related bills. They shall divide equally the children's medical insurance premiums. Both parties agree not to incur an uninsured and unreimbursed cost in excess of $200 without first notifying and receiving consent to the treatment from the other party, except in the event of an emergency. Both parties agree that such consent shall not be unreasonably withheld.

Life insurance provisions are typical and an important part of protection for the children. If you are not already insured, however, check to make sure you are insurable for a reasonable cost before agreeing to maintain coverage. For example, if you are a smoker over age forty-five, coverage may be prohibitively expensive or impossible to acquire. A term policy is the cheapest form of life insurance because you can obtain a higher death benefit for a lower amount of money. Term insurance does not accumulate cash value, however. Like car or homeowners insurance, once the policy period expires, you have to renew your coverage. If you simply let it lapse, and you die after the lapse, it does you no good. That's why it's important to make sure that the policies stay in effect each year.

To keep the policies in force past the age of majority, you must agree in writing to make it enforceable by the court.

(e) Life Insurance. The parties shall each maintain the life insurance (or another policy with an equivalent death benefit) that they currently have in place naming the minor child(ren) as irrevocable beneficiaries until they reach the age of twenty-four years. Each party agrees to mail proof that such insurance is in place to the other party on an annual basis, upon thirty days' written request by the other party.

In the event of death of the WIFE without the agreed and required insurance in effect, the HUSBAND or the child(ren) shall have a preferred debt claim against the estate of the WIFE in the amount equal to the amount of insurance that should have been in full force and effect as well as the reasonable cost, including attorney's fees, of establishing such claim.

In the event of the death of the HUSBAND without the agreed and required insurance in effect, the WIFE or the child(ren) shall have a preferred debt claim against the estate of the HUSBAND in the amount equal to the amount of insurance that should have been in full force and effect as well as the reasonable cost, including attorney's fees, of establishing such claim.

The Federal Kidnapping Prevention Act helps parents locate children who have been "kidnapped" by another parent. You have to specify that it applies in your case, or there may be some question about whether the federal law or state law applies. Including the language of the Act ensures you can apply both.

(f) **Federal Parental Kidnapping Prevention Act Statement.** The parties agree that the Federal Parental Kidnapping Prevention Act (28 USC 1738A) applies in their case and represent as follows:

1. Due notice has been given to all custody claimants;
2. There are no custody proceedings elsewhere previously, or at this time;
3. _____ *(your state)* has jurisdiction over this matter under state law by virtue of the fact that it is the home state of the child(ren), and has historically been the home state of the child(ren);
4. Custody jurisdiction is based upon the conditions set forth in 28 USC 1738A(c)(2) as (your state) is the home state of the child(ren), no other state has current jurisdiction over the child(ren), and it is in the best interests of the child(ren) to assert jurisdiction at this time in *(your state).*

Relocation becomes more of an issue every year, as our society becomes more and more mobile. It's important to address the possibility of relocation even if you're not planning to relocate at this time. Things change and people move on. If you can establish some ground rules from the beginning, you may be able to avoid conflict later.

(g) **Relocation.** The parties agree that if either party wishes to relocate more than thirty miles from his or her present residence that the party wishing to do so shall notify the other party in writing at least ninety days in advance of the planned relocation. Each party agrees to use his or her best efforts to negotiate a reasonable modification of visitations and expenses related to the exercise of his or her individual rights as pertains to the best interests of the child(ren). If an agreement cannot be reached, then the issue shall be submitted to the court for determination.

Unless otherwise specified, the person with whom the children live is the person who is permitted by law to claim the children as exemptions on his or her tax return. For tax planning purposes, it may make sense to give the exemption to the noncustodial parent in exchange for something else, especially if the custodial parent is in a low tax bracket.

Whether the head of household designation may be claimed if the right to claim the children has been waived by the custodial parent has been the source of some controversy recently. Prior IRS Code permitted claiming of head of household even if you'd waived the right to claim a child who lives with you. Recent changes have mandated that the person claiming as head of household must claim at least one child to qualify for head of household. For example, if you have two children, you could each claim one child and the residential parent would still qualify for the head of household tax designation.

Head of household designation for tax purposes places you in a lower tax bracket than "single" or "married filing separately" and so it is worthwhile to claim as head of household if you qualify by law.

Because tax law can change with the wind, consult your tax advisor prior to claiming head of household on your taxes.

(h) **Tax Exemption.** The parties agree that they shall each claim one exemption on their respective taxes for each of their two minor children. The father shall be entitled to claim the younger child, and the mother shall be entitled to claim the older child. The mother shall be entitled to claim as "head of household" for IRS purposes under the current custodial arrangements.

—or—

The parties agree that they shall alternate claiming the exemption for the minor child on their tax returns, with the mother claiming the child in the even-numbered years and the father claiming the child in the odd-numbered years. The father shall be entitled to claim as "head of household" for IRS purposes under the current custodial arrangements.

Courts cannot provide for support of children who are over the age of majority in that state. Some states use eighteen, some use age twenty-one. If you intend to make provisions for financial contributions to your children's college educations part of your agreement, you need to specify how much each of you will be required to provide, which expenses it will cover, and whether there are any limitations as to how much both of you will contribute. A typical provision might limit the maximum amount that each parent contributes as 50 percent of the cost of room, board, tuition, and books at a good state college, for the year your children are expected to enter college.

You may also want to designate the same amount of financial assistance to your children if they wish to pursue technical career training instead of high school. You may also wish to limit the time during which you are obligated to pay, i.e., "This provision terminates when the child reaches his/her twenty-fourth birthday."

(i) College Education. The parties agreed that they shall share the minor children's college or post–high school educational expenses for room, board, tuition, books, $100 per month spending money, and any airline transportation equally (or 60/40, or 70/30, or one parent pays all). The parties agree that this amount is limited to the estimated expenses for room, board, tuition, and books at [name college here, often a local state university] for each year that each child will be attending college. The parties also agree that these expenses are in addition to any child support that may be due.

The parties' obligation to pay these expenses shall terminate for each of the minor children: at the age of twenty-four years, after graduation from college or a post–high school educational program, or in the event the child stops attending college or the chosen post–high school educational program for more than two semesters consecutively, whichever event is first to occur.

Be specific about how the real estate, if any, is to be split, who is responsible for mortgage payments, whether the house needs to be refinanced, and move-out dates.

If there are provisions for sale, be specific as to how price reductions will be negotiated, and counteroffers by prospective buyers will be handled.

3. REAL PROPERTY

The (HUSBAND/WIFE) shall be responsible to pay for the mortgage, taxes, insurance, utilities, upkeep, maintenance, and any and all other expenses associated with (his/her) ownership of the home. The (HUSBAND/WIFE) agrees to indemnify and hold the other party harmless with respect to payment of these obligations.

—or—

The parties agree that the home shall be sold as soon as possible. They will cooperate in securing a listing agreement through a mutually acceptable Realtor. In the event the parties are unable to select a Realtor, they shall each select a Realtor, and the two Realtors selected by the parties shall recommend one Realtor to represent them for the sale. The parties agree to abide by the Realtor's recommendations for a listing price, and both agree to accept any price that comes within 5 percent of the asking price. Price reductions, if necessary, shall be negotiated by agreement.

In the event that the home cannot be sold for what the parties agree is a reasonable price, either party may purchase the home from the other at 95 percent of the then-current asking price. The party purchasing the home shall secure financing in his or her own name solely. Net equity shall be calculated as: asking price less 5 percent minus any mortgages, taxes, liens, closing costs, and ordinary costs of sale, including attorney's fees for the seller. The party seeking to buy the home shall pay the outstanding mortgages, taxes, liens, closing costs, and ordinary costs of sale, including attorney's fees, as well as 50 percent of the net equity to the other party.

The parties agree that the court may maintain jurisdiction over the provisions for the sale of the home in the event that the parties are unable to sell the home within a reasonable time, if they are unable to agree on an acceptable reduction in the listing price, or any other issues with respect to the sale of the home.

—or—

The parties agree that the husband/wife shall have sole right, title and interest in and to the home located at _____. He/she shall attempt to refinance the mortgage(s) into his or her own name solely, but in the event that he/she is unable to do so after making three reasonable, good-faith attempts, the refinance provision will no longer be required. In the event of a failure to refinance the home, the husband/wife shall be responsible for the mortgage, taxes, insurance, and any and all other expenses associated with the home and shall indemnify and hold the [other party] harmless on these expenses.

The parties agree that the net equity in the property shall be calculated by hiring an MAI certified appraiser to appraise the home, and that the appraiser's valuation shall be considered to be the value of the home. From the value of the home, the parties shall subtract the balance of any mortgages, taxes, or liens on the home, as well as the husband/wife's refinancing fees and closing costs for the refinancing loan to determine the net equity. The husband/wife shall pay the [other party] 50 percent of the net equity (choose one or determine your own time frame: at the time of the refinance, within ____ years, when child graduates from high school, etc.).

If a repayment time is chosen that is later than the time of the refinance— e.g., in five years—you may wish to have the "selling" party's interests secured on the land records with a mortgage or other notice of lien.

If pension assets are involved, make sure that your rights are secured. If the pensions are being split, this is typically done via Qualified Domestic Relations Order, a special type of court order your lawyer can prepare. Even if you do your divorce yourself, you should probably have a lawyer draft the QDRO. Oftentimes, companies will provide sample QDROs that you can use as a guide if you are determined to do it yourself.

Pensions and 401ks are often the largest assets that a couple owns. Don't forget to include them as part of your negotiations.

4. PENSION

The parties agree that each shall retain his or her own pension and IRA accounts, and each waives any right, title, and interest he or she may have in the other's pension or IRA accounts.

—or—

The parties agree that the wife shall receive 50 percent of the husband's defined benefit pension through [company of employment] valued as of the date of the divorce. The wife's interest in said defined benefit pension shall be secured by a Qualified Domestic Relations Order. The wife's attorney shall be responsible for preparation of the QDRO, and the court shall retain jurisdiction over this provision of the agreement in order to effectuate the QDRO's processing.

The husband shall receive 50 percent of the wife's 401k plan through [company of employment]. The husband's interest in the 401k plan shall be secured by a Qualified Domestic Relations Order. The husband's attorney shall be responsible for preparation of the QDRO, and the court shall retain jurisdiction over this provision of the agreement in order to effectuate the QDRO's processing.

Include a specific schedule of who gets what if you are concerned that the division of personal property will not go smoothly on the "honor system" set forth in the provision below.

5. DIVISION OF PERSONAL PROPERTY

(a) **Household Items.** The parties have divided between them, to their mutual satisfaction, the personal effects, household furniture and furnishings, and other articles of personal property that have heretofore been used by them in common, except as otherwise expressly provided herein.

—or—

The parties agree that the wife shall keep the living room, bedroom, and dining room furniture and the contents of those rooms, as well as her personal effects, half of the kitchen items, and the hutch given to her by her grandmother. The husband shall keep the washer and dryer, family room furniture and contents, large-screen color TV, and Nintendo, as well as his personal effects and half of the kitchen items.

(b) **Automobiles.** The HUSBAND shall have sole ownership and title to the _____ automobile. The WIFE shall execute any papers necessary to transfer ownership and registration of said vehicle to the HUSBAND within ten (10) days of executing this agreement. All outstanding payments due on said automobile, if any, shall be the sole obligation of the HUS-BAND, and the HUSBAND hereby agrees to indemnify and hold the WIFE free and harmless from any payment of any amounts due on said automobile and any liabilities stemming from his ownership of the vehicle. If the WIFE shall be required for any reason to make any payment concerning the vehicle, the HUSBAND shall indemnify the WIFE forthwith.

The WIFE shall have sole right, title and interest in and to the _____ automobile. The HUSBAND shall execute any papers necessary to transfer ownership and registration of said vehicle to the WIFE within ten (10) days of executing this agreement. All outstanding payments due on said automobile, if any, shall be the sole obligation of the WIFE, and the WIFE hereby agrees to indemnify and hold the HUSBAND free and harmless from any payment of any amounts due on said automobile and from any liability arising from her ownership of the vehicle. If the HUSBAND shall be required for any reason to make any payment concerning the vehicle, the WIFE shall indemnify the HUSBAND forthwith.

If you are making specific provisions for division of bank accounts, include account numbers and approximate balances as to who gets what so there is no confusion. If you have already divided your accounts, you can simply reflect the up-to-date balances on the financial statement you provide to the court as part of your final divorce.

(c) **Bank Accounts.** The parties agree they have divided their bank accounts and other cash assets except as otherwise specifically provided herein.

6. PAYMENT AND LIABILITY FOR DEBTS

(a) **Responsibility for Payment.** The WIFE shall be responsible for all debts listed on her financial affidavit, and shall indemnify and hold the HUSBAND harmless thereon. The HUSBAND shall be responsible for all debts listed on his financial affidavit, and shall indemnify and hold the WIFE harmless thereon.

The parties agree and covenant that they shall pay any and all debts that they incur, that each shall not look to the other party, nor will the other party be responsible for any such debts or obligations of any nature whatsoever from this date forward.

Filing for bankruptcy erases most of your debts, with alimony, child support, some taxes, and all student loans being the most notable exceptions. If you and your spouse are jointly responsible for credit card debts and one of you agrees to pay for all of the joint debt, if that person files for bankruptcy, the other person could end up having to pay that debt—even though the court order specifically said that the bankrupt spouse was supposed to pay it. Therefore, if bankruptcy is a possible concern, be sure that you classify any joint debts taken on by your spouse as "in the nature of alimony and support" so that they won't be dischargeable in bankruptcy, leaving you on the hook.

(b) Bankruptcy. The parties agree that they intend that the specific debts and liabilities assumed by each herein shall be nondischargeable under 523(a) (5) of the Bankruptcy Code, and that each party shall make the payments required under this Agreement and hold the other harmless for payment thereof. The obligations assumed herein are necessary for the parties' support. They are in the nature of alimony and support.

(c) Tax Matters. For certain calendar years, the parties have filed or will file joint federal tax returns. Additionally, the parties may have filed joint state tax returns.

In the event of any review or audit by the Internal Revenue Service, the Department of Revenue Services, or other governmental agency of any such joint return, each party shall cooperate with the other and his or her agents with such review or audit and shall furnish whatever information and documents, including but not limited to amended returns, as are reasonably requested of him or her by the other or his or her agents.

In any such review or audit of any such joint return of the parties:

(i) The WIFE shall be fully and solely liable and responsible for any taxes, assessments, penalties, and interest (collectively "liability") attributed to the WIFE's income and deductions, which may be assessed against the HUSBAND and WIFE. The HUSBAND shall be fully and solely liable and responsible for any other taxes, assessments, penalties, and interest (collectively "liability") that may be assessed against the HUSBAND's income and deductions.

(ii) The WIFE shall pay for the defense of any claim of liability attributed to the WIFE's income and deductions. The HUSBAND shall pay for the defense of any claim of liability attributed to the HUSBAND's income and deductions.

Make sure that your agreement is full and final settlement of all claims between you. Once this litigation is finished, you should be as separate as possible. An example of an action that can be brought after a divorce unless a Mutual Release clause is included is for damages caused by injuries incurred in a domestic violence assault. Be sure you mutually understand that the divorce agreement settles everything and that something doesn't come back to haunt you later.

7. MUTUAL RELEASE

Subject to the provisions of this Agreement, each party has released and discharged and by these presents does for himself or herself, and his or her heirs, legal representatives, executors, administrators, and assigns, release and discharge the other from any and all causes of action, claims, rights, or demands whatsoever, in law or equity, which either of the parties had or now has against the other, except any or all cause or causes of action for dissolution of the marriage.

8. ATTORNEY'S FEES

The HUSBAND and WIFE agree to assume responsibility for his or her own attorney's fees in full and for any attorney's fees with respect to this Agreement.

Although in most states estate rights are automatically relinquished as part of the divorce, you don't want to take any chances that your estate is encumbered by a former spouse making a claim. The divorce does not affect your children's rights of inheritance from you.

9. RELEASE OF RIGHTS IN EACH OTHER'S ESTATE

Neither party has any right to share in the estate of the other or to be appointed executor or administrator of the other's estate. This is a mutual waiver of each party's rights to receive his or her statutory share of the other's estate.

This next provision ensures that there will be no claim of side agreements after the divorce.

10. ENTIRE AGREEMENT

This Agreement constitutes the entire understanding of the parties. There are no representations or warranties other than those expressly herein set forth. Neither party shall request of any court hearing an action for a divorce or a dissolution of the marriage between the parties any greater or different rights or dispositions than provided herein. This Agreement shall be considered as a final and full settlement between the parties and considered as such.

In the event that your spouse moves out of state, you'll want to make sure that your agreement is interpreted under the laws of your state, not your spouse's new state.

11. LAW OF *(YOUR JURISDICTION)* TO GOVERN

It is understood and agreed that this Agreement is entered into under the laws of the state of *(your state)*, and in construction of execution of the same, wherever and whenever undertaken, the laws of the state of *(your state)* shall be deemed to apply and prevail.

If additional documents need to be signed after the divorce, then both of you agree to cooperate. Typical additional documents are car titles, deeds, insurance forms, and waivers of death benefits on pensions.

12. EXECUTION OF ADDITIONAL DOCUMENTS

Each party shall sign and deliver to the other any additional writings or documents that may be necessary to enforce or carry out the purposes of this Agreement.

Providing that all modifications must be in writing assures you that your spouse can't try to claim that you agreed to something that wasn't put in writing.

13. MODIFICATION

A modification of any of the provisions of this Agreement shall be effective if made in writing and executed with the same formality of this Agreement.

As part of the court proceedings you'll both submit financial statements as to your assets, liabilities, and earnings as of the date of your divorce. This provision protects you in the event you find out your spouse was not truthful on his or her affidavit, and you need to reopen your case later.

14. FINANCIAL AFFIDAVITS

The parties represent that they have each made a full and complete disclosure to each other as evidenced by the financial affidavits attached hereto or filed with this Agreement. It is expressly understood that the terms of this Agreement and the financial negotiations and arrangements contained herein were made upon the representations made in those affidavits. It is further understood and agreed that the parties hereto relied upon said representations in executing this Agreement.

The parties further represent that no undisclosed substantial change of circumstances has occurred in his or her respective financial condition since the signing of the financial affidavits.

Each party has accurately advised the other as to his or her respective income, assets, liabilities, property, and estate to the satisfaction of the other party. Each party agrees that he/she has had the opportunity to review, among other things, the financial affidavits exchanged between the parties.

You want to be certain that both of you acknowledge that you've both been involved in the negotiations and that you've signed the Agreement without coercion, duress, or undue influence.

15. VOLUNTARY EXECUTION

Alternative paragraphs
(Both parties represented by attorney)

The *(client)* is represented by *(lawyer)* and the spouse is represented by *(lawyer)*. Both parties agree that the provisions of this Agreement and their legal effect are fully understood by each of them, that each party acknowledges the Agreement is fair and equitable, that it is being entered into voluntarily and that it is not the result of any force, duress, or undue influence.

—or—

(one party represented by attorney, other party pro se)

It is clearly understood by the WIFE and the HUSBAND that the Law Firm of *(lawyer)* is representing the *(client)* interest in preparation of this Agreement and any further proceedings regarding a dissolution of the marriage relationship. The *(spouse)* has been specifically advised to retain independent counsel but has expressly chosen not to do so. He/she has, however, been involved in the negotiation of this Agreement and is satisfied with the same. He/she has fully read the Agreement and understands its provisions and is signing it as his/her voluntary act and deed.

For all agreements: Both parties agree that the provisions of this Agreement and their legal effect are fully understood by each of them, that each party acknowledges that the Agreement is fair and equitable, and that it is being entered into voluntarily and that it is not the result of any force, duress, or undue influence.

IN WITNESS WHEREOF, the parties have set their hands and seals in triplicate originals of this Agreement, each of which constitutes an original, this *(date)*

WIFE _____

HUSBAND _____

(Agreement should be notarized)

ASSET AND LIABILITY CHECKLIST

Use this checklist to make sure you've accounted for all of your assets, both in your financial disclosures and in assessing your fair share of any settlement.

ASSETS

Personal property

❏   Furniture

❏   Antiques/heirlooms/artworks/collections

❏   China, silver, crystal

❏   Jewelry, furs

❏   Stereo equipment

❏   Pets

❏   Sporting equipment

❏   Vehicles

  • Automobiles (Who holds title? You, your spouse, or jointly?)

  • Trucks

  • Motorcycles, recreational vehicles, planes, snowmobiles

❏   Stocks and stock options, bonds, mutual funds

❏   Money owed to you or your spouse

❏   Cash and bank accounts, CDs

❏   Life insurance (cash surrender value)

❏   Retirement plans

  • IRA

  • 401k plan

  • Defined benefit plan

  • Annuity

  • Keogh plan

❏   Real estate

  • Residence

  • Rental property (owned by either spouse)

  • Vacant land

  • Vacation property

  • Other (time share, etc.)

❏   Business interests

  • Interest in a closely held corporation

  • Partnership interest

❏   Anticipated tax refund

❏   Other assets, such as

  • Tax-sheltered investments

- Pending lawsuits
- Patents, trademarks, copyrights

LIABILITIES

Be sure to account for payment of all liabilities in your settlement agreement, and be sure to include any payments you must make into your budget planning.

- ❏ Mortgage on residence, 2nd mortgages
- ❏ Mortgage on other real estate
- ❏ Loans
- ❏ Loans from
  - Retirement plan
  - Insurance policy
  - Relative or friend
- ❏ Medical/dental bills
- ❏ Credit card accounts
- ❏ Tax liabilities

EXPENSE INVENTORY

Be sure you've accurately portrayed your expenses both in your court-required financial disclosures and in your personal budget calculations.

- ❏ Home mortgage payments (specify whether the amount includes taxes and homeowners insurance)
- ❏ Second mortgage and/or home equity loan
- ❏ Real property insurance (if not included above)
- ❏ Real property taxes (if not included above)
- ❏ Homeowner's association fees/condo fees
- ❏ Home maintenance costs
- ❏ Rent
- ❏ Renter's insurance
- ❏ Food, restaurant meals, and household supplies
- ❏ Utilities
- ❏ Dry cleaning
- ❏ Clothing
- ❏ Uninsured medical and dental fees, and prescription costs
- ❏ Insurance premiums

- Life
- Disability
- Medical and dental
❑ Child care expenses
   - Day care costs, nursery school
   - Baby-sitter costs
   - Camp
❑ Visitation expenses
   - Long distance telephone calls
   - Transportation
   - Entertainment
   - Meals
   - Other
❑ Support payments required by prior divorce
❑ School expenses for yourself and/or children
   - Tuition
   - Books and supplies
   - Transportation, parking
   - Dormitory
   - Lab fees and activity fees
   - Meals
   - Field trips
   - Uniforms
   - Other
❑ Entertainment
❑ Children's summer activities
❑ Children's lessons
   - Dance, music, sports, etc.
   - Religious school
❑ Children's allowances
❑ Children's tutoring, club dues
❑ Automobile
   - Gas
   - Maintenance and repairs
   - Insurance
❑ Gifts

- ❑ Incidentals
    - Pocket money
    - Grooming
    - Newspapers, magazines, books
- ❑ Pet care, vet
- ❑ Vacations
- ❑ Other expenses

SAMPLE DEPOSITION QUESTIONS

What is your legal name?

Where are you living now?

How old are you?

What is your date of birth?

How is your health?

How is your spouse's health?

Has your health always been good?

Have you ever had any health problems that required hospitalization? When? For what?

Were you ever married previously? Cause of breakdown?

Do you have any children? Are you required to support them? Where do they live?

Did you bring any assets to the marriage? Did you bring any debt? Did your spouse?

How old were you when you got married? Started living together?

What is your educational background? Have you furthered your education since you got married?

How far did you go in school? When and where?

What job did you hold when you got out of school?

What has been your work history?

What has been your history at your job? What has been your history of salary, job title, and promotions? What do you intend to do now that you've been laid off? (Have you collected unemployment? How much?)

Would you say you contributed to your marriage in a nonfinancial way? How? Did your spouse (e.g., work on the house)?

Did anyone in your family contribute either money or in a nonfinancial way to your marriage? To your property? What kinds of contributions did they make? When? How much?

Where did the money come from to buy your home? Who paid the closing costs and real estate commissions? When was that? Do you want to take possession of the home and live there now? Why not?

Have you received during the course of your marriage any funds or any gifts from your parents or siblings or other relatives or friends? Loans? Gifts?

During the course of your marriage have you received any other gifts from any other individual? For any reason? Other men? Other women? Loans? What kinds of things?

Have you given any gifts worth over $50 to anyone who is not a blood relation to you? Bought anything for anyone?

Do you have any bank accounts with anyone besides your spouse? What bank? What are the circumstances?

During your marriage, have you gone on any trips not involving work with a man (other than your husband), or a woman? Where? When? With whom? Under what circumstances?

Have you gone on any business trips since the date of your marriage? What purpose? Where, how long? Did anyone accompany you?

Why do you feel your marriage broke down? Was your spouse a good wife/husband? Was she/he supportive? What were the problems? How did they arise?

How would you describe your spouse? Did she/he do anything to contribute to the breakdown of the marriage?

How do you feel you contributed to the breakdown of your marriage?

Were you ever unfaithful to your spouse? Did you ever have a sexual relationship with a man or woman other than your husband/wife since the date of your marriage?

How long have you known him or her? How did you meet? Under what circumstances? How did your relationship develop? When did it become more serious? Why?

Did you ever have any other relationships with other men or women during your marriage? Prior to your marriage but during the time you were living together?

Were you ever untruthful to your spouse about your whereabouts?

Relationship with men/women?

Have you ever had an affair with a coworker? Neighbor?

Have you had a sexually transmitted disease since the date of your marriage? Since living with your husband/wife?

Do you feel your husband or wife contributed to the breakdown of your marriage? How? How would you describe your spouse?

Why did you allege that he or she had been intolerably cruel to you as a basis for your divorce cross-complaint?

Has your spouse, to your knowledge, had an affair with another man or woman since the date of your marriage? Who, what, where, when, and how did you find out about it?

Did you ever go to marriage counseling? When? With whom? For how long, and what was the result? Did you ever suggest counseling?

Did your spouse suggest counseling? Why didn't you go?

Were there any incidents of violence during the course of your marriage? Perpetrated by whom? Under what circumstances? When? Did your spouse ever hit you?

While you were living together as husband and wife, how was money handled and how were the family bills paid? Who paid the mortgage, who kept the money, where did each person's paycheck go? Did you maintain joint finances, separate finances, or both? How were things allocated?

Who do you intend to call as a witness in your behalf in the event of a trial? Against your spouse?

What is your current employment? What is your current salary? Are you ever eligible for overtime work? How is eligibility determined? What portion of overtime is discretionary? Do you ever refuse overtime?

Do you have a retirement plan? Do you have to make contributions to it? How does it work? How much is it worth? How do you collect? When do you collect? Are there ever other times you can collect, under other circumstances? When you do collect, how much will you get? Is this in addition to Social Security?

Do you have any bank accounts now? Where is each account, and how much is in each? Are they joint or sole?

Have you sold any assets or disposed of any assets since this divorce action began?

Have you paid any monies toward anyone's support other than your own or your spouse's or child's since you were married? Paid anyone's rent, utilities, credit card bills, bought groceries, etc.? Whose? Who have you given money to, and for what?

Do you drink alcoholic beverages or take nonprescription drugs? How much? How frequently?

Have you ever been under any kind of psychiatric treatment? When, where, how much, who paid, what diagnosis?

Since the date of your marriage, would you say that you or your spouse has contributed more financially to the marriage? In what way? What about nonfinancial contributions? What types of things?

Have you been in any kind of accident since the date of your marriage? Do you have any lawsuits pending of any kind?

RESOURCES

USEFUL LEGAL WEB SITES

Legal Self-Help and Research

The premier self-help law site is run by Nolo Press, *http://www.nolo.com,* a company dedicated for the past thirty years to helping individuals navigate the sometimes murky waters of the law. At the Nolo site, you can find do-it-yourself books and forms kits for things such as divorce and estate planning, and in addition, it's a comprehensive, informative site on many divorce-related topics. Nolo Press is known for its accuracy, and its products are typically very trustworthy.

A huge database of legal topics to help with your research can be found at Cornell Law School's great legal research site, found at http://www.law.cornell.edu. For a direct link to the law of each of the 50 states, check out http://www.secure.law.cornell.edu/topics/Table_Divorce.htm.

A comprehensive site with links to attorney and legal-research-oriented topics can be found at http://www.alllaw.com. Another site at http://www.findlaw.com is a comprehensive online library of legal resources dedicated to making legal information on the Internet easy to find.

Check out your lawyer at http://www.lawyers.com, a site sponsored by Martindale Hubbell, the nation's leading directory of lawyers. Attorneys are listed by specialty and geographic area, among other choices. Because Martindale is a paid subscription service, however, many smaller firms aren't listed. LawInfo.com at http://www.lawinfo.com offers referral lists of lawyers, private investigators, and other law-related professionals as well as a law dictionary, online bookstore, message boards, and legal links.

vORCE INFORMATION WEB SITES

ites to join discussion groups, find out general information
nd read articles of interest.

http://www.vix.com/crc is the site for the Children's Rights Council, a
nonprofit organization dedicated to assuring that both parents have continuing contact with their children after divorce. It features articles, research,
links, and contact information for local chapters.

http://www.divorcecentral.com includes links to divorce laws of each
state and a searchable databank of divorce professionals.

http://www.divorcecare.com features a searchable database of divorce
support groups.

http://www.divorceinfo.com is a clearinghouse for a wealth of divorce
information, including articles and research.

http://www.helphorizons.com offers numerous psychology-related articles on divorce.

American Academy of Matrimonial Lawyers: http://www.aaml.org.

Divorce Source: http://www.divorcesource.com includes calendars for
divorce planning, people locators, financial calculators, each state's laws,
and discussion groups.

Because the Internet changes daily, consider typing in key divorce
words such as "divorce mediation," "child custody," "child support" along
with the name of your state to get state-specific information.

DOMESTIC VIOLENCE WEB SITES

The American Bar Association Commission on Domestic Violence
has developed two brochures on developing a safety plan, one for adults, and
one for children. Copies are available from http://www.abanet.org/domviol.

WEB SITES FEATURING ASSET SEARCHES

Many asset searches charge a fee for their services. Be sure to inquire
about the fees prior to utilizing such services. Because online businesses are
difficult to monitor, be very wary. Neither the authors nor the publisher of
Your Divorce Advisor endorse or encourage the use of such services, except
for those offered by Lexis and Westlaw. If you decide to use a service and
would like to provide feedback (positive or negative), we'd love to include it

on our Web site. If you have other suggestions for sites you've used, we'd love to hear them. E-mail us at info@yourdivorceadvisor.com.

PUBLIC RECORDS DATABASES

Public records database search: http://www.choicepoint.com and http://www.knowx.com charges pay-as-you-go; http://www.1800ussearch. com offers a background-oriented public records search (such as where someone's lived, and whether they lived with someone else) for $20–$40.

Criminal Records database search: http://www.crimcheck.com costs $25–$45.

You can also try public records database, asset, and people searches through Lexis and Westlaw and a number of other sites, including http://www.firstinc.com/freesearches.htm, http://www.specinvsvc.com, http://www.recordsbureau.com. WebGator Investigative Resources, at http://www.inil.com/users/dguss/wgator.htm, is an exhaustive site with links to such personal information as obituaries, court records, state parole and prison information, unclaimed property, and vital records, to name a few.

Source Resources is an online investigation services, which, for a fee, will find out almost anything, on almost anyone, including sending an investigator in person to check land records or court documents. You can find Source Resources at http://www.sourceresources.com.

FINDING PEOPLE

You can find the name and address of the person behind the phone number with online reverse telephone directories, including http://www. infospace.com/info/reverse.htm and http://www.reversephonedirectory. com.

The United States Post Office offers a zip code directory which works well for finding a specific address from partial information. You can access the service at http://www.framed.usps.com/ncsc/lookups/lookup_zip+4. html.

Government Information

Social Security Administration: http://www.ssa.gov. You can use this site to check your and your spouse's Social Security benefits and estimate your retirement income.

IRS Address and Internet Address: http://www.irs.ustreas.gov/prod/ cover.html is a humorous interactive IRS magazine-style site with articles, statistics, IRS forms, and publications. Be sure and download IRS Publication 504 on information for divorced individuals.

CHILDREN'S ISSUES AND CUSTODY SITE

Custody Planning

Create your own calendar with http://www.myevents.com, an Internet calendar which you can create and use online. It's easy to navigate and includes lots of graphics, which makes it fun to share with your kids. Printouts make it easy to keep everyone's schedule straight.

You may also wish to check out the Children's Rights Council, dedicated to maintaining parental contact between divorced parents and their children at http://www.vix.com/crc.

Life Insurance

Find reasonable life insurance quotes through http://www.insureclick. com, http://www.intelliquote.com, or http://www.quotesmith.com.

Unravel the mystery of different types of life insurance products available at http://www.insure.com and http://www.insweb.com.

College Planning

Help your child shop for schools at http://www.review.com, sponsored by Princeton Review, the test prep company. Kaplan also has a decent site at http://www.kaplan.com.

Organize your children's college applications through http://www. collegequest.com and register for SAT's at College Boards On-Line at http://www.collegeboard.com.

Comprehensive financial aid information can be found at http://www. finaid.org. This site also includes tips for maximizing your eligibility, financial calculators, and loan comparisons.

If the financial aid numbers are too daunting, investigate scholarships at http://www.fastweb.com.

How much must you put aside now for your children's college education? Financial calculators can help you calculate this in a matter of minutes. Below are several of the best and most comprehensive financial calculator sites.

HELPFUL FINANCIAL PLANNING SITES
Financial Calculators

How much will your savings be worth in 10 years? How much must you put aside now for your children's college education? How can you figure out a budget? How long will it take to pay off your debt? Financial calculators can help you figure out all this in a matter of minutes. Below are several of the best and most comprehensive financial calculator sites:

http://www.financenter.com
http://www.money.com even includes a relocation calculator
http://www.moneycentral.com
http://www.quicken.com
http://www.smartmoney.com

Taxes, taxes, taxes

Start with the source itself: the Internal Revenue Service. The IRS has a surprisingly easy-to-use and straightforward site. You can download forms, search advice sections, and even e-mail questions at http://irs.ustreas.gov.

Other useful tax planning and tip sites include http://www.taxcut.com, http://www.turbotax.com/taxcenter, and http://www.willyancey.com.

Online Loans and Banking:

Find just about every personal finance topic on http://www.bankrate.com, from car loans, credit cards, mortgages, and money market funds.

Check out the best rate for mortgages in all 50 states at http://www.bestrate.com.

Apply for mortgages online at http://www.e-loan.com and http://www.quickenmortgage.com.

Quicken.com can even link you to a great real estate search site, http://www.realtor.com when you're ready for that new house or condo purchase.

Citibank's online bank is full service, from online banking to loans and financial calculators. Find it at http://www.citibank.com.

Financial Planning

Decipher financial terms and learn the basics of financial planning at http://www.personalwealth.com, http://www.ivillagemoneylife.com.

Basic financial planning starts at http://www.moneycentral.msn.com, Microsoft's financial planning site.

Learn the basics of investing at http://www.investoreducation.org.

IRA's

Find the pros and cons of Roth IRA's at http://www.rothira.com.

Estate Planning

Your divorce will make your wills obsolete. Make a new estate plan as soon as you're able.

Get a referral to a qualified estate planning lawyer at http://www.actec. org, the official Web site of the American College of Trust and Estate Counsel. Double check your pick at http://www.lawyers.com to see if she or he is listed with Martindale Hubbell, the leading publisher of legal directories. Lawyers are listed by geographical area and specialty.

Prepare for your appointment with the estate planner by using the forms and tips on http://www.rushforth.org/planning.

Don't forget Nolo Press's do-it-yourself estate planning kits and information, available at http://www.nolo.com.

California Estate Planning information can be found at http://www. castlelaw.com, a site sponsored by a major California estate planning firm.

ASSET VALUATION SITES

By using these Web sites, you can start to prepare your financial disclosure statements.

Automobiles

The Kelly Blue Book is the standard source for valuing automobiles, and the site is easy to use. Find it at http://www.kbb.com.

Stocks and Other Investments:

You can use these sites to keep track of your investments, and to get up-to-the-minute values on your stocks and mutual funds:

http://www.excite.com provides easy access to stocks and investments, and permits you to personalize a portfolio online.

http://www.investor.msn.com is a comprehensive money management site focused on stocks and investments.

Top sites for stockbrokers and online trading can be found at: http://www.schwab.com, http://www.dljdirect.com, http://www.e-trade.com and http://www.discoverbrokerage.com and Value Line, one of the top companies devoted to stock analysis, at http://www.valueline.com. Find bond information at http://www.investinginbonds.com. You can use these sites to estimate the current values of your stocks, bonds, and mutual funds. Use the history features to decide which are worth keeping, which are worth giving up, and which need to be sold.

For tracking and selecting mutual funds, try http://www.morningstar.com, the ratings people, http://www.fundsinteractive.com, and http://www.forbes.com/funds. To know when to sell, try Fund Alarm, at http://www.fundalarm.com.

Real Estate Sites

Online sites may be helpful in determining an estimate of your house's value, but always seek out a qualified appraiser before you make any final decisions about your divorce.

Get a ballpark value of your home at http://www.owners.com.

Find that new house at http://www.homescout.com, http://www.coldwellbanker.com or http://www.realtor.com, and figure out how to buy it with help from Nolo Press's site by searching "buying a house" at http://www.nolo.com. Check out the neighborhood at http://www.homeadvisor.com.

Arrange your move and notify the post office and your magazine subscriptions of your new address with http://www.movecentral.com.

CREDIT REPORTS
Experian, NCAC
P.O. Box 2106
Allen, TX 75013-2106
1-888-397-3742
http://www.experian.com

Trans Union
P.O. Box 2000
Chester, PA 19022
1-800-916-8800 customer service
1-800-888-4213 order credit report
http://www.transunion.com

Equifax
P.O. Box 105496
Atlanta, GA 30348-5496
1-800-997-2493
http://www.equifax.com

COMPUTERIZED DATABASES
You can use computerized databases such as Lexis and Westlaw (available online, for a fee) and CD-Roms such as LawDesk to search for the names of lawyers, judges, and expert witnesses to see the results in those cases. Simply type the person's name into the search field, and see if their name appears in any cases. You can then read that judge's decisions or the cases that attorney was involved in.

ADDITIONAL IRS INFORMATION
Free tax services: To find out what services are available, get Publication 910, *Guide to Free Tax Services.* It contains a list of free tax publications and an index of tax topics. It also describes other free tax information services, including tax education and assistance programs.
Phone:

- Call 1-800-829-3676 to order current and prior year forms, instructions, and publications.

- Call the IRS with your tax questions at 1-800-829-1040.
- Call 1-800-829-4477 to listen to TeleTax's prerecorded messages covering various tax topics.

Walk-in: You can pick up certain forms, instructions, and publications at many post offices, libraries, and IRS offices. Some libraries and IRS offices have an extensive collection of products available to print from a CD-ROM or photocopy from reproducible proofs.

Mail: You can send your order for forms, instructions, and publications to the Distribution Center nearest to you and receive a response in seven to fifteen workdays after your request is received. Find the address that applies to your part of the country.

- Western part of United States
  Western Area Distribution Center
  Rancho Cordova, CA 95743-0001
- Central part of United States
  Central Area Distribution Center
  P.O. Box 8903
  Bloomington, IL 61702-8903
- Eastern part of United States and foreign addresses
  Eastern Area Distribution Center
  P.O. Box 85074
  Richmond, VA 23261-5074

CD-ROM: You can order IRS Publication 1796, Federal Tax Products on CD-ROM, and obtain:

- Current tax forms, instructions, and publications
- Prior-year tax forms, instructions, and publications
- Popular tax forms that may be filled in electronically, printed out for submission, and saved for record keeping
- Internal Revenue Bulletins

The CD-ROM can be purchased from National Technical Information Service (NTIS) for $25 by calling 1-877-233-6767 or for $21 on the Internet at www.irs.ustreas.gov/cdorders. The first release is available in mid-December 2000 and the final release is available in late January 2001.

RECOMMENDED BOOKS

Brodt, Armin. *The Single Father: A Dad's Guide to Parenting Without a Partner* (New York: Abbeville Press, 1999). A book geared to the male experience during divorce, with tips and information about issues ranging from maintaining a relationship with your children through setting up a new kitchen. A lot of solid information in one place.

Fisher, Roger, and William Ury. *Getting to Yes: Negotiating Agreement Without Giving In* (Boston: Houghton Mifflin, 1981). A renowned sourcebook for tips on negotiating strategies aimed at maximizing positive outcomes and effecting settlements.

Friedman, James T. *The Divorce Handbook* (New York: Random House, 1999). Detailed consideration of the legal process, in question-and-answer format.

Garrity, Carla B., and Mitchell A. Baris. *Caught in the Middle: Protecting the Children of High Conflict Divorce* (New York: Lexington, 1994). A concise explanation of ways to keep children from becoming embroiled in parental conflict after divorce.

Gold, Lois. *Between Love and Hate: A Guide to Civilized Divorce* (New York: Plume/Penguin, 1992). Thoughtful analysis of the psychological issues in divorce, with emphasis on children, handling conflict, and negotiating to avoid adversarial stances. Useful information about constructing parenting plans.

Krantzler, Mel, and Pat Krantzler. *The New Creative Divorce* (Holbrook, MS: Adams Media, 1998). Thorough overview of the psychological process of divorce.

McKay, Matthew, Peter Rogers, Joan Blades, and Richard Go___ vorce Book (Oakland, CA: New Harbinger, 1999). Addresses lega___ chological issues, with a focus on constructive solutions to the problems of divorce.

Ostman, Ellen D. *Dear Client: A Complete Handbook for Understanding and Surviving Your Legal Divorce Process* (Tampa, FL: Axelrod, 1996). Resource for copies of actual forms such as interrogatories and injunctions, checklists, copies of testimony transcripts. Also full of statistics on marriages and divorces.

Pruett, Kyle D. *Father Need: Why Father Care Is as Essential as Mother Care* (New York: Free Press, 2000). Earthy writing and a cogent analysis utilizing research and clinical examples combined to describe the many faces of fatherhood, and its importance to the men and their children.

Quinn, Jane Bryant. *Making the Most of Your Money* (New York: Simon & Schuster, 1999). Comprehensive, easy-to-understand financial guide that covers basic issues like how to balance a checkbook to advanced issues like how to allocate your investment portfolio. Essential reading to gain financial expertise.

Ricci, Isolina. *Mom's House, Dad's House* (Revised, New York: Fireside, 1997). This user-friendly book was one of the first, and is still one of the best, descriptions about how to put together a shared parenting plan and make it work for all people involved.

Sitarz, Daniel. *Divorce Laws of the United States* (St. Peters, MO: Nova, 1999). Summary of divorce laws of each state, listed state by state.

Smith, Gayle Rosenwald, and Sally Abrahms. *What Every Woman Should Know About Divorce and Custody* (New York: Perigee, 1998). Readable treatment of some of the psychological and a few of the legal issues of divorce, but focus is primarily women and children.

BOOKS FOR CHILDREN

At Daddy's on Saturdays. Linda W. Girard. Morton Grove, Ill.: Albert, Whitman, 1987.

Daddy, Daddy, Be There. Candy Dawson Boyd and Floyd Cooper. New York: Philomel, 1995.

Daddy Day, Daughter Day. Larry King and Chaia King. Beverly Hills, Calif.: Dove Kids, 1997.

Dinosaurs Divorce: A Guide for Changing Families. Laurence Brown and Marc Brown. Boston: Little, Brown, 1986.

Divorce Is Not the End of the World. Zoe Stern, Evan Stern, and Ellen Sue Stern. Berkeley, Calif.: Tricycle, 1997.

The Divorce Workbook: A Guide for Kids and Their Families. Sally B. Ives. Burlington, Vt.: Waterfront Books, 1988.

Father and Son. Lauture Denize. New York: Philomel, 1992.

How It Feels When Parents Divorce. Jill Krementz. New York: Knopf, 1988.

Why Are We Getting a Divorce? Peter Mayle. San Francisco: Harmony Books, 1988.

REFERENCES

CHAPTER 2

Buchanan, C., E. E. Maccoby, and S. M. Dornbusch. *Adolescents After Divorce* (Cambridge: Harvard University Press, 1996).

CHAPTER 3

Dillon, P. A., and R. E. Emery. "Divorce Mediation and Resolution of Child Custody Disputes: Long-Term Effects." *American Journal of Orthopsychiatry*, 66 (1996): 131–40.

Emery, R. E. *Renegotiating Family Relationships: Divorce, Child Custody and Mediation.* New York: Guilford Press, 1994.

Kelly, J. B. "Is Mediation Less Expensive?: Comparison of Mediated and Adversarial Divorce Costs." *Mediation Quarterly* 8 (1990): 15–26.

———. *Mediated and Adversarial Divorce Resolution Process: An Analysis of Postdivorce Outcomes.* Final report prepared for the Fund for Research in Dispute Resolution. Corte Madera, Calif.: Northern California Mediation Services, 1990.

Kitzmann, K. M. and R. E. Emery. "Child and Family Coping One Year After Mediated and Litigated Child Custody Disputes." *Journal of Family Psychology* 8 (1994): 150–59.

Kressel, K. and D. Pruitt, eds. *Mediation Research: The Process and Effectiveness of Third Party Interventions.* San Francisco: Jossey-Bass, 1987.

CHAPTER 4

Fisher, R. and W. Ury. *Getting to Yes; Negotiating Agreement Without Giving In.* Boston: Houghton Mifflin, 1981.

CHAPTER 6

Pruett, M. Kline. *Divorce in Legal Context: Outcomes for Children.* Final report presented to the Smith Richardson Foundation, Inc., 1998.

CHAPTER 7

Amato, P. R. "Children's Adjustment to Divorce: Theories, Hypotheses, and Empirical Support." *Journal of Marriage and the Family* 55 (1993): 23–28.

Emery, R. *Marriage, Divorce, and Children's Adjustment.* Newbury Park, CA: Sage Publishing Co., 1988.

Grych, J. H., and F. D. Fincham. "Children's Adaptation to Divorce: From Description to Explanation." In I. N. Sandler and S. A. Wolchik (eds.), *Handbook of Children's Coping with Common Stressors: Linking Theory and Intervention.* New York: Plenum, 1997.

Hetherington, M. E., and E. A. Blechman. *Stress, Coping, and Resiliency in Children and Families.* Hillsdale, NJ: Lawrence Erlbaum Associates, 1996.

Hetherington, M. E., G. Clingempeel, et al. "Coping with Marital Transitions: A Family Systems Perspective." *Monographs of the Society for Research in Child Development* 57 (1992).

Johnston, J. R., and L. E. G. Campbell. *Impasses of Divorce: The Dynamics and Resolution of Family Conflict.* New York: Free Press, 1995.

Johnston, J. R. and V. Roseby. *In the Name of the Child: A Developmental Approach to Understanding and Helping Children of Conflicting and Violent Divorce.* New York: Free Press, 1997.

Kelly, J. B. "Current Research on Children's Post-Divorce Adjustment: No Simple Answers." *Conciliation Courts Review* 31 (1993): 29–49.

———. "Longer-Term Adjustment in Children of Divorce: Converging Findings and Invocations for Practice." *Journal of Family Psychology* 2 (1988): 119–40.

Kline (Pruett), M., J. R. Johnston, and J. M. Tschann. "The Long Shadow of Marital Conflict: A Model of Children's Postdivorce Adjustment." *Journal of Marriage and the Family* 53 (1991): 297–310.

Kline (Pruett), M., J. M. Tschann, and J. R. Johnston. "Children's Adjustment in Joint and Sole Custody Families." *Developmental Psychology* 25 (1989): 430–38.

Maccoby, E. E., and R. H. Mnookin. *Dividing the Child: Social and Legal Dimensions of Custody.* Cambridge: Harvard University Press, 1992.

Tschann, J. M., J. R. Johnston, and M. Kline (Pruett), et al. "Family Process and Children's Functioning During Divorce." *Journal of Marriage and the Family* 51 (1989): 431–44.

Wallerstein, J. S., et al. *The Unexpected Legacy of Divorce.* New York: Hyperion, 2000.

Wallerstein, J. S., and S. Blakeslee. *Second Chances: Men, Women and Children After a Decade.* Boston: Houghton Mifflin, 1996.

Wallerstein, J. S., and J. B. Kelly. *Surviving the Breakup.* New York: Basic Books, 1980.

CHAPTER 8

Ahrons, C. R., and R. H. Rogers. *Divorcing Families.* New York: Norton, 1987.

Hodges, W. F. *Interventions for Children of Divorce: Custody, Access and Psychotherapy, 3rd ed.* New York: Wiley, 1991.

Lamb, M. E. and Kelly, J. B. Using child development research to make appropriate custody and access decisions for young children. *Family and Conciliation Courts Review,* in press.

Pruett, K. D., and M. Kline Pruett. "Only God Decides: Young Children's Perceptions of Divorce." *Journal of the American Academy of Child and Adolescent Psychiatry* 38 (1999): 1544–50.

Pruett, K. D., M. Kline, and K. HoganBruen, "Joint Custody and Shared Parenting: Research and Interventions." In K. D. Pruett and M. Kline Pruett, eds. *Child Custody Issues: Child Psychiatric Clinics of North America Monograph.* Philadelphia: W. B. Saunders Company, 1998.

Pruett, M. Kline, and K. D. Pruett. "Fathers, Divorce, and Their Children." In K. D. Pruett and M. Kline Pruett, eds., in *Child Custody Issues. Child Psychiatric Clinics of North America Monograph.* Philadelphia: W. B. Saunders Company, 1998.

Pruett, M. Kline, and C. Santangelo. "Joint Custody and Empirical Knowledge: The Estranged Bedfellows of Divorce." In R. M. Galatzer-Levy and L. Kraus, eds., in *The Scientific Basis for Custody Decisions.* New York: Wiley, 1999.

Solomon, J., and C. George. "The Effects on Attachment of Overnight Visitation in Divorced and Separated Families: A Longitudinal Follow-up." In J. Solomon and C. George, eds., in *Attachment and Disorganization*. New York: Guilford, 1999.

Spokane County Bar Association. *Child-Centered Residential Schedules*. Spokane, WA, December 1996.

Whiteside, M. F. *An Integrative Review of the Literature Pertinent to Custody of Children Five Years of Age or Younger*. Executive Summary to the Statewide Office of Family Court Services, San Francisco, Calif. (April). Ann Arbor, Center for the Family, 1996.

CHAPTER 9

Bow, J. N., and F. A. Quinnell. *Summary of Psychologists' Current Practices and Procedures in Child Custody Evaluations*. Hawthorn Center Report, State of Michigan Department of Community Health, 1999.

CHAPTER 10

Barrett, O. W., C. L. Miller-Perrin, and R. D. Perrin. *Family Violence Across the Life Span: An Introduction*. Thousand Oaks, Calif.: Sage, 1997.

Crosby, Philip C. *Custody of Vaughn: Emphasizing the Importance of Domestic Violence in Child Custody Cases. B.U. Law Review* 77 (1997): 483.

Davidson, H. *The Impact of Domestic Violence on Children: A Report to the President of the American Bar Association*. Chicago: American Bar Association, October 1994.

Kurtz, Lynne R. "Protecting New York's Children: An Argument for the Creation of a Rebuttable Presumption Against Awarding a Spouse Abuser Custody of a Child." *Albany Law Review* 60 (1997): 1345.

Jaffe, P., D. Wolfe, and S. K. Wilson. *Children of Battered Women*. Newbury Park, Calif.: Sage, 1990.

McCloskey, L. A., A. J. Figueredo, and M. P. Koss. "The Effects of Systemic Family Violence on Children's Mental Health." *Child Development* 66 (1995): 1239–61.

Osofsky, J. "The Effects of Exposure to Violence on Young Children." *American Psychologist* 50 (1995): 782–88.

Walker, L. *The Battered Woman's Syndrome*. New York: Springer, 1984.

INDEX

ABOUT THE AUTHORS

Marsha Kline Pruett, Ph.D., M.S.L., is Research Scientist in the Law and Psychiatry Division of the Connecticut Mental Health Center at the Yale School of Medicine, Department of Psychiatry and the Yale Child Study Center. She has served as the Director of Child and Adolescent Programs at The Consultation Center, a nationally regarded Yale-affiliated center for prevention and intervention research and programming. Her clinical psychology degree is from the University of California, Berkeley, with additional master's degrees in law from Yale, and in education from the University of Pennsylvania. She has eighteen years of clinical experience with individuals, couples, families, and children, and has been trained in both Family Therapy and Divorce Mediation. She is noted nationally for her research regarding child adjustment to divorce, joint custody, school interventions, and work/family conflicts.

Dr. Kline Pruett was a member of the original team of investigators headed by Judith Wallerstein and Janet Johnston, with whom she spearheaded early research on joint custody and marital conflict in California. Since then, she has been Primary Investigator on numerous state and federal grants, and is also known nationally for the development, implementation, and evaluation of preventive interventions. Her writings include numerous original articles published in scientific journals. She has directed the Culture of Litigation Project, which investigates the process of divorce, and its impact on families with children under the age of six. Currently, she is directing the Collaborative Divorce Project, which offers families with young children in Connecticut a model approach to working with lawyers, judges, family services, and mental health professionals to obtain a timely and cost-effective divorce that maximizes children's contact with both parents through parenting plans designed by the parents, along with assistance from an intervention team. This project also examines the impact of the intervention on children's well-being, and on the legal and psychological costs to the family. A gifted lecturer and teacher, she has spoken to audiences large and small throughout the country, and served as expert commentator on both local and national radio and television news programs.

Dr. Kline Pruett lives in Guilford, Connecticut, with her husband, the nationally renowned child psychiatrist Kyle Pruett, M.D., and their toddler, the irrepressible Olivia Zoey. She also has two adult stepdaughters.

Diana Mercer is founder of Peace Talks Divorce Mediation Services in Los Angeles, California, and a partner in the law firm of Noyes & Mercer, P.C., which focuses its practice exclusively on family law. Mercer is a family lawyer who has shifted her focus from divorce litigation to family law mediation. She is a graduate of Indiana University School of Law, where she received the American Jurisprudence Award for Excellence. She received her undergraduate degree from Indiana University in Economics and French, and she is a member of the Mortar Board Honor Society for service and academics.

In addition to her skills as a seasoned trial attorney, Mercer is a former professor in the graduate studies program at the University of Bridgeport. She is a member of the American, California, Connecticut, Los Angeles, and Beverly Hills Bar Associations and the Academy of Family Mediators, and has lectured on Children's Records Law, Child Support Collection, Equitable Division of Marital Assets, Children's Attorneys and Guardians, and Child Custody. She has been published in the Connecticut *Family Lawyer* journal, has written numerous articles on divorce and child custody, and her comments appear frequently in the *Los Angeles Times, New York Times,* and *New Haven Register.*

Mercer serves as a mediator in the Alternative Dispute Resolution Program in the Los Angeles Superior Court, and as a Special Master to the family court and the Regional Family Trial Contested Custody Court in Connecticut. She is also an Attorney Trial Referee for the Connecticut Superior Court.

She currently lives in Los Angeles, California, with her husband.